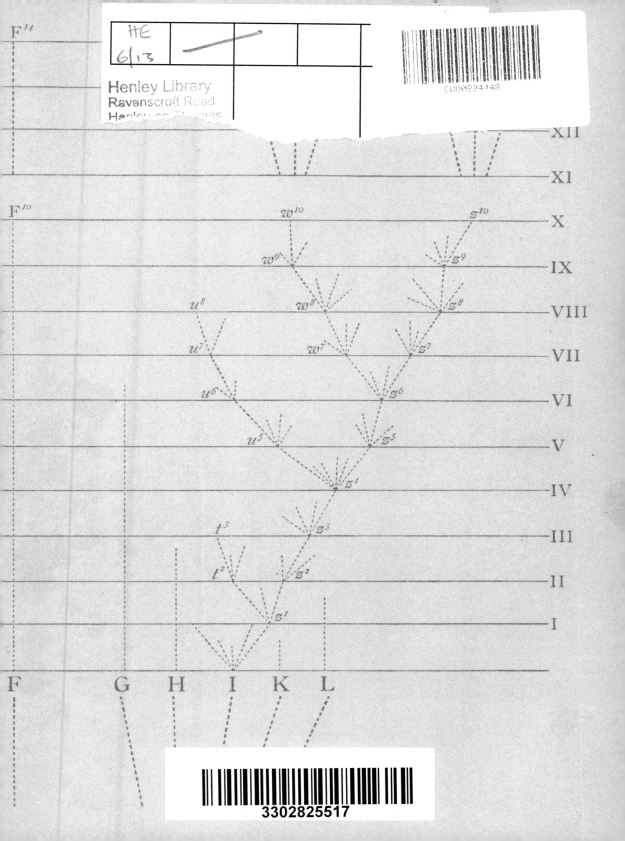

WEEDS
WEEDING
(& DARWIN)

WEEDS, WEEDING (& DARWIN)

The Gardener's Guide

FRANCES LINCOLN LIMITED
PUBLISHERS

Frances Lincoln Limited
www.franceslincoln.com

Weeds, Weeding (& Darwin): The Gardener's Guide
Copyright © Frances Lincoln Limited 2013
Text copyright © Willie Edmonds 2013
Photographs copyright © Willie Edmonds 2013 except those listed on page 287

First Frances Lincoln edition 2013

A catalogue record for this book is available from the British Library.

978-0-7112-3365-2

Printed and bound in Shenzhen, Guangdong, China by C&C Offset Printing

1 2 3 4 5 6 7 8 9

Commissioned and edited by Jane Crawley
Designed by Anne Wilson

PAGE 1 Blackberries hanging over the garden fence.
PREVIOUS PAGE Dandelions taking over.
ABOVE The author wrestling with a dandelion.
RIGHT Himalayan balsam in menacing mode.

Contents

I
Nature's garden selection

Just what are weeds? 'Plants growing where they are not wanted' is the standard answer given to gardeners. Glib as this may sound, the key point that any plant can act as a weed and that anybody may determine what, where, when and why is easily grasped. Even so, such a definition could hardly be less adequate.

Whether we are tending flowers or growing food, we choose to cultivate particular plants to the exclusion of all others which might get in the way or become spoiling nuisances. A massive wilderness of undesirables lies out there and we have to be on our guard. Potentially, we might say, these undesirables could include all but a tiny proportion of the plant kingdom. But let's not beat about that proverbial bush. We all know the principal culprits hanging about over the garden fence or on the edges of fields, waiting for the slightest chance to move in. Think of dandelions, docks, nettles and brambles, just for a start.

LEFT Dürer's most unusual masterpiece, *Great Piece of Turf*, 1503, provides a neat introduction to the world of weeds. The prime nuisances may change over the years but their collective intrusion into our affairs persists to this day, whether in our gardens or fields. Much helped by this eye-level view, we see how weeds come to the fore when turf grass is left ungrazed or unmown. There they are, in this case: salad burnet, dandelion, plantain, hound's tongue and daisies, with a shoot of yarrow left lying over them.

And let's face it too, many of these common intruders can be really 'bad' – *mauvaises herbes* or *malas herbas* as French or Spanish speakers say. Between them the unwanted guests will obstruct, crowd out, entwine, strangle, smother (below ground as well as above), steal space and light, take needed moisture and nutrients, sting, prick, scratch, injure, poison, spread disease and infestation, uglify and wreak havoc in all kinds of ways over and above just being unwanted. Folklore has it that a good few of these dubious plants are the work of the devil: devil's grip, devil's nettle, devil's plague, devil's helmet, to name but a few. Human survival, let alone garden survival, has depended all along on our struggle to contain this enemy and keep the wilderness sufficiently at bay.

On the other hand – and be warned this whole saga is riven with contradiction – these bad guys invariably have their 'good' (beneficial to us) sides too. Remember the above four examples. They each have valued uses, cherished herbal properties and other niches where we appreciate them as wild flowers.

It is true that in our present-day urban and cocooned existence, weeds are low down the list of perceived threats to everyday life – in contrast, say, with four centuries back. In those more down-to-earth times it was only natural for Shakespeare to make frequent reference to all kinds of troublesome plants as these were a constant threat to the well-being of his audiences. Weeds provided him with potent metaphors:

...O thou weed!
Who art so lovely fair and smell'st so sweet
That the sense aches at thee, would thou hadst ne'er been born.

Thus Othello rages over the sleeping Desdemona. These days, to call someone a 'weed', as may happen in the school playground, is to insult them for being an ineffectual weakling rather than to damn them for their evil duplicity.

Today, in our own back gardens, most of us implicitly acknowledge the tough challenge of unwanted plants by spending more time on weeding than on any other task – apart, maybe, from lawn-mowing which, anyway, happens partly to serve as a form of weed control. Even so, we often tend to weed surreptitiously, as if embarrassed by having such blemishes in the first place. True, the more vigilant and regularly attentive we are to general garden care, the less weeding there is to do in the long run, but there is no simple escape from the task. Frankly, to be responsible for any garden is to be stuck on some kind of weeding treadmill, like it or not. Whether this always has to be a chore is another matter.

Unfavoured by us, weeds are the plants which nature selects for our gardens – the outstanding survivors of the plant world, both of nature's struggles and of our own struggles with nature. Their life force is formidable – they will return week after week throughout the year. Leave a garden to its own devices for a growing season and nature's select locals soon take over. So, as remarkable survivors and as plants provided and selected for us by nature, can our old garden foes tell us something about 'Natural Selection', Charles Darwin's central concept in *On the Origin of Species*? And can Darwin, too, throw light on the nature of weeds and how we might deal with them?

'Survival of the fittest' is probably what first springs to most of our minds when trying to grasp the notion of natural selection. In fact, this famous aphorism was coined by Herbert Spencer, the distinguished social philosopher of that time, who introduced it to Darwin after reading the first edition of *On the Origin of Species*. It was subsequently used by Darwin in later editions, one suspects a little reluctantly, though he was most gracious to Spencer. The latter's addition vividly evokes the harsh competition of the natural world, the law of the jungle if you like, even though he intended 'fittest' to convey 'most suitable' rather than 'most physically fit'. But, whichever way we understand it, 'survival of the fittest', an impressive survivor in its own right, does not, on closer examination, take us very far.

Obviously, those life forms most fitted to survive would be the ones most likely to survive. But would the tough ones always win? Weeds, mercifully, point to a different answer. They demonstrate that their success does not depend on superior vigour alone. Many of them may indeed be 'weedy specimens' in the colloquial use of the term. The weaker weeds, of course, win out by being phenomenally prolific. Many others are just enduring mediocrities, while a few can be utter brutes. Weeds succeed, more especially, by having extraordinary capacities to come back from or adapt to the mini-extinctions which we repeatedly try to inflict on them. This is a resilience which has already come about through the long-term trials of nature and is what weed fitness, if we can call it that, is all about.

The rascals – and it is so easy to personalise these plants, just as Darwin did with the plants on which he conducted his detailed observations – variously outsmart and challenge us, whether as tearaway seeding annuals, as lingering biennials or as persistent perennials. They quite often succeed by combining these lifestyles. The ways and means by which weeds gain advantage over us or, could we but admit it, how they actually take advantage of us, highlight astonishing botanical ingenuity.

Plants have been honing their survival strategies from earliest beginnings of more than a billion years ago, slowly changing (and barely at all in the first half of this time) from the simplest forms to becoming the most sophisticated operators. All those especially challenging plants which we have come to know as weeds straddle across this evolutionary development and it turns out that together they provide a remarkable representative showcase of what has happened in all. So here is an entirely new presentation of weeds in

WEEDS, WEEDING (& DARWIN)

the form of an evolutionary story, based too on recent DNA-based refinements to plant classification. Darwin himself completes the picture for us as a selection of pertinent details from his life and work are woven into the story. And so, impertinently, this introduction now proceeds where Darwin left off – with the concluding paragraph from *On the Origin of Species* (first edition):

> It is interesting to contemplate an entangled bank, clothed with many plants of many kinds, with birds singing in the bushes, with various insects flitting about, and with worms crawling through the damp earth, and to reflect that these elaborately constructed forms, so different from each other, and dependent on each other in so complex a manner have all been produced by laws acting around us. These laws, taken in the largest sense, being Growth with Reproduction; Inheritance which is almost implied by reproduction; Variability from the indirect and direct action of the conditions of life, and from use and disuse: a Ratio of increase so high as to lead to a Struggle for Life, and as a consequence to Natural Selection, entailing Divergence of Character and the Extinction of less-improved forms. Thus, from the war of nature, from famine and death, the most exalted object which we are capable of conceiving, namely the production of higher animals, directly follows. There is grandeur in this view of life, with its several powers, having been originally breathed into a few forms or into one; and that, whilst this planet has gone cycling on according to the fixed law of gravity, from so simple a beginning endless forms most beautiful and most wonderful have been, and are being evolved.

This picture of 'an entangled bank' is immediately engaging. In reality it is much easier to imagine than to come across with all its diverse elements on display in such close proximity. Even so, for most of us nowadays it can still readily conjure up a wide rising verge beside a country lane or pathway, and one backed by a rather overgrown hedgerow. This bank, with its thriving little ecology, acts as a natural wildlife haven, whereas on either side there is likely to be human disturbance – people and maybe vehicles passing along the track, while over the top of the bank there could well be some cultivation or pasturage.

LEFT Charles Darwin at 54, four years after the publication of *On the Origin of Species*. Meticulous observation of plants, including weeds, played a significant part in this work. Once this book was completed, botany became Darwin's prime scientific focus, and for the rest of his life living in the village of Downe in North Kent. The majority (seven) of his subsequent books were about plants.

BELOW *Still Life* by Trajan Hughes, 1732. This painting now hangs in Down House, Darwin's old home, by the village of Downe. Darwin would have appreciated how it encapsulates the essence of his 'entangled bank' scenario: a display of a wide range of wildlife interacting around a foxglove in flower. A fine sight for naturalists but not such a pretty picture for the gardener.

As it happens, such a site is a key to our understanding of weeds, for there is a good chance that a significant proportion of those 'many plants of many kinds' will be our classic offenders (brambles, nettles, docks and dandelions) – plants which have survived previous periodic human disturbance and which are also well suited to entangling, rapidly spreading out and colonising any nearby newly exposed ground created by farmers or by us gardeners. As well as plants just sending out new shoots all over the place, there will be plenty of seeds finding all sorts of ways of dispersing themselves far and wide. Any people, animals or vehicles going along the route will be unwittingly assisting this spread.

It is a little unnerving to realise that here are plants which have a natural affinity with us, which congregate around our dwellings, which follow us wherever we go – even across the world – lining our travel routes if they possibly can (those 'flowers of the wayside') and interfering in pretty well all our outdoor activities, if given half a chance. Whether we like it or not, weeds come to be our companion plants, playing all kinds of subtle and not-so-subtle roles in relation to us.

Attracted as common weeds are to our way of life, we should recognise that they are also known to be the very same kinds of plant which are the first to move into naturally disturbed sites such as soil exposed by melting glaciers, landslides or various kinds of erosion. We can think of them as nature's front-line colonisers, or pioneers, if that makes us feel a little less paranoid. Certainly we associate them with wasteland – areas laid waste by us and then, as likely as not, recolonised by nature.

Most of us consciously confront such plants most regularly and most annoyingly in our gardens. This scenario is the principal focus of this guide. But we should not forget that weeds are vitally relevant in relation to farming and especially to crop production and it is this commercial interest which is responsible for most of the scientific research on weed habits and control.

Ironically gardens play a key role in the proliferation of weeds by unavoidably importing them – whether from seeds being brought in on the breeze, being walked in on footwear, being woken up after years of dormancy, or from other unwitting actions by ourselves. Then sometimes gardens will also export their own prized specimens as garden escapes. Australians and New Zealanders most especially can tell of many fine foreign plants brought into their gardens only soon to become horrific weeds wreaking havoc on the native landscape.

In the following chapters we shall see how Darwin's 'laws acting around us' contribute to the remarkable success of nature's garden selection – a phenomenon we cannot but come to respect and even hold in awe, despite much cursing and moments of despair on the way. Without further ado, therefore, let's meet one hundred prime weeds in all their 'forms most wonderful' … and most terrible … and learn, if we can, how to deal with them.

2
One hundred weeds to know

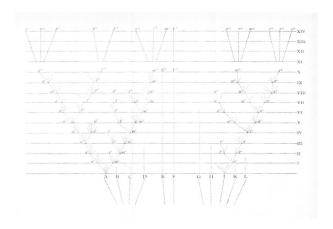

'Know your enemy!' This was the counsel of the Taoist military strategist, Sun Tzu, in Ancient China. He added, 'If you know your enemies and know yourself you can win a hundred battles without a single loss'.

The aim here is to lay bare one hundred typical garden villains to win those one hundred battles. Not necessarily 'without a single loss', but as decisively as is possible for the time being. In this chapter one hundred weed candidates are identified, described and analysed. Almost as many other plants with weed-like tendencies receive a mention too. The idea is to include all the more usual suspects and a varied selection of others, including one or two which, at first, you may be a little surprised to see here. Even so, it's quite possible that a key culprit particular to your own garden or surroundings has been missed. In that case, a good local flora guide should help with identifying it and its family and there should then be a strong chance of finding relevant information about a close relative in the list.

The relationship of one plant with another in an ever branching network is fundamental to this book. Hence the diagram above – which happens to be Darwin's sole illustration

LEFT Old garden enemies taunting us with a wildflower display of pure delight.

in *On the Origin of Species*. Fortunately, we now have the help of a new 'Tree of Plant Evolution' produced by the scientists at Kew in 2010 for a book, *The Art of Plant Evolution*, published to celebrate the major Darwin anniversary in 2009. The publishers have kindly given permission for it to be used here as well (see pages overleaf).

This particular tree is a significant rearrangement and an exciting new development arising from major advances in DNA analysis during the last twenty years or so. The 'Major branches' each take on a distinctly new character, a newly adjusted relationship with each other and some new descriptive names (from 'Basal Angiosperms: Minor Groups' to 'Core Angiosperms: Asterids').

Each one of these 'major branches' represents a collection of related plant 'orders' which are indicated at the branch tips. These orders themselves embrace groups of connected 'families', which, in turn, embrace groups of connected 'genera'. Then, of course, genera, divide into 'species' by which we know and name each distinctly different plant.

'Major branch'—Order—Family—Genus—Species

In adopting this tree we have slotted in the numbers by which we sequence our chosen one hundred weeds. The numbers refer to the weeds whose common names are listed opposite. Acknowledging the tree's evolutionary framework, we clamber up the tree from one of its lowest major branches, 'Algae', right up to its most developed uppermost branch tips with the dandelions to be found among the asterales.

Although we dare to present a one-to-a-hundred sequence, this cannot in any way indicate a clear temporal succession of emerging plants. For example, we meet the grasses quite early on as Weed 14 while in fact they arrived relatively recently in parallel with the higher core eudicots which are to be found in our 80s or so. In fact, we find ourselves hopping all the time across a host of semi-parallel developments. We follow the main branches one by one, though on one occasion we rashly jump across a whole major branch to another and back again to make a particular point of interest to our narrative. Even so, the whole tree covers a vast time. Green algae are believed to have appeared at least a billion years ago. More recently, we see that the arrival of the daisy family comes at least 100 million years after that of the buttercups. The whole evolution of plants is truly wondrous and that just of our weeds goes some way to providing a spectacular select illustration of it.

To put a name to a weed is to take the first step in dealing with it. But what name? In this chapter each weed is first introduced by its scientific (botanical) name. This is the internationally recognised two-part (binomial) Latin name officially assigned to that plant following the system created by the Swedish botanist Carl Linnaeus in the mid-eighteenth century. These identify separate species, each one with its genus name followed by a species epithet. For example, *Hyacinthoides non-scripta* where *Hyacinthoides* is the genus name (meaning 'like a hyacinth') and *non-scripta* (meaning 'not written in law') is the species epithet. Such names are always written in italic with just the first letter of the first part being in upper case. After the botanical name in our weed titles (that is, for all the flowering plants starting from Weed 6) we include the family name – the one always with the suffix 'aceae' and then what we believe to be the plant's best known English common name. In this case 'bluebell'. In just a few of our examples, there may be two, three or more closely associated species which are best considered together. For these we use 'spp.' for the second part of the botanical name.

Be prepared for a host of statistics, sometimes quite bizarre. Numbers abound in our plant profiles: numbers of sepals, petals, stamens, carpels, fruits and seeds per plant. Linnaeus based his classification system on counting sexual parts. As gardeners we are often interested in germination rates, months of seed dormancy, years of seed viability, distances of seed dispersal, vegetative extension per season and so on. Darwin did his share of meticulous counting of seeds, seedlings and suchlike. Since his time, counting chromosomes has become important and now we are looking into vast numbers of genes.

Altogether there are over 400,000 possible weeds, given that that is the estimated total number of known plant species worldwide. Of course, only the minutest fraction of these ever comes to be in any way bothersome to us. In Australia, which has a weed problem like no other, over 1,700 national weeds have been officially declared, a large proportion of which are garden escapes into the wild. So these one hundred chosen examples of ours are a pretty select few.

Knowing a weed also means knowing what it looks like and so illustrations of each of our one hundred cited examples are important. But bear in mind that any plant can look quite different according to its stage of growth, its growing conditions, its genetic make-up and, quite simply, its natural proneness to variation. Also a plant, like anything else, can look so different from different angles and distances. And then many plants are thought of as weeds simply because they do not make a pretty picture. They rarely stand out alone to be seen; more often they are half visible in an entangled mess.

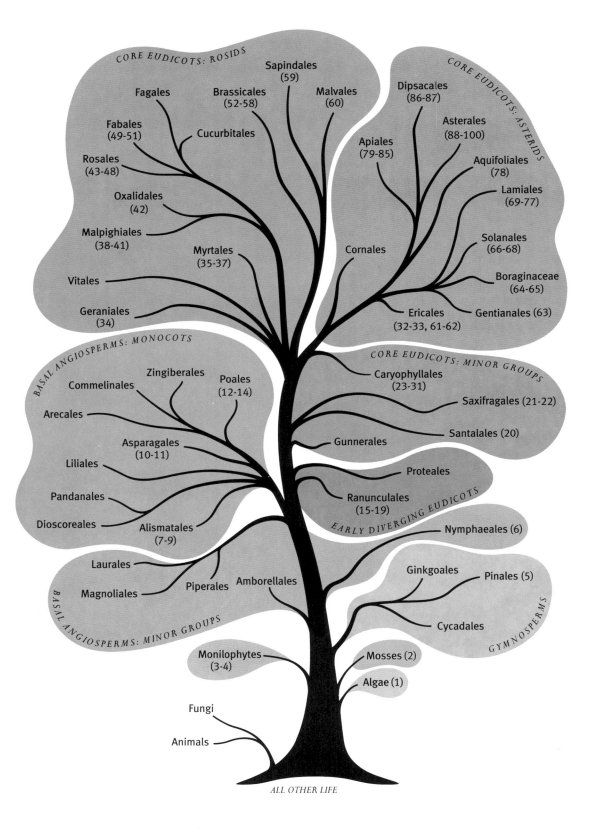

CORE EUDICOTS: ROSIDS

Sapindales (59)

Fagales

Brassicales (52-58)

Malvales (60)

Cucurbitales

Fabales (49-51)

Rosales (43-48)

Oxalidales (42)

Malpighiales (38-41)

Myrtales (35-37)

Vitales

Geraniales (34)

CORE EUDICOTS: ASTERIDS

Dipsacales (86-87)

Asterales (88-100)

Apiales (79-85)

Aquifoliales (78)

Lamiales (69-77)

Solanales (66-68)

Cornales

Boraginaceae (64-65)

Ericales (32-33, 61-62)

Gentianales (63)

BASAL ANGIOSPERMS: MONOCOTS

Zingiberales

Poales (12-14)

Commelinales

Arecales

Asparagales (10-11)

Liliales

Pandanales

Dioscoreales

Alismatales (7-9)

CORE EUDICOTS: MINOR GROUPS

Caryophyllales (23-31)

Saxifragales (21-22)

Santalales (20)

Gunnerales

Proteales

Ranunculales (15-19)

EARLY DIVERGING EUDICOTS

Nymphaeales (6)

Laurales

Magnoliales

Piperales

Amborellales

Ginkgoales

Pinales (5)

Cycadales

GYMNOSPERMS

BASAL ANGIOSPERMS: MINOR GROUPS

Monilophytes (3-4)

Mosses (2)

Algae (1)

Fungi

Animals

ALL OTHER LIFE

The Kew 'Tree of Plant Evolution' showing the numbers of the one hundred weeds on the branch of their appropriate orders and within their coloured 'major branch'.

1	Blanket Weed	35	Evening Primrose	69	Mint
2	Moss	36	Rosebay Willowherb	70	Red Dead Nettle
3	Horsetail	37	Purple Loosestrife	71	Ground Ivy
4	Bracken	38	Wild Pansy	72	Self-heal
5	'Leylandii'	39	Spurge	73	Plantain
6	Water Lily	40	Dog's Mercury	74	Speedwell
7	Pondweed	41	Perforate Saint John's Wort	75	Foxglove
8	Duckweed	42	Wood Sorrel	76	Mullein
9	Arum Lily	43	Bramble	77	Butterfly Bush
10	Stinking Iris	44	Parsley Piert	78	Holly
11	Bluebell	45	Creeping Cinquefoil	79	Ivy
12	Sedge	46	Nettle	80	Cow Parsley
13	Rush	47	Mind-your-own-business	81	Ground Elder
14	Grass	48	Pellitory of the Wall	82	Wild Carrot
15	Buttercup	49	White Clover	83	Fool's Parsley
16	Celandine	50	Gorse	84	Hemlock
17	Poppy	51	Kudzu Vine	85	Hogweed
18	Fumitory	52	Shepherd's Purse	86	Valerian
19	Barberry	53	Thale-cress	87	Teasel
20	Mistletoe	54	Hairy Bittercress	88	Campanula
21	Stonecrop	55	Charlock	89	Thistle
22	New Zealand Pigmy Weed	56	Wild Radish	90	Sow-thistle
23	Dock	57	Garlic Mustard	91	Burdock
24	Sheep Sorrel	58	Horseradish	92	Golden Rod
25	Fat-hen	59	Sycamore	93	Groundsel
26	Chickweed	60	Mallow	94	Ragwort
27	Pigweed	61	Rhododendron 'Ponticum'	95	Daisy
28	Japanese Knotweed	62	Himalayan Balsam	96	Sunflower
29	Russian Vine	63	Cleavers	97	Yarrow
30	Sundew	64	Comfrey	98	Dandelion
31	Prickly Pear	65	Forget-me-not	99	Hawkweed
32	Primrose	66	Bindweed		
33	Scarlet Pimpernel	67	Black Nightshade	*and...*	
34	Geranium	68	Thorn Apple	100	Weeds Anon

From earliest beginnings

Our first four weeds are those which come from three short branches at the base of the tree. Relatively small branches they may be, but the weeds that occupy them – green alga, moss, horsetail and bracken – are each capable of making major onslaughts on our gardens.

I

Spirogyra spp.
Blanket Weed / Filamentous Alga

Green alga first appeared more than a billion years ago, seemingly out of nowhere, to start greening the waters of our planet. It is still here. It is the villain that torments us by greening our ponds, coming apparently out of nowhere too, in one of its most ubiquitous modern guises, spirogyra – a genus with some 400 known species worldwide. Any ditch or natural pond is likely to contain a dozen or more of these. It is the real invasive curse of so many garden ponds, water butts and bird baths. Spyrogyra signals stagnation, the suppression of other water life and that part of the garden in retreat. And it calls for radical action.

But first let us relish its awesome significance a little more. Yes, 'from so simple a beginning', of green slimy matter just like this, 'endless forms most beautiful and most wonderful' did indeed evolve – including all plants and every objectionable weed.

'I believe', said Charles Darwin in the conclusion to the *Origin* (the abbreviated form of his title which he came to adopt), 'that animals are descended from at most four or five progenitors, and plants from an equal or lesser number.' Then he added, 'Analogy would lead me one step farther, namely, to the belief that all animals and plants are descended from some one prototype'. While going on to qualify this analogy, Darwin referred to 'lower algae' as quite possibly being both animal and plant, or at least the progenitors of both kingdoms.

RIGHT Spirogyra making a bid to blanket a garden pond, and at the same time generating patches of bubbling scum.

WEEDS, WEEDING (& DARWIN)

Now DNA analysis indicates that animals appear to diverge from fungi which arise before algae from a bacteria-like pool. Green alga – green from its chlorophyll content which enables photosynthesis (the process of harnessing light energy to convert into chemical energy) – therefore has to be close to the beginning of all plant life.

With more far-reaching scrutiny of the fossil record and with advanced microscopic studies of basic life forms, we are able to go a long way towards deducing what may have happened so long ago. Current research strongly indicates that green alga emerged with the fusing and symbiotic liaison of different bacteria cells, including chloroplasts, the greening light-responsive components. But who knows how many times this revolutionary fusion may have occurred independently…or not?

We generally experience spirogyra as a dreaded boring slime, though, if you like, you can see the beauteous charm of 'water silk' or 'mermaid's tresses', as these two common names suggest. But certainly its microscopic structures are striking, showing strings (filaments) of adjacent cells with spiralling chloroplasts (hence its genus name). But, to the naked eye, it is generally uninteresting.

Spirogyra reproduces in two ways: asexually by mitosis (cell division), especially stimulated when filaments fragment, as they readily do when they go beyond a certain length; and also by sexual 'conjugation' when filaments touch each other up, so to speak, in early summer and form bridging channels (appearing like ladder steps) between cells enabling them to fuse the material from both sides to create 'zygospores'. Such embryonic spores will also sometimes form between adjacent cells of a single filament. The new creations free themselves and sink to the bottom of the water lying in wait until the following spring before eventually germinating for the next generation of this confounded weed to rise up again. Meanwhile, as the water warms, the first generation takes over the pond surface in late summer, if given half a chance.

Especially disconcerting is the speed with which spirogyra spreads through an abrupt explosion of cell division and conjugation and suddenly arises from apparent hiding. No doubt birds play their part, not to mention we humans, in the continual widespread redistribution.

So there we are: a 'so simple a beginning' still here today, and most unwelcome in our gardens.

WHAT TO DO
- Scoop out – twisting around a stick, hoe or rake. Or skim off with a wide fish net.
- Take preventive measures:
  Insert a sheath of barley straw, or a bunch of lavender stalks into the pond to absorb CO_2.
  Take out extraneous organic matter – dead leaves and suchlike – to reduce CO_2 and nutrients.
  Introduce other plants (lilies etc.) to reduce light penetrating the water.
  Possibly apply algacides – but very gradually.
  Avoid too shallow water (note how bird baths green up almost immediately).
  Aerate with a fountain.
  Dim the lighting by providing some shade to reduce the rate of photosynthesis.
  Or, if inclined to more advanced technical solutions, seek out UV light or ultrasound treatments of circulating water.

2

Rhytidiadelphus squarrosus
Springy Turf Moss

The lawn covered in moss. What a bugbear that is too! The troublesome impact of early plant evolution on our gardens grows apace.

Bryophytes (i.e. mosses, liverworts and hornworts) were among the first plants to colonise land extensively about 400 million years ago. They occupy the next branch up from algae at the base of our evolutionary tree, a small one compared with what later succeeded it but a very distinctive one. About 1,000 bryophyte species have currently been identified in Great Britain and Ireland. As if to demonstrate Darwinian niche-adaptive speciation, a great many of the species are closely associated with very specialised sites: different positions on specific trees, on rotting wood in differing states of decay, with varying woodland light conditions and soil varieties, and so on. Of course there are some species which have taken off in a big way. In its lush sphagnum form, moss today clothes one per cent of the earth's land surface (equivalent to half the area of the USA as North Americans grandiosely assert).

Most specific to garden lawns is *Rhytidiadelphus squarrosus* (Springy Turf Moss). If you have ambitions for the perfect green sward, this is just what you do not want. It can subvert a lawn in sizeable patches like no other weed, especially in spring and autumn when light levels are lower and there is likely to be more moisture about. Mosses like this one are adept at holding water like a sponge (as if to be an aquatic plant surviving outside a pond) but they can also easily withstand drying out, throughout a hot summer for instance, to be able to rehydrate instantly at any time from a shower of rain.

Mosses like this can spread at an amazing rate both by pushing out their branching feathery stems indefinitely and by producing and showering spores (at the rate of 50 million per capsule). This latter 'sexual' process comes about in two stages known in the trade as 'alternation of generations'. The first and more substantial 'gametophyte' generation consists of those short feathery stems which fertilise each other on touch. This fertilisation creates a second generation of 'sporophytes' which are those stalks topped with beak-like capsules with the spores inside to be released for spawning the next generation of gametophytes.

With this armoury for putting itself about, moss is always going to be one of the first colonisers of second-grade open spaces as long as it is not too dry or unremittingly bright. Just as moss took over the grasslands of the northern European plains at the end of the last ice age and supposedly caused the demise of mammoths, so lawns are still susceptible to moss ascendancy at the end of our winters. Then, with the grass relatively weakened, the ground compacted from being trodden while damp, and with light levels relatively low, everything conspires for a flush of moss. Again in autumn, after a dry summer, when the grass is threadbare and light levels reduce, it readily returns. For all its apparent softness, such moss is as tough as old boots, or at least well able to withstand much trampling from them.

For certain, *Rhytidiadelphus sqarrosus* will not be the only moss around your garden and its surrounds. Any slightly damp or semi-shaded corner will attract an appropriate moss or two, with north-facing roofs making especially favoured havens. It is all part of the rich tapestry of nature's work around any dwelling and significantly contributes to a cottagey charm.

WHAT TO DO (in spring and autumn especially)
- Scarify (deeply scratch) and rake it out to allow grass to regain the upper hand.
- Mow not too low. Shaving grass weakens it and makes way for moss.
- Apply moss-killer compounds containing ferrous sulphate (before expected rain).
- Apply nitrogenous fertilisers to grass or a moss killer which includes them, like ferrous ammonium sulphate (again before rain).
- Improve drainage by spiking the ground with a fork or a tining machine.
- Reduce shadiness by trimming and thinning adjacent shrubs and trees.
- Re-seed grass with more shade-tolerant varieties.
- Or... love it. Introduce a 'mossery', a fashionable feature in Darwin's time.

BELOW Samuel Palmer, *A Cow-Lodge with a Mossy Roof* , *c*.1828–9. Samuel Palmer (1805–81) was a close contemporary of Darwin (1809–82). His most inspirational time was spent at Shoreham in Kent, only seven miles from Darwin's home at Downe, although by the time Darwin and his family moved there in 1842, Palmer had already moved on. Both men were enthralled by the natural world of this locality though their passions were worlds apart. Palmer, a romantic visionary, clung to a timeless view of his surroundings whereas Darwin constantly sought to explain the small changes he observed day to day (and therefore had to be happening so substantially through millennia). Moss has changed relatively little over 400 million years. Palmer evidently took more interest in it than Darwin did.

3

Equisetum arvense
Field Horsetail

If you are unfortunate enough to have horsetails in your garden, console yourself for a moment that you have the most extraordinary survivors – plants found in that very early branch, the monilophytes, as are the ferns as well. Here is true primeval grit manifesting itself in some of the earliest plants. With this grit they hoisted themselves fully off the ground for the first time – silica-fortified node (stalk segment) by silica-fortified node – nearly 400 million years ago.

Horsetails stand out for their unique primitive form and lifestyle. A lifestyle so unique as to make them one of the most unwelcome garden guests of all. They are particularly at home in acidic and damp soils, but that does not stop them from installing themselves in all sorts of other places too.

There is fossil evidence of horsetails from the Devonian geological period. They appeared to luxuriate through the long lush Carboniferous period and then to survive a prolonged drought before succumbing to 100 million years of hungry herbivorous dinosaurs. Perhaps they pulled through by ever reselecting themselves to become ever more inedible, as indeed they are now to all grazing animals. Grittiness from a high silica content ensures this. Traditionally, we have taken advantage of this abrasiveness to use stems to scour pots and pans and to polish metal too. Now it also has an even classier status for being known to hold traces of gold, cadmium, zinc and other notable minerals.

On first examination and earlier in its season, it is intriguingly cute with its regular whorls of thin stalk-like leaves which are aptly described by other local names like 'bottle brush', 'horse pipes', 'snake grass' and 'poor man's pine'. But we are talking about a persistent perennial invader adept at mingling and cannily unobtrusive at first, with a lush mid-summer growth spurt and, most disturbingly, with a massive underground network in the form of rhizomes (spreading underground stems). These take the form of hairy blackish threads which extend horizontally and vertically in successive layers down a metre and more – and at such a pace. A 10 centimetre rhizome was once seen to have extended 64 metres in a year.

And then there is spore production which takes place at the beginning of the annual above-ground lifecycle with the emergence of pale cone-bearing stems often described as 'stove-pipe'-like. These last for just ten days (and are a weird and wonderful sight well worth looking out for) during which time each cone can release 100,000 spores, which germinate quickly on a damp surface but where survival is most precarious and unlikely. Even so, it only needs one to slip through.

WHAT TO DO

- Throwing up your arms in despair is an understandable first reaction. Weedkillers will often just wipe out all other plants to give horsetails an even freer rein.
- A concerted combined approach over several years is the only chance of reducing (if not eradicating) horsetail infestation. This might include repeated cultivation; persistent cutting of both spore-bearing and vegetative shoots; continual mowing (will work); extended exclusion of light by the toughest mulching membranes or whatever; improved drainage to induce dessication; application of lime to reduce acidity and enhanced soil structure and fertility to promote stronger competitors to supplant the horsetails.

4

Pteridium aquilinum
Bracken

Following horsetails, also on the monilophytes branch albeit a few million years later in the Carboniferous geological period, came ferns even more luxuriantly living it up – and literally upwards too – when much of our land mass was hovering over the equator and its hot steamy conditions. These are among the first plants able to lift themselves wholesale off the ground with a vascular structure – in effect a simple wick which both supports and transports water upwards.

Today, we have bracken to contend with. Its branching stem can rise a couple of metres to overshadow all other undergrowth and so become one of the world's most dominating and most unwanted plants, covering all continents bar Antarctica. It has even taken over three per cent of the surface area of Britain and is still spreading aggressively, especially over grassy uplands. If that is not enough, what we see is only a fraction of the plant's bio-mass which primarily consists of a massive root system, with rhizomes in action again.

The roots go both deep and wide. If the soil allows they can descend a metre or so, becoming denser and thicker to serve as storage organs. The rhizomes (the horizontally extending shoots) are slimmer and will constantly break out of the soil surface with frond buds. A single bracken plant can extend itself to create a clone up to 400 metres in width. So it presents a huge underground invasive threat. What hope, then, of removing it? Especially when single living clones have been found (in Finland) to date back to the Iron Age.

Fronds uncurl crozier-like (and disarmingly elegant) from the emergent buds in early summer and, if damaged, they are immediately supplanted by back-up dormant buds at their base. Although each frond sheds spores in their multi-millions, these require highly delicate conditions to generate new plants and so are largely wasted – just as with the field horsetails. In our gardens, bracken needs to be watched in marginal or wilder areas but because it is so conspicuous it rarely gets a toe-hold in cultivated beds. But take note! For sheer nastiness, bracken is virtually unsurpassable. It is a rampant pasture coloniser; a coarse brute whose tough stems readily cut hands giving it a tug; severely toxic and known to cause stomach cancers if fronds are eaten (as they are by Japanese people); a producer of spores which are highly carcinogenic to us all; a cause of ulceration and blood loss in cattle, and of

RIGHT Bracken here is encroaching into the longer grass area of a large garden. It has a place but for how long?

WEEDS, WEEDING (& DARWIN)

blindness in sheep, though they usually shun it and let it take over their pasture; the habitat of sheep ticks which transmit Lyme disease; and it is repellent to birds and other wild life.

As Darwin latterly commented, it is so nasty that, 'no plant is so little attacked by enemies as the common bracken-fern'. But it can be useful. It is harvested as cattle litter in areas where straw is scarce. Stacked and rotted, it can provide a useful soil conditioner and a garden mulch with special weed-inhibiting properties. And now it is being investigated as a source of bio-fuel. Vile weed and possible eco-saviour, a schizophrenic plant indeed.

WHAT TO DO

- In flower beds, pull out any showing shoots. They probably arrived with compost.
- In wilder garden areas, control by repeated mowing or strimming through summer to prevent any significant growth.
- Bruise emerging fronds, causing them to bleed and weaken, with a roller or a lawnmower with a roller, or a specialist 'bruising' machine.
- Repeatedly slash cut, especially before August.
- But do not burn. This only stimulates a vigorous comeback.

Gymnosperms

Now to a distinctly more substantial branch, that of the 'naked seed' gymnosperms. Having seeds for the first time enables plants to proliferate more freely – a capacity later to be a major asset for weeds. Gymnosperm seeds are 'naked' in the sense of not being enclosed by a fruit wall. The plant group comprises conifers, ginkgos and cycads. It is only among the conifers that we find a relatively small spot of bother.

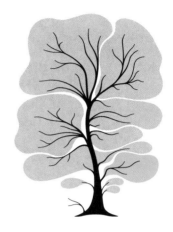

5

X *Cupressocyparis leylandii*
Leyland Cypress

Usually known just as 'Leylandii', this hedging plant jarringly appears right here as a sole representative of the gymnosperms.

Strange, isn't it, that we somehow express our mixed feelings about this one by generally referring to it just by its second Latin name? We appreciate this cypress for its fast hedge-growing qualities, for its windbreak uses and also as a fine specimen tree in itself, but then at the same time just the name of our representative, Leylandii, can evoke a knee-jerk horror: that of a neighbour's ragged overgrown hedge blocking out sunlight and obscuring distant views. 'Unwanted' barely begins to cover the feelings that this one sometimes arouses and, it has to be admitted, there can a strong element of snobbish disdain too. A weed? Perhaps too contemptible on occasion to be called even that. But here it is, a strong candidate in our list of plants capable of being truly problematic.

And note the X in front of this one's full name. It indicates what was thought to be a particularly clever hybrid cross not just between two species but between two different genera. The cross was originally achieved in 1888 when female cones of *Cupressus macrocarpa* were successfully fertilised with the pollen of *Chamaecyparis nootkatensis* on

RIGHT A wall of Leylandii is now an all-too-familiar and unbecoming feature of many a rural landscape. Unknown in Darwin's time, here it is blocking most of his former view towards Downe village.

WEEDS, WEEDING (& DARWIN)

the Leighton Hall Estate in Powys, Wales. 'What was thought to be' now looks as if it was no more than that. Current molecular examination of the two genera indicates they could well be one and the same genus. Somehow it was the proprietor of the estate, CJ Leyland, whose name got attached to the hybrid and whose name still stands in everyday usage.

Successive similar crosses refined the quality of this new wonder hedging plant which can grow a metre a year to make quick and effective screens and windbreaks and nurserymen rich (the plant being very easy to mass produce from cuttings). Soon it also made neighbours fall out. So bad have neighbour relations occasionally become that violence has ensued, with even a murder in 2001 (in Powys too). The problem was acknowledged in Part VIII of the Anti-social Behaviour Act 2003, also known as 'the Leylandii Law', which gave local authorities the power to reduce the height of such obstructing hedges.

A conifer carefully manipulated by us turns out to be the one to give us most trouble while also providing an invaluable asset. So is there a lesson here? At least we might remind ourselves that this innovation was an outcome of the heady times of horticultural enterprise during Darwin's century, and that it was to the ingenuity of plant breeders in creating new garden plants that Darwin looked first in the opening chapter of the *Origin*.

WHAT TO DO
- First try a charm offensive on your neighbours. Invite them to see your side.
- If that does not work, ask your council to have the hedge lowered.
- If you have a Leylandii hedge (and it can be fine), make sure it is pruned every year at a comfortably accessible height. And perhaps use some of the more interesting varieties, 'Castlewellan Gold', for example.

AND THEN, flowering plants burst upon the scene –'the new weeds'! The most stunning breakthrough in plant evolution was the arrival of angiosperms, the flowering plants, in the lower Cretaceous period around 140 million years ago. Here were dramatically different plants, marked out, most especially, by a new ultra-sophisticated reproductive system requiring flowers – in essence, one involving the process of pollination and all that goes with it.

The idea of pollination, as is well known, absolutely hooked Darwin – as did, of course, the host of new insects on which the new plants, too, became symbiotically dependent. There was sufficient uncovering of fossil evidence in Darwin's time for him to realise that the breakthrough had been sudden and spectacular but he stayed puzzled, indeed increasingly exasperated, as to just why and how. In a letter of 1879 to his great friend, Joseph Hooker, the director of the Royal Botanic Gardens at Kew, he complained that 'the rapid development, as far as we can judge of all higher plants within recent geological history is an abominable mystery'.

This 'abominable mystery' has remained in the air virtually to this day. But in the last few years, as well as some fine new fossil discoveries, there has been a flush of scientific papers offering a whole raft of possible explanations, no doubt spurred on by the big 2009 Darwin anniversary celebration. It is now agreed that the 'mystery' is not nearly as inexplicable as it was. One such paper was from Sherwin Carlquist, a research botanist at the Santa Barbara Botanic Garden. He titles it, as if just for us, 'Weeds that re-invented weediness: flowering plants are the new weeds, able to keep re-inventing new forms and wood patterns'. As he elaborated, 'using juvenile tendencies' … they (the first angiosperms) are the 'new kids on the block, the weedy newcomers that change and adapt rapidly'. Need we say more, except to introduce the first band of the newcomers.

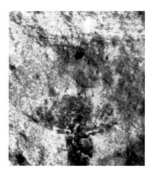

ABOVE For us to have a peep at what one of those earliest flowers, 'new weeds', actually looked like in the form of a trace on a piece of stone is a rare and amazing privilege, and especially as we have only been able to do so in the last very few years. Here is a photograph of *Bevhalstia pebja*, a fossil plant discovered in a Sussex quarry. It is itself an extreme rarity among plant fossils for portraying the outline of a cup-like form, one of just 8 mm across. It is tempting to see this as a precursor to the buttercup whose family is already known to be among the more 'primitive' of the flowering plants. In actual fact, it is more likely to be an aquatic plant, possibly something more closely related to the first water lilies.

Basal Angiosperms: Minor Groups

Here we are with a few remnants of the earliest flowering plants in their first significant branching. A pretty odd mixed bag they are too, as the clunking title given to the whole branch suggests. Laurels, magnolias, pepper (the spice) and water lilies have very little in common, let alone any obvious shared ancestor. The DNA people admit that these are 'simply grouped together at the base of the phylogenetic tree by being excluded from the rest of the flowering plants'. Lumped and dumped there, it seems. But among them, most definitely, is our next weed candidate.

Plant families now take on a special significance. Weed names will be shown with their family names and the name of the order to which they belong will appear up the side of the page.

6

Nuphar luteum
NYMPHAEACEAE
Water Lily

The simple water lily – the 'brandy bottle', yellow one – is weedily prolific and half clogs up many a murky watercourse, inhibiting boating and even swimming. And then in the garden pond many of its flashier cousins are known for attempting total takeovers. So, surprise surprise, even the innocent water lily can manifest the insidious qualities of weediness and incidentally show us how elastic the concept of a weed can be.

WHAT DO TO
• Constantly divide and reduce waterlilies of every kind to avoid pond take-overs.

Nymphaeales

Basal Angiosperms: Monocots

Now we join our first truly distinctive group of substantial size. This one is singular on three counts:

- It is much the largest branch we have joined so far.
- It is monophyletic (i.e. all its species share a single ancestor), unlike the previous basal angiosperm groupings which we have just visited.
- All the represented species are monocots, i.e. distinctive by having single cotyledons (seed leaves) and a shared range of associated characteristics.

Traditionally botanists neatly divided angiosperms into two subclasses: monocotyledonae (monocots) and dicotyledonae (dicots). Now, with recent DNA revelations, this division does not appear to be so simple. A revised ordering sees the monocots as just one of several major angiosperm branches (as the arrangement of these major branches on the tree makes evident), albeit one claiming almost a quarter of all flowering species – and a fair share of eligible weeds.

7

Potamogeton spp.
POTAMOGETONACEAE
Pondweed

With an ornamental pond, your garden becomes complete – a satisfying ecological entity. But look out! This pond can also generate weeds like no other area. The contained space ensures that the water rapidly warms up in summer and the plants will grow like mad, quickly becoming overcrowded and weed-like. The pond is a great attraction, too, for birds to cool themselves and have a drink while bringing in (and taking out) additional material on their feet and feathers to add to the chaotic vegetation. 'I do not believe that botanists are aware how charged the mud of ponds is with seeds', Darwin emphatically pointed out after doing his own tests on such mud.

WEEDS, WEEDING (& DARWIN)

It therefore does not come as much of a surprise to find that there is a regular aquatic plant named simply 'Pondweed' (*Potamogeton*, which comes in many different species). Darwin happened to comment about this one: 'even small fish swallow seeds of moderate size as of...Potamogeton'.

Quite nice it is too, in moderation and for a while. Varieties will often be on sale at aquatic centres. Its floating pale green oval-shaped leaf pads complement those of water lilies. But, wait for it, this one multiplies vigorously and can easily turn into quite a mess.

Much the same can be said about several other standard 'pondweed' plants like:
- *Elodea canadensis* (Canadian Pondweed). A submerged plant and a much recommended oxygenator.
- *Aponogeton distachios* (Cape Pondweed)
- *Lagarosiphon major* (Curled Pondweed)
- *Elodea nuttallii* (Nuttall's Pondweed) and others all belonging to this same plant group. Of course, there are many other anonymous plants which just appear and get dismissed as 'pond weeds'.

N.B. As if the above were not enough, when we meet the core eudicots (at Weed 22) we will find further aquatic weeds which are highly alarming as pond escapees.

WHAT DO TO
- Note that all of the above 'pondweeds' can play a useful supporting role in your pond but that they need to be watched and restrained from total takeovers.

RIGHT Pondweed playing an integral role in the wildlife of a natural pond. Has it a part to play in a garden pond as well, or will it be just a weed? That's the challenge for gardeners to resolve.

Alismatales

8

Lemna spp.

ARACEAE
Duckweed

Spot the dots! Bits of duckweed, you may recall, were spotted right at the beginning of this story, dotted around the green algae photographed for Weed 1. You can spot a sprinkling of them in almost any pond at some time or other and even as extras in the photos of aquatic plants in the *RHS Gardeners' Encyclopedia of Plants & Flowers*. If you forget about your pond for a few days, you may be astonished to suddenly find it totally covered by the stuff, as if overnight someone had spread a dainty dappled-green tablecloth over the water.

'Duckweed', it becomes clear, is a collective noun for vast numbers of tiny floating plants which can assemble together in various densities. It is tempting to patronise them as plantlets, but in their 2–3 mm diameter sizes they are already impressively mature plants. Single duckweeds have the dubious honour of being the smallest of all flowering plants. The ones we are meeting, the *Lemnae*, are in the middle range of duckweed sizes having the basic measurement given above. There is an even smalller genus, *Wolfia*, which is only 0.5 mm wide.

Look closely at just one *Lemna* and you will see an impressive organism. What looks like a tiny leaf, or a bunch of three tiny rounded leaves, is in fact its basic structure known as a 'thallus', in effect a miniscule raft with a rudder-like single root and with a mother

WEEDS, WEEDING (& DARWIN)

Alismatales

segment from which two daughter segments grow out from buds. All this ensures an ongoing process of vegetative reproduction by which it can double its colony size every two to three days. That sounds alarming but somehow the colony size seems to ebb and flow without always overwhelming everything else. Then rather mysteriously, it will sometimes disappear as fast as it arrives.

The flower is much harder to spot. It appears on the thallus towards its edges: two stamen with pollen laden anthers atop and, above an ovary, a single stile supporting a cup-shaped stigma, and that is all – no petals or sepals. Barely visible flashes of white from the anthers signal the flowering. As if to satisfy Darwin posthumously, it was worked out that an elaborate rigmarole ensures cross-pollination even when the sexual parts are so close to each other on one plant. Seeds and fragments of thallus fall to the pond floor to ensure a next generation arising at the end of a freezing winter.

As we have been gently hinting so far, the presence of duckweed is by no means all bad. In addition to the saving grace of could-look-worse and so on, it is known that a covering of duck weed in midsummer can act as a defence against the sun overheating the water and as a barrier mitigating rapid evaporation. Also *Lemna* has a high protein content. In certain parts of the world it is farmed for livestock and human consumption. There is an implication that this is an as yet largely untapped food resource. *Lemna* is used quite extensively for 'bioremediation' of polluted water and is also used in assessing toxicity of chemicals. And then *Lemna* has been adapted by molecular biologists to 'express' proteins of pharmaceutical interest. Apparently a dramatic advance.

However, all this cannot compensate for the times when duckweed takes over ponds and forever comes back despite all of our efforts.

WHAT TO DO

- Perhaps introduce carp into you pond. They feast on duckweed and as likely as not will eliminate it. But note that carp also feast on much else and are incompatible with wild life like frogs, newts and so on.
- Scoop out regularly to minimise its presence rather than eliminate.
- Apply 'Duckweed Control'. This is a product for biological control. It contains a bacterial culture which removes nutrients from the water and so makes life more difficult for duckweed (and presumably for other pondweeds).

LEFT Duckweed is our smallest weed by far but, unfortunately, that does not stop vast colonies of it taking over garden ponds.

Alismatales

9

Arum maculatum
ARACEAE
Arum Lily / Cuckoo Pint

At last out of the water comes the arum lily, alias cuckoo pint or lords and ladies. This is a plant which the gardeners at Kew single out as one of their most nuisance weeds.

Strange indeed that arum lily belongs to the same family as the duckweed above. A plant like this which wraps a cloak ('spathe') around its flowering structure has to be suspicious. The suspicion arises right from the start as this oddball plant will often be the first to emerge

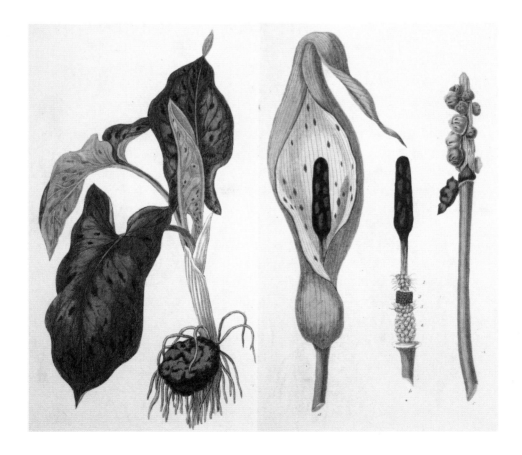

WEEDS, WEEDING (& DARWIN)

Alismatales

out of bare ground in the new year, looking to all intents and purposes like the first weed with its nondescript bunch of semi-rolled-up leaves. Usually we can relax, knowing that the cheeky new arrival will soon be overtaken by much else. But then, some months later comes a much more serious alarm: a head of deadly poisonous red berries appears.

What happened in the meantime? A bizarre flower emerged on a 'spadix' (a poker-like form as is shown here). We have to say here that the spathe total wraparound worried Darwin, and at that critical moment in May 1842 while he was staying with his in-laws and going on to make that first 'pencil sketch' of his theory. He was much exercised that the spathe looked as if it would prevent insects from carrying away pollen to enable cross-fertilisation elsewhere. Thirty years later he triumphantly wrote up his findings in his book *The effects of Cross-and Self-Fertilisation in the vegetable kingdom*. What it took for midges to do their job and for Darwin to find out were both extraordinary. He explained:

The spathes of **Arum maculatum** are furnished with filaments apparently adapted to prevent the exit of insects…. On examining several spathes, from thirty to sixty minute Diptera [midges] belonging to three species were found in some of them; and many of these insects were lying dead at the bottom, as if they had been permanently entrapped. In order to discover whether the living ones could escape and carry pollen to another plant, I tied in the spring of 1842 a fine muslin bag tightly round a spathe; and on returning in an hour's time several little flies were crawling about on the inner surface of the bag. I then gathered a spathe and breathed hard into it; several flies soon crawled out, and all without exception were dusted with **arum** pollen. These flies quickly flew away, and I distinctly saw three of them fly to another plant about a yard off; they alighted on the inner or concave surface of the spathe, and suddenly flew down into the flower. I then opened this flower, and although not a single anther had burst, several grains of pollen were lying at the bottom, which must have been brought from another plant by one of these flies or by some other insect. In another flower little flies were crawling about, and I saw them leave pollen on the stigmas.

WHAT TO DO
- Read the above Darwin description a second time to fully appreciate the cunning both of the arum lily and of Darwin in unravelling it.
- Find an arum with a spathe to try your own observations.
- And, of course, keep this freak under firm control.

LEFT The ever bizarre arum lily as pictured in Stephenson's *Medical Botany*, 1834.

Alismatales

10

Iris foetidissima
IRIDACEAE
Stinking Iris

We seem to know this iris by its scientific name and by a common name in almost equal measure, as if to emphasise its wavering status: part respectable old-time garden player, part prestigious subtle-coloured speciality, part wild-flower visitor and part out-and-out rogue. While arum lilies are sometimes pilloried for having a moment of smelling of rotten flesh, these irises claim to smell of roast beef, although one herbal speaks of 'a lothsome smell or stinke'. It is that outrageous streak which interests us here – the

WEEDS, WEEDING (& DARWIN)

indomitable capacity to strike out anywhere and everywhere and to hoodwink us that it is still an honourable companion. That said, this character does take care of the shady, rubble-strewn, negligible-soil areas. It will also take care of too many other parts of the garden, if allowed, but not in an overwhelming way (and so getting away with it again, with our quiet cognisance of its background presence). Like the arum, it has a later appealing flush of red berries, this time cheering up the late autumn and winter with the fruits attractively bursting out of a large pod.

WHAT TO DO
• Perhaps keep in moderation if you wish. But be ruthless with it, if needs be.

Not forgetting from the family:
• *Iris pseudocorus*. The yellow flag and great hanger-on of ponds, if allowed. A classic of the wild where it is probably best left.
• *Crocosmia aurea* (Montbretia). A South African import, which for many of us has had its time: over familiar, over garish and over extending itself, to the extent of being a dubious garden escapee as well.

And then from the closely related Amaryllidaceae:
• *Agapanthus praecox*. An amazing plant on all counts. Another native of the Cape, it found its way to Britain in the mid seventeenth century to be much prized to this day even to the extent that an image of its flower has been used on the RHS membership cards. But in Australia and New Zealand it has done so well as to become a pervasive wayside weed and thus fervently unwanted in many gardens as an aggressive commoner. Beware the agapanthus Down Under!

LEFT Iris reveals all. An exquisite flower typically let down by ragged unsightly foliage, and a slug in residence too.

Asparagales

II

Hyacinthoides non–scripta

IRIDACEAE
Bluebell

Bluebells in flower are simply glorious, and most especially when seen en masse in woodland on a bright late-spring day. So why not just bring a few of the charmers into the garden to brighten up the base of a tree, all in the finest gardening tradition of reflecting nature? Why not? A first answer to this question is that of the law. The Wildlife and Countryside Act 1981 made the bluebell a protected species. This was followed by an

amendment in 1998 making it an offence to trade in wild common bluebell bulbs or seeds. It is shameful that such legislation was deemed necessary but at the same time it is gratifying that this simple plant should acquire prized status. Even though it is now easy to find bluebells propagated and marketed by reputable nurserymen, it is hard not to feel disapproval in the air regarding bluebells in gardens.

Many gardeners share this distaste, if not profound irritation, for a rather different reason. To put it bluntly, bluebells can be dreadful weeds, ones which come and come again in all the spots we really do not want them. Not only that, they resolutely resist being tugged out when the leaves come through. Swollen bulbs at the base of the leaves and a mop of fibrous rootlets firmly secure the plant into the ground. All right, the period of blooming gives some reward, but not for long. Much longer and distinctly tiresome is the gradual die-back of the leaves lying across the ground in unsightly patches.

If left to their own devices, bluebells readily go on to generate multiple offshoot bulbs and to set quantities of all-too-viable seed. It is win-win all the way for bluebells in the garden unless persistent and consistent action is taken (see below).

To deepen the aggravation *Hyancinthoides hispanica*, the Spanish bluebell, has appeared on the scene. Who can have thought of introducing and promoting this as the new-must-have plant to brighten up the border in that tricky in-between-seasons time? A large number of us fell for this imposing stouter variation on the common bluebell whose flowers stand assertively upright. But, oh dear, it has changed the face of bluebells in many gardens, hybridising all too readily with the natives and creating an even more vigorous stock and, therefore, a more invasive one. From gardens the hybrids have found their way out onto verges and back into the woods. Talk of genies out of bottles, here seems to be a greater threat than the Wildlife and Countryside Act of 1981 ever envisaged.

WHAT TO DO

- Dig up and destroy all Spanish bluebell-affected plants if you want to try and stay native.
- Use a fork or a long narrow trowel to take out all new plants as they emerge and do not be deceived that they could be more interesting bulbs. Likewise destroy – perhaps in a bin full of water.

LEFT Who could ever think this flower unwanted in a garden? Here under a tree in late spring it plays the perfect part. But it is not so welcome when it all too readily finds its way into those beds across the lawn.

Asparagales

12

Carex pendula
CYPERACEAE
Pendulous Sedge / Hanging Sedge

Both the next two candidates, a sedge and a rush, as often as not get labelled 'marginals', generally referring to their association with waterside situations. Their common names appear to be marginal too (with two equally valid choices for each species, making it difficult to know which one to use) and, most significantly for us, a question mark arises as to their marginality as regards our current expectations of gardens.

Carex pendula pushes itself onto this list just as it pushed itself into gardens only later to find itself pushed out again to hang around the other side of the garden wall. It is a native of Western Europe and in recent years it has appeared to become a native of many a garden, no doubt marketed by garden centres as a robust ornamental grass (though it is not a grass) when such things were in strong fashion. When its flowers are in full pendulous bloom, the plant is certainly attractive but, compared with most of the grasses of comparable size, it lacks finesse. Its asset, if you like, is that it can tough it out as a perennial evergreen piece, and claim some architectural stature too. It can be useful for taking care of a relatively shady space. But is that enough? This sedge's place in the garden therefore hangs in the balance. If allowed to stay, it will continue to push out its rhizomatous roots and hang out its seeds to multiply with disconcerting persistence. Be warned! We have reason to be wary of it as one species of the sedge family, *Cyperus rotundus* (purple nut sedge) was, in America in 1977, declared 'the world's worst weed'.

WHAT TO DO
- Be prepared for a ruthless decision to reduce radically or even remove.
- Think imaginatively for an alternative. *Carex oshimensis* is a variegated sedge with an RHS Award of Garden Merit.

Poales

RIGHT Pendulous sedge gracefully going to seed. But how far this vigorous plant merits significant garden space through the year is another question.

WEEDS, WEEDING (& DARWIN)

WEEDS, WEEDING (& DARWIN)

I3

Juncus communis
JUNCACEAE
Common Rush / Soft Rush

A modest tuft of 'rush' beside a garden pond can look just right. To include a representative of the rush family in a garden also demonstrates the diversity of your plant collection, and the common or soft rush does this with as much aplomb and charm as any other members of this family (which have their own eclectic range of members: hard rush, frog marsh rush, sharp-flowered rush, blunt field rush, jointed rush, and so on). Its dull-green tubular leaves with their spongy interiors and their neat little flowering beards sprouting midway up them are together so characteristically distinctive and yet look comfortable with most other plants around them.

But a patch of this rush elsewhere in the garden is that classic dreaded indicator of a potential major problem: poor drainage or even severe water-logging.

WHAT TO DO
- Either address the drainage issue...
- Or exploit the site and go to town with rushes of all kinds. But we warned! Hard rush (*Juncus inflexus*) has an exceptional seed output per plant with a count of 200,000 – 234,000 (Hill).

LEFT Common rush is gently untidy and brings a soft naturalness to the edge of a garden pond. Its presence is a reminder that the natural world has much to contribute to gardens including, sometimes, offering strong signals that attention to better drainage may be needed when it appears away from ponds.

Poales

14

POACEAE
Grass

In this entry alone we are treating a vast family as an entity in itself, though focusing primarily on turf grasses. And let's note straightaway that, while grasses appear quite early on in this evolutionary story, they are relative newcomers. They are more recent manifestations of the monocots in that they developed in tandem with grazing animals – in the last 20 million years or so.

Quite simply there is an awful lot of grass. Continuous 'grassland' of one kind and another covers nearly a third of the world's land surface and, of course, scatterings of a wide variety of grasses also extend much further. There are just over 10,000 species in the whole grass family, including those to be found in turf, all the cereals and the taller and more robust specimens like bamboos. It is hardly surprising that some grass will turn out to be troublesome at times. It will be troublesome too for playing host to a good many other plants which can be nuisances. Albrecht Dürer illustrated this beautifully for us way back at the beginning of the sixteenth century (see page 6).

Then take a look at a traditional garden lawn where the grass is generally mown. What a lot of laborious attention this entails. If we fail to mow a lawn for a few weeks in the growing season it will quickly go to flower and become a scruffy weed-like mess or even eventually look like Dürer's turf. In fact Darwin did just this in an experiment on his lawn which we will come to in the next chapter.

But obviously lawns are by no means all problematic. They are, after all, a much prized defining characteristic of the typical British garden, providing that key backdrop space which sets off everything else while making room for us to walk about and enjoy, to go about and weed, to sit or even lie down and relax, as well as itself serving as an inviting children's playground. Good lawns have their precise edges but, aha, these are, in effect frontiers which need to be guarded. When some of their constituent grasses and allies cross their own frontiers into flower or other beds, they invariably look out of place and cry out to be removed. When we take action, most of us most of the time do not easily distinguish one turf grass from another and certainly not to the extent of readily being able to name them all. We have the excuse that there are so many, but three species deserve briefly to be highlighted here: annual meadow grass, couch grass and rye grass.

Poales

Poa annua
Annual Meadow Grass

Annual meadow grass is no mere annual. It is an 'ephemeral' (the botanical term for a plant with a short life cycle which can be completed many times in a growing season). Shepherd's purse, thale cress, groundsel and chickweed are other particularly notorious examples (we will be meeting them later). Most of them will linger and grow on for some time once finding their spot but they will have let go their first seeds within a month or so from themselves first emerging.

Annual meadow grass is itself spurred on in the race to multiply by self-fertilising and sometimes even by bypassing sexual fertilisation altogether. It is one of the first and most common grasses to appear as seedlings and is relatively easy and satisfying to spot and identify, being 'a loosely tufted plant with hairless leaves, often transversely crinkled when young and with a boat-like tip', as Edward Salisbury neatly summarises. As he also points out, identifiable as they are, young seedlings can often get away with it by having purplish inflorescences (arrangements of flowers)which act as a camouflage against many soils. In its defence, we can say that this one is an adept pioneer, one of the first little plants to move into a newly worked piece of ground, and then quite prepared to make way for something else.

WHAT TO DO
- Remove on first sight (while peering hard not to miss any).
- Watch where you tread. Seeds readily stick to boots.

LEFT Annual meadow grass characteristically appearing where it is not wanted, and already shedding seeds early in the season for a next generation to follow fast on its heels.

Poales

Elytrigia repens
Couch Grass / Twitch

Mention of couch invariably comes with a sharp intake of breath, and it is those tough, almost wiry, rhizomatous roots which especially give the game away and raise levels of despair.

Seemingly entrenched in a raspberry bed, couch leaves reveal themselves relatively innocently, as on the left below, and there on the right is what had lain underneath them or rather just what could be forked out without going too far in harming the raspberry roots. Not only will these rhizomes penetrate and entwine into other root networks with their sharp tips but they can penetrate plant tissue itself, notoriously going into a potato and out the other side.

WHAT TO DO
- Regular cultivation will wear them out, but that is not so easy once they have found the base of a fruit bush.

Lolium spp.
Rye Grasses

The standard rye grass, *Lolium perenne*, is a recommended ingredient for well-trodden back lawns and sports fields. Sometimes its known resilience will be too much for its own good, overpowering other grasses and creating an unseemly coarse appearance. It is 'well hard' as they say. Beware!

And we should not forget *Lolium temulentum* or darnel, the 'tares' scourge of biblical times and of Shakespeare's as a polluter of wheat crops. 'Want ye corn for bread? 'tis full of Darnel; do ye like the taste?' is how the bard references it in *Henry V1*. Now, as Salisbury proclaimed in the 1960s, it is virtually extinct in cornfields, largely due to effective fine screening of seeds.

WHAT TO DO
- Enjoy feeling smug that darnel is no longer with us as a menace.
- Only introduce rye grass in extreme moderation in gardens unless you treat your lawn as a football pitch.

LEFT Couch grass and an exposed display of its pernicious rhizomes dug out of the ground.
RIGHT Rye grass is the notorious hard-wearing lawn grass used for well trampled back lawns. But sometimes it can be a little too enduring to the detriment of other grasses and garden plants.

Poales

Early Diverging Eudicots

These are the first true ('eu') dicotyledonous flowering plants. For us, the principal component of the early diverging eudicots is the ranunculale order, and, as one might expect, its main family is the ranunculaceae, the buttercups. We also meet papaveraceae, the poppy family, and its subfamily fumaraceae, and, rather more curiously, berberidaceae. So, on to our next weed.

15

Ranunculus repens
RANUNCULACEAE
Creeping Buttercup

A single flower of *Ranunculus repens,* if you stop to look at it closely, is quite breathtaking in its simple beauty. Its golden glow innocently encapsulates summer sunshine, radiating purity and perfection. And, to bring us a little more down to earth, a fatty glisten ensures that this gem is deliciously evocative of fresh farm butter – hence its most commonly used

RIGHT A creeping buttercup flower is as alluring as can be.

WEEDS, WEEDING (& DARWIN)

name. Yet, as we all too readily know, this enchanter will also act up as a most persistent and pernicious garden interferer. 'Devil's guts', 'granny threads', 'ram's claws', 'sitfast' and 'tether toad' – to give but a few of this weed's historic common names – together give us a vivid picture of an exceptionally tenacious character.

All this, already, for a small plant which is traditionally denoted 'primitive', that is a plant reckoned to be among those having the fewest known ancestors. The basic simplicity of its flower structure is why so often we are asked to draw it at our first botany lesson. Here it is in cross section showing those concentric whorls of sepals, petals and stamens around a spiralled cluster of carpels each tipped with a stigma and enclosing an ovary.

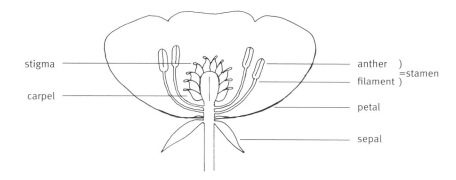

Bear with us now for an extended introduction to this jewel-cum-menace. It is by far the most detailed of our plant profiles as it sets the background to all its successors and also happens to touch upon a key moment of Darwin's life and work.

To start with, and intriguingly for our whole story, we note that 'great numbers of the *Ranunculus repens*' flowering 'in a field of wretchedly sterile clay' happened to catch and hold Darwin's attention at a most timely moment. They appear to be his first recorded natural history observation at Down House in Kent, made within a month or so of moving into his new home in the autumn of 1842. Of course, there had to be something special about these particular buttercups. But before being diverted into discussing an anomaly, we should outline carefully this plant's already remarkable regular characteristics.

Having a particular attraction to damp compacted ground like that 'wretchedly sterile clay', *Ranunculus repens* is often to be found in trodden garden margins and in trampled lawns, from where it will creep readily into flower beds. Once into open fertile soil worked by us, the villains luxuriate. This buttercup is an opportunist par excellence.

Ranunculales

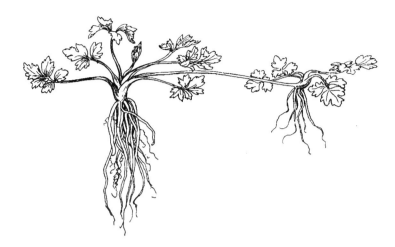

First, early in the year there are those shrunken rosettes of leaves already claiming their own patches of ground, as often as not in a little cluster of their own. These leaves emerge from a thickened stem which is secured into the soil with a mop of stout root strands. These easily resist our first attempts to tug them out. What is more, the roots secrete toxins and appear to deplete the soil of potassium, thereby inhibiting the growth of nearby competitors. The compact little plants are well able to withstand trampling and compaction while gradually expanding, with a succession of new leaf tips emerging from the 'apical meristem' (central growing tip).

Eventually, if allowed, there rises a branching stalk with buds which then open into a small array of flowers. Each of the flower parts – sepals, petals, stamens and carpels – in their concentric whorls are, in effect, modified leaves. Not all buttercup plants flower, perhaps wisely, so to speak conserving their energies, but most of those which do flower invite insect cross-pollination. If that does not work out, self-pollination can take place too. The fertilisation success rate of this 'primitive flower' is an unusually strong one. Each flower – and here we go with the inevitable painstakingly researched statistics – produces 20–30 seeds, each flowering shoot produces 140 seeds, and each plant produces an average of 687 seeds a season (Garden Organic).

Then those plentiful seeds disperse, somehow all too freely and perhaps most notoriously through the assistance of grazing animals, even though buttercups are not particularly palatable and are apt to give sheep and cattle diarrhoea. All the same, there is no better way to introduce a crop of the finest buttercups around your roses or into a kitchen garden than to apply some farmyard or stable manure.

Yet even though they may be extremely plentiful, thoroughly dispersed and well ripened, the seeds are not ready to germinate straightaway. In fact, they are deeply dormant at first

WEEDS, WEEDING (& DARWIN)

and need a varied period of 'after-ripening' which will then lead to sporadic seedling emergence. This can occur throughout the year, even during a frost. They can also wait, buried in a reserve soil 'seed bank' for up to seven years, ready to seize any opportunity that might arise from fresh turning of the ground. Even that is not necessarily the end of it. Seed from excavations dated at 80 years is reported to have germinated. The capacity to spin out germination over days, weeks, months, years and even decades gives creeping buttercups and, as we shall see, many other weeds an enormous survival advantage.

While parent plants might be knocked out by extreme conditions of drought, flooding, freeze-ups, predation or whatever, their lying-in-wait seeds ensure the continuity of the plant population. Furthermore, each buttercup seed is genetically unique as a consequence of the shuffling of parental genetic material and the random combinations of 'gametes' (fertilising cells) and this provides a major extra advantage for species survival. The inherited diversity of sexually produced offspring leads to genetic flexibility and a good chance of there being an exceptional variant somewhere that is able to survive an extinction event to set going a new line of suitably adapted plants.

Well, it was the sight of buttercup variants, in fact ones with double and even treble rows of petals, which especially aroused Darwin's curiosity during his first weeks at his new country home in late September 1842. To appreciate why this phenomenon grabbed the attention of the young family man, it is worthwhile stopping for a moment to look at what was happening in his life just then.

Eager to be away from the bustle, noise and grime of central London (and the increasing disturbances from rioting early Chartists at the end of his street), Darwin had taken his wife and two young children to spend much of the summer of 1842 at his in-laws in Staffordshire. There, apart from trying to secure a loan from his father to enable that move out of London and apart from becoming absorbed in a spell of 'botanising' and making an excursion to North Wales, he used a couple of weeks of peace and quiet to pencil a first brief sketch of his 'species theory' – thirty-five scrawled folio pages in all.

In this 'sketch', as he called it, he outlined how variation and selection occurred under domestication and then he elaborated on the less pronounced variation arising in nature. He alluded to the idea that plants and animals might be 'unsettled' by changing environmental conditions or by different species somehow mixing, but came to the conclusion that there was still a major problem in finding a convincing explanation of variation. Anyway, we can sense that he needed to sort out his ideas in this preliminary outline in order to put the whole question aside for a while, for he had more than enough other pressing concerns, like house-hunting and so on. But at the back of his mind, he undoubtedly remained acutely sensitised to the issue of 'variation', and to explaining its whys and wherefores.

Ranunculales

Returning to London, Darwin looked around the outskirts and within a month bought and moved into Down House just outside the village of Downe on the North Downs of Kent. Eight days later his wife Emma gave birth to a daughter who then only lived for three weeks. And in the midst of all this, he spotted those distinctively different buttercups. Further domestic turmoil followed, including the hassle of alterations to the house and garden to fit their particular needs and the distraction of relatives coming to stay. On top of all that he had set himself to write yet one more book from his notes from the *Beagle* voyage, that on 'Volcanic Islands'. Throughout this, the niggling puzzle of the double-flowered buttercups must have stayed with him because, after prolonged pondering and some further investigation, he took it upon himself a whole year later to contribute to a discussion in the *Gardeners' Chronicle* about double flowers. He sent in an example of a *Gentiana* and described its half-formed extra parts and then reinforced his point by mentioning the buttercups:

> I may mention that late last autumn, I found on an adjoining field of wretchedly sterile clay, great numbers of the *Ranunculus repens*, producing semi-double flowers, some having three, some additional rows of petals. The partial or entire sterility of double flowers is generally attributed to their doubleness; but is not this putting the effect before the cause?

He went on to suggest that this sterility could well be induced by environmental factors, ominously citing here the 'wretchedly sterile clay' and including the example of alpine plants being known to be infertile when transplanted to lowlands. So perhaps, he again suggested, resources freed up by the unused reproductive parts were being diverted into producing the extra petals, rather than the extra petals themselves disabling reproduction. In fact, Darwin came presciently close to our current understanding. This is that as the flower parts are merely modified leaves, it only takes a tiny tweak in the modification process for a potential stamen to become an extra petal instead, with consequent fertility loss. Even so, we are still left wondering with Darwin on how and why the change is prompted in the first place. The editor of the *Gardeners' Chronicle* actually added a footnote asserting that, while his correspondent's hypothesis seemed as acceptable as any other, it was known in the trade that multiple-petalled flowers especially luxuriated in

RIGHT The buttercup meadow just beyond the Down House back garden completes an idyllic summer scene. Here is meadow buttercup (*Ranunculus acris*) characteristically offering even more charm with its taller flowers and finer foliage than its creeping cousin – and with an invasive spread too.

fertile gardens, thereby throwing doubts on Darwin's suggestion that the double-flowered plants were a consequence of infertile soil.

Unfortunately for Darwin's vision of 'modification through descent', here was an example of a variation dead-end, enforced by the sterility. After posting off that article to the *Gardeners' Chronicle* to which he became a frequent contributor, he spent the following winter turning the 'pencilled sketch' of his species theory into a full-blown finely-reasoned 230-page exposition only for it then to be left on a shelf yet again (but with a note to his wife this time requesting that it be published if anything should happen to him and putting aside £400 pounds for the purpose). The issue of sterility, arising particularly with hybrid variants, came up forcefully in this second major essay. No doubt the disturbing example of those double-flowered buttercups was niggling away at the back of his mind and continued to do so. They certainly resurfaced twenty-five years later to be cited in his two-volume tome, *The variation of animals and plants under domestication* (1868).

So, back to our own story of *Ranunculus repens*, how can sterile buttercups multiply in great numbers? This, of course, is where the 'creeping' comes in, and such creeping is certainly not limited to *R. repens* with sterility problems. Putting itself about by vegetative means is the vital second string to this character's reproductive armoury.

Instead of using rhizomes (spreading roots) as we have seen so far with bracken and horsetails, creeping buttercup makes use of ground-level stolons (runners). These horizontal stalks push out along the ground and then put down their own sets of adventitious roots (repeats of those tenacious little mops) at a succession of nodal points. Hence an impressive radiation of daughter plants emerges from a parent plant. Once new plantlets begin to establish, the connecting stolons wither away to enable the daughters to become independent entities and mothers-to-be of a further tribe. Here, for example, is a diagrammatic illustration of one plant's spread into a colony of 34 daughter plants through a season.

The 34 new clones in the diagram cover about half a square metre. The parent plant also flowered as did 22 of its offspring. The recorder of this cloning event in 1942 was Edward Salisbury who, the following year, became Director of the Royal Botanic Gardens at Kew (and a direct heir to Joseph Hooker). 'Weeds' were his speciality and the subject of a lifetime of dedicated research. His name appears frequently through this whole survey. Just now we have to add that nineteen years after mapping that clonal spread, Salisbury claimed one buttercup could clone a colony of two square metres in a season. All right, even then it is possible that more plantlets might be emerging from the seeds of one plant, but the spaced-out cloned ones have been shown to have a greater survival rate than lots

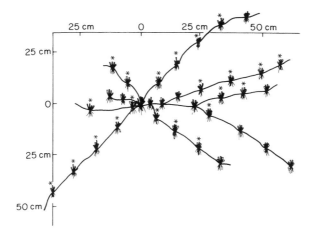

of closely packed seedlings. The creeping habit appears to be particularly induced by intense grazing, mowing or trampling. Left entirely to itself, *Ranunculus repens* tends to go for a more erect and static habit.

With such formidable sexual and cloning reproductive capabilities, and with such an impressive range of other adaptive resources, there's no stopping this 'primitive' plant. When it really comes down to it, seeds are the creeping buttercup's best survival option during drought, whereas wet conditions favour vegetative extension. And in just any old conditions, where better to creep or seed than into newly disturbed ground, that is anywhere we actively garden or tread. No wonder *Ranunculus repens* is always with us: flattened rosette; sunshine flower; abundant seeds; staggered dormancy; capacity for variation and stolon creep.

WHAT TO DO

- Salute this buttercup's cameo role at a pivotal moment in the life and work of the great man.
- Dig out with a fork to make sure all the root shoots come out too. Mercifully, creeping buttercups are conspicuous from the early stages and can be taken out almost as easily as they arrive. But watch out, especially, for their creeping from lawns (where they might be partially welcome) onto flower beds (where they are as good-as-never acceptable).
- Treat on lawns with nitrogen-rich feed-and-weed compounds if they have become too much of a good thing, or if you are determined on a pure grass sward.
- But certainly **do not dig in**. This will virtually assure a later successional crop.

Ranunculales

16

Ranunculus ficaria
RANUNCULACEAE
Lesser Celandine

Yes, perhaps surprisingly at first, the celandine is very much part of the buttercup family. It has the air of being even more 'primitive' than the standard buttercups, but perhaps we can think that because it is one of the first spring flowers to arrive. Its multiple bulbils are the source of its major invasive character and its shining green leaves rapidly create a tiresome despoiling carpet effect on the early-year virgin soil – vying, along with arum lilies (Weed 13), for the first major weed invasion of the year.

LEFT Lesser celandine, another beguiling member of the buttercup family and one capable of being an even more troublesome weed and right at the very beginning of the season.

RIGHT Beware! Poppies are very seductive and most adept at mixing in uninvited.

WHAT TO DO
- Hand fork out as much as possible, but be careful not to disturb other up and coming bulbs.
- Or leave be, as they soon disappear again without any surface trace for the rest of the year. Disturbing them ensures the bulbils drop off and spread about even more.
- Otherwise try, if you can, almost daily topping of emerging leaves over that short early season.

Ranunculales

WEEDS, WEEDING (& DARWIN)

17

Papaver rhoeas
PAPAVERACEAE
Common Poppy

Here, in this list, is our first annual weed, albeit one that will often over-winter. The flowers attract plenty of insects for cross-pollination but it has been observed that the cross-pollinators often will be beaten to it by self-pollination, with anthers dropping their pollen naturally and relatively early. These stars of cornfields are also well able to pop up in any disturbed ground where a large reserve of seeds can stay in a viable state for well over five years. Isolated plants are known to produce up to half a million seeds which, being miniscule, can disperse from the characteristic capsules some distance with a summer breeze.

Papaver dubium (Long-headed Poppy) is a little more distinctive than the above, as indicated by its range of other common names: blaver, blind eyes, cock's head, headache and yedwark. The long head is its elongated fruit and seed capsule. It is self-fertile but its

Ranunculales

anthers are positioned below the stigma, ensuring that insects promote cross-pollination – again another seemingly cunning advantageous adaptation.

WHAT TO DO

- The issue for gardeners is whether or not to welcome common poppies for a short guest appearance. It is probably best to take the hint that your garden is poppy-suitable (generally indicative of a pH 6–8) and sow more striking hybrid varieties like 'ladybird' and 'shirley' poppies or, if you really fall for them, the newer much-marketed, extravagantly-petalled varieties of opium poppy.

18

Fumaria officinalis
FUMARACEAE
Common Fumitory

Any plant whose name includes the epithet 'common' is unlikely to be welcomed into the garden. Common fumitory, a northern European native annual which belongs to a sub-family of the papaveraceae, is just such a case. Like the poppies, common fumitory plays a taunting game with us. It first appears with a delicate spray of dissected leaves as if promising to be something rather special. Its mauvish flowers then make quite a show, but somehow it is just not up to the mark for the garden. It is too ready to arrive uninvited, too fleeting, too formless and its colouring too unharmonious. We want it out.

Darwin also discovered that there was something not quite right about this plant, or rather something distinctly abnormal. It must have niggled at the back of his mind for a good few years because eventually in 1874 he found himself writing to *Nature* about it in the early days of that journal which had been founded in 1869. He pitched into a correspondence noting that, 'many years ago I watched perseveringly the flowers of

ABOVE Common fumitory – perhaps just too much of an unspectacular commoner for the garden.

Fumaria officinalis and *parviflora*, and never saw them visited by a single insect; and I concluded from reasons which I will not here give (as I cannot find my original notes), that they were frequented during the night by small moths. Insects are not necessary for the fertilisation of *Fumaria officinalis*; for I covered up a plant, and it produced as many seeds as an uncovered one which grew near.' So, common fumitory has a secret night life, and one which is not absolutely necessary for its reproduction! We realise too, as Darwin hinted at earlier in his published *Nature* letter, that there is something about the 'mauvish' colour which may have been a turn-off to insects in daylight (as well as to us). Then, when we learn that, whatever the circumstances, a single plant produces an average of 15,000 seeds, no wonder we have to be wary of this one.

Not only that, we need to be watchful of its close cousin *Corydalis lutea*, a lover of flint walls and sometimes referred to as yellow fumitory. But with this corydalis 'aid of insects is indispensable', as Darwin noted.

WHAT TO DO
- Have no qualms about removing. But note corydalis has many garden treasures.

19

Berberis darwinii
BERBERIDACEAE
Darwin's Barberry

Here, over the page, is *Berberis darwinii*, a prize-winning spring-flowering shrub in an English garden. It is our final example from the ranunculales and, to most of us, what a surprise to find it here, grouped with 'primitive' buttercups and then paraded as a weed.* How can this be possible for such a glorious garden plant esteemed for its orange-yellow flowers set against a glossy, dark green foliage of holly-like leaves, and one prestigiously named after Charles Darwin?

Its story can only be something to do with what came out of that famous voyage. 'We were driven into Chloe by some very bad weather', wrote Darwin to his Cambridge botanist mentor and voyage recruiter, John Stevens Henslow. And there, on that volcanic island off Chile, Darwin discovered this most distinctive bush. A sample came back to Kew, where the then director, William Hooker (Joseph's father), named this new discovery in honour of its English discoverer.

Ranunculales

Not surprisingly, mid-nineteenth-century nurserymen in Europe quickly realised the plant's potential and started to propagate and market it seriously. And hardly surprising again that in the last century *Berberis darwinii* won an RHS Award of Garden Merit which it has retained to this day.

Obviously here was a plant worth marketing for all it was worth, and therefore exporting. So, among other parts of the world, it reached New Zealand. Evidently it relished coming back to the southern hemisphere and thrived so well that it flew over the garden fence, soon to become a major scourge of the native landscape. Local birds gorged on its berries only to scatter seeds encrusted with fertiliser far and wide. It even found itself under the canopy of native forests.

Here we are with a role reversal: gardens are the centre of attention more for exporting plants (which themselves were originally brought in from abroad) to become nuisance weeds in the wild than for importing plants from the wild that become nuisance weeds in the garden. Either way gardeners get the blame. So serious are the problems this berberis has created for New Zealand's native habitats that the national government has had it classified as an 'unwanted organism', meaning that it can no longer be propagated, distributed or sold.

Darwin was not to know of this subsequent problematic spread of the plant he collected from that island off Chile, but he did uncannily comment in *Origin* that 'the endemic productions of New Zealand, for instance are ... now rapidly yielding before the advancing legions of plants and animals introduced from Europe'. He was well ahead of his times in realising the extent and significance of migrations of other species following in the wake of early colonial settlers. But in fact, according to claims made by today's conservationists in New Zealand, native plants have held their own quite well and apparently have 'yielded' hardly at all to the many foreign invaders. You can sense that the conservationists have a professional and patriotic pride in the resilience of their own flora in standing up to outside competition. Even so, Darwin's barberry has been changing many parts of the New Zealand landscape in a drastic way and is not unlike gorse in its prickly yellow and dark-green takeover of hillsides. And, of course, New Zealand remains in a great number of ways a showcase for the alarming effects of 'eco-imperialism' – a phenomenon we shall meet again several times in this story.

As a footnote, we should mention that Darwin's barberry is not the only berberis to go out of control. In the north-east of the United States *Berberis thunbergii* has gained notoriety for aggressively invading fields, pastures and even woodland margins. Also, it has to be said that the berberis genus itself finds itself unwanted by many gardeners because the spikes are so horrendous to work around. In the United Kingdom, though, *Berberis darwinii* is very much the favoured exception.

* At the time of writing, it looks as if a future readjustment of the 'evolutionary tree' placings, might see berberidaceae moved to a higher branch to join the caryophyllales. For the time being it is still officially lodged with the ranunculales.

WHAT TO DO
- In Chile: enjoy as a native plant.
- In Britain/Europe: enjoy as a handsome garden shrub or hedging plant.
- In New Zealand: take note that it is classed as an 'unwanted organism', and take inspiration from the residents and conservationist volunteers of Stewart Island where an 'Eradication Crew' have been uprooting it in a concerted effort with every resource at their disposal and look set to be ridding it totally from the island off the very south of their country.

Ranunculales

Core Eudicots: Minor Groups

Core eudicots cover all the rest of the angiosperms (flowering plants) on our evolutionary tree. Their 'core' status indicates that they are considered to be the principal representatives of all the eudicots. Their main attribute is simply that they are not monocots. Generally they have two cotyledons (seed leaves), but this is not necessarily always the case.

Compared with the two major branches at the top of the tree, the branching in this section is 'minor' and consists of four separate branches bundled together. Gunnerales at the base, santalales and saxifragales which are just conjoined, and then caryophyllales which is linked to the major branch above for the asterids. Right now, we skip over the gunnerales to meet the parasitical mistletoe in the santalales.

20

Viscum album
SANTALACEAE
Mistletoe

A highly toxic plant which can live and feed on up to 200 different tree and shrub species, is capable of reducing its host's normal growth and sometimes even totally overwhelming it, must, you might think, rank high in the weed stakes. Mistletoe demands an explanation. Darwin thought so too, and right there on page three of his introduction to *On the Origin of Species*. Bear with his long sentences again, but in a short paragraph:

> In the case of the mistletoe, which draws its nourishment from certain trees, which has seeds that must be transported by certain birds, and which has flowers with separate sexes absolutely requiring the agency of certain insects to bring pollen from one flower to the other, it is equally preposterous to account for the structure

Santalales

of the parasite, with its relations to several distinct organic beings, by the effects of external conditions, or of habit, or of the volition of the plant itself. It is, therefore, of the highest importance to gain a clear insight into the means of modification and co-adaptation.

For Darwin, the 'clear insight' challenge was to explain how a plant could come to operate in such a bizarre, multi-dependent complex way which took idiosyncrasy to its furthest extreme. That he could even entertain the idea of plant 'volition' is telling of how far he felt he was up against it. Even so, he made it clear that the gaining of 'a clear insight into the means of modification and co-adaptation' was the fundamental objective of his whole research project. In effect, the mistletoe enigma provided him with an arresting lead-in.

Today, we too can be thrown by the odd-ball nature of mistletoe and be unsure what to make of it. Gerard, the sixteenth-century herbalist who was ever ready to speak of medicinal or culinary attributes, writes elegantly about mistletoe's convoluted form and growing habits but makes no mention of its having any special properties of help or indeed hindrance to us. So are we just left with a Yuletide decoration with a spurious romantic pull?

For gardeners in particular, mistletoe will normally be a welcome curiosity rather than an unwanted threat. But it is a parasite nonetheless, and that idea unsettles. In the background lurks the uncomfortable feeling that it is in the nature of all weeds to be parasitical upon our gardens and gardening efforts – to the extent of taunting and persecuting us with what feels like an evil volition too.

All said and done, mistletoe is a plant out on a limb, for sure.

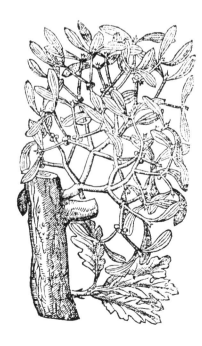

WHAT TO DO
* The above said, enjoy!

RIGHT The elegant woodcut illustration of mistletoe in Johnson's edition of Gerard's *Herbal*, which was first published in 1597.

Santalales

21

Sedum album
CRASSULACEAE
Stonecrop

We come to succulent sedums. *Sedum album,* the white flowered one, and *Sedum acre,* the yellow flowered one, both make excellent introductions to this thick-skinned, fleshy-leaved set of plants. Both settle in easily but then go on for a steady expansive creep. *S. acre* is the standard native one which looks best as an outside-the-garden native, classically topping a low-lying wall. *S. album* has slightly more refined flowers and leaves. Hence it is the one we are more likely to introduce into the garden, perhaps to get an alpine bed going, often to regret it a year or two later when it has gone everywhere – a ground-covering plant par excellence spreading relentlessly over beds and stony paths with equal facility. More than the softer leaved ground-cover plants like *Ajuga reptans*, ivy and periwinkle, stonecrop really does cover the ground without a single bare space – and, it has to be said, in a pleasant pebbly way. So simple it is, compared with mistletoe, that there is little more to say.

WHAT TO DO
- Be prepared to scrape it back drastically or even take it out once it has done its pioneering work. Let it stimulate you to seek more spectacular sedums: *S. spectabile* and its many varieties, why not?

LEFT Stonecrop all too naturally encroaching onto paving.

22

Crassula helmsii

CRASSULACEAE

Australian Swamp Stonecrop / New Zealand Pigmy Weed

In the same family, crassulaceae, we now switch from all-out ground cover back again to all-out water cover. 'Australian swamp stonecrop' and 'New Zealand pigmy weed', the two common names for *Crassula helmsii*, together conjure up a pretty disturbing picture. This aquatic plant was introduced into Britain from Australasia in 1911 as a desirable new oxygenating plant for ponds. It served this purpose quite well and with the added cachet of being something exotic

from the other side of the world. Then, inevitably, it found its way into the wild where it has been spreading rapidly and where its water-covering capacity was certainly not so welcome. Dense mats of the pigmy, fleshy leaves have been out-competing native aquatic plants, filling up drainage ditches and blocking waterways.

It is important to note here that the same story has been repeated five times: exotic foreigners for garden ponds which have escaped to cause havoc – all within the last thirty years or so. The problem was acknowledged by the British government who set up the Non-Native Species Secretariat (NNSS) in 2008 with the co-sponsorship of other key organisations like the Royal Horticultural Society. They singled out five aquatic plants including the one introduced above:

Myriophyllum aquaticum (Parrot's Feather) from South America
Azolla filicules (Water Fern) from the American tropics
Ludwigia grandiflora (Water Primrose) from South America
Hydrocotyle ranunculoides (Floating Pennywort) from North America

WHAT TO DO

- Join the NNSS campaign to 'Be Plant Wise' and 'don't dump aquatic plants into the wild'. They emphasise that these plants can often regenerate from a tiny fragment of a

Saxifragales

millimetre or two. Do not ever dispose of such plants outside your garden. Walk out with cleaned boots and so on and so on.

- Take note of the versatility of the saxifragales, the home of the last two weed entries. Not only does this order host the stonecrops and its saxifrage fellow 'alpines', but it also includes gooseberries – prickly awkward devils, but a special favourite of the Darwin family who sought out every variety they could find. In the cause of science? It does not look like it this time.

NOW WE COME to our next small branch, the caryophyllales.

This branch, which edges towards the major asterid branch above it, comprises a mixed bag of 11,000 species which contrast with those on our previous branches by not having any woody elements at all and by containing 'betalain', a beetroot-coloured pigment. This telltale colouring percolates plants (especially their leaf ribs) which range from those with lush spinachy leaves to the tough-skinned cacti and the sticky insectivorous plants. Within this group, the weed 'anti' ratchets up a good notch or two. But let us still put this in proportion: out of that 11,000, we are talking about little more than a dozen awkward customers, of which ten are represented here, including such horrors as dock, fat-hen, Japanese knotweed and prickly pear.

23

Rumex crispus
POLYGONACEAE
Curly Leafed Dock / Yellow Leafed Dock

Rumex obtusifolius
POLYGONACEAE
Broad Leafed Dock

Ubiquitous, obtrusive, deeply dug-in, coarse in appearance and excessively proliferating, docks exude defiance. They are definitely among the weed big guns. Not one dock but two – two distinct species – in a dastardly double act. Even their first leaves as they emerge from the ground look alien and out of proportion to the surrounding foliage. Then, when they become more mature upright plants, they can look ragged and rust worn while, at the same time, showering shoals of seeds and extending their tap roots. They push their way into gardens, though this is nothing compared with their threat to pasture. Together the duo have the dubious honour of being highlighted as two of the five 'injurious weeds' (along with ragwort, creeping thistle and spear thistle) specified for strict containment in the Weeds Act 1959.

R. crispus is so named and recognised from the crisp wavy margins of its leaves which narrow towards the base of the stalk and tend to be shorter than those of *R. obtusifolius.* It is said to be the most common of the two, thriving almost anywhere, including more marginal terrains like shingle beaches. It is earlier to flower and so its same-year seedlings themselves get a chance to bloom and seed before the season is out. Although it is usually classed as a perennial, mature plants can die exhausted after a flowering fling, although, of course, they merely make way for successors.

BELOW Curly leafed dock – the one with narrower leaves with crisp curled margins.

Caryophyllales

R. Obtusifolius, duly named from its foliage configuration where broader leaves successively sprout from the stem at obtuse angles from each other, can also grow anywhere and is especially the villain of grassland. It is notoriously egged on by slurry which can burn off the grass enough to allow its fresh seed content to get away in an enriched patch of soil. Likewise, it homes in on trodden areas by gates and where cattle congregate. It comes into flower in June so that the double act neatly extends the dock season; and it is not so susceptible to keeling over after a good flowering. And what a flowering! And what proliferation of deep roots too! The latter only further encouraged to go deeper by cutting or grazing of the foliage.

Not sure that you can always tell the difference? That is hardly surprising as the two closely related species readily cross-fertilise. First-generation hybrids have extra vigour

BELOW Broad leafed dock – the other one with broader leaves appearing successively at obtuse angles to each other.

and when these naturally back-cross with either parent second generation hybrids emerge with both exceptional seed production and viability. These then have the edge to become super-invaders of all those slightest-bit disturbed patches of field or garden. Here is testimony to the power of heterogeneity. It was something unknown to Darwin though it certainly owes something to the extended experiments with hybridisation which he, among others, set in motion.

These genetic riches, unsurprisingly too, help the scoring of record numbers: up to 60,000 seeds per *plant*, with a claim of 88 per cent germination; five million asserted for the number of dock seeds per acre; and more chilling still is the claim that the seeds can remain viable for up to 70 years.

Behind the gross figures is intense alarm at the precariousness of keeping this monster under control. The documented research on this particular threat to pasture is one of the most extensive on any weed and, it has to be said, is full of contrary figures and viewpoints, with wildly varying claims of seed production, of germination rates, of potassium requirements, of whether flooding acts as a restraint or the reverse, and especially with regard to capacities for regeneration.

Geoff Hamilton, an eminent former TV garden presenter, once nailed a dock root to a shed door and had it exposed to full sun, frost and winds for two years. Then he planted it, only to see it spring into new life, 'as if the rest had done it good'. Tradition has it that rhubarb (from the same family as the docks) when propagated by division does best when its roots are exposed to the frost for a while before replanting. The sharp shock generates the sugars and gets things going just as it does with exposed dock roots – so don't leave them about!

And what about those seeds? We know they are dispersed not just from falling or being blown away, but also in manure, along rivers, by birds, attached to animals (including especially us humans by way of our footwear, clothes, vehicles and so on). Also the fine seeds easily fall in with other seeds that are being saved for resowing for standard farm crops. So we are unwittingly major dock distributors, as we must have been since way back.

Our ancient association with dock is documented from pollen found in Neolithic and other excavations. Its name, derived from the Anglo-Saxon *docce*, also tells of antiquity. Then, as a true Brit, it has followed us around the world, and even found relative favour in the New World as 'not a bad weed', valued there more than here for its medicinal properties.

In New Zealand a dock plant came to Darwin's attention. This was in the Bay of Islands (during the latter part of his voyage) where he observed ants interacting with aphids on a dock leaf. He reported the incident in his journal and then twenty-four years later repeated and commented on it in the chapter about instinct in the *Origin*: 'I removed all the ants from a group of about a dozen aphides on a dock plant, and prevented their attendance for several hours.' Already Darwin was alert to the interdependence of organisms which he so eloquently summarised in contemplating that 'entangled bank'. Dock, we now know well, is a nourishing host to an abundance of insects and unseemly fungi, all contributing to its often tawdry appearance. Weeds, like all plants, are never unencumbered. But dock appears to be exceptionally infested – and infesting.

In his *Journal of the voyage of HMS Beagle* Darwin noted one more shocking detail about dock in New Zealand. 'The common dock is also widely disseminated, and will, I fear, for ever remain a proof of the rascality of an Englishman, who sold the seeds for those of the tobacco plant.' A few New Zealanders curse this incident to this day.

So, has dock any saving graces? Of course. As an integral part of nature's bounty, it is absolutely part and parcel of those many corners of unattended ground where it does no harm whatsoever. Along with nettles, it is a welcome indicator of lush fertility. And the juicy leaf of Doctor Dock is the renowned and effective relief for nettle stings. Some claim it to be the ingredient of a tonic, not to mention of a laxative too – as they will or have done of almost every weed at some time or other.

WHAT TO DO

- In the average moderately sized garden docks are easily spotted early and should be no problem to fork out or even simply knock out, except, notoriously, in paving. But in longer grass or wilder areas they can be a tough challenge. And deciding on the best strategy can be an even tougher challenge, for the jury again appears to be out. Essentially there are four options to weigh up.
- The first is simply to get in quick and decapitate young plants within forty days of seedlings first appearing. Grazing by cattle and sheep (but not horses) at this stage will go some way towards this. After that forty-day point the root has enough food reserves to enable foliage to come back. If you miss that opportunity, there are further courses.
- Either follow the optimistic advice of a new lobby who are cautiously saying 'it-is-generally agreed' that spudding (chopping and lifting out) the underground parts at 7.5 cm below the surface will provide the knock-out blow. In fact the stem will reach down to a good 5 cm below ground and then there is a transition zone before real root is met. So, if the root is genuinely decapitated below this transition zone and if this point remains well enough buried to receive no light, that should be it.
- Or follow the old guard who wag their fingers, warning that it only takes a tiny fragment of root left in the ground to set off new shoots, and who settle for nothing

WEEDS, WEEDING (& DARWIN)

less than total extraction by RIP (removal of individual plants). Fortunately the advocates of this policy have now provided the ultimate tool, the 'Lazy Dog Fork', an ingenious invention which can quite easily prise out whole roots. Such one-by-one removal in a field can be a long slog, but a rewarding one. Then make sure to thoroughly dispose of all plant parts by burning or whatever. (This third option also leads to a further dilemma because the roots contract and are easier to prise out just as the plants set seed. So is it worth the risk of waiting until then? Your choice again.

- And, in any case, be wise (invariably after the event for most of us) and do not over graze, especially with horses, as this creates thin patches accessible to dock seeds and seedlings.

24

Rumex acetosella
POLYGONACEAE
Sheep Sorrel

This one is to be noted because in many respects it looks like a slimline version of the docks and because it appears to sneak into (and stay around) gardens. Perhaps it can get away with it because it is not quite as obtrusive as its dock cousins. It is known for its high oxalic and acetic acid content which is said to affect milk and reduce yields. We need to be wary of sheep sorrel because not only does it have dock-like tap roots but it also spreads through rhizomes in compensation for less good viable seed production. Finally, we should note that this plant is an indicator of a sour soil.

WHAT TO DO
- Sweeten the soil with an application of lime.

ABOVE A stem of sheep sorrel intruding into a row of potatoes along with some groundsel. Neither can do much harm at this stage, it seems.

Caryophyllales

25

Chenopodium album
CHENOPODIACEAE
Fat-hen

From perennial sorrel we shift the spinachy mode to two challenging annuals: fat-hen and chickweed. Fat-hen (alias goosefoot, lamb's quarters or muckweed) is very much a farmyard and dung-heap weed. No bones about this one; fat-hen flourishes on fertile ground. Hence its particular affiliation with newly manured allotments and gardens.

Like its perennial cousins, it, too, is prone to invigorating hybridisation with its closer relatives, be they separate species or whatever. This also results in their coming in a great variety of plant and leaf forms which, too, can easily vary according to the types of soil and growing conditions. In the farming world certain varieties have come to the fore because they have shown resistance to standard herbicides – straightforward unnatural selection.

Rich in vitamin C, fat-hen provides valuable nutrition for us and for livestock. From Neolithic times to the sixteenth century we apparently ate it as a vegetable until we discovered spinach and cabbage. The seeds were supposedly ground into flour. Unfortunately fat-hen is also appetising to pests like aphids and plays host to troublesome viruses as well.

The seeds, which provide food for that plump fowl and other farmland birds, are the extraordinary phenomenon of this weed. The recorded numbers per plant range from 10 to 164, 691. Then each plant has several different kinds of seed, essentially black ones (the majority) and some brown ones. The black seed is hard coated, with some having a rough and others a smooth surface, and so takes longer to germinate, whereas the browns have a softer coating and germinate more quickly, while still producing plants with the same proportion of black and brown seeds.

Fat-hen seed left around in undisturbed soil for 20 and 39 years has been found to have 65 per cent and 9 per cent germination rates respectively. Seed from archaeological sites has germinated after 100 years and more. Apparently viable seeds of fat-hen have been extracted from adobe walls of 143-year-old Mexican buildings. And so the statistics roll on.

How, then, do we experience this quite different champion in our gardens? A long season certainly. Seedlings emerge to try their luck throughout the growing time but have their prime flush from May to July. The earlier ones tend to become larger and leafier than the later ones but the big fruition and showering of seeds tends to coincide with the

RIGHT Fat-hen boldly staking a claim among some celeriac plants, and alarmingly in full seed too.

WEEDS, WEEDING (& DARWIN)

main vegetable crops, which is just the time when it is also all too easy to let go of the weeding. Compared with so many, fat-hen is a relatively tame weed, but it makes up for its innocuousness by putting itself about in abundance and repeatedly so.

WHAT TO DO

- Hoe. A prime candidate for sustained hoeing or hand weeding.
- Pull or fork out the larger specimens which have escaped the hoe.
- Feed the mature plants (which you should not have allowed to get that far) to chickens. They like the seeds but not necessarily as a first choice.

26

Stellaria medea
CARYOPHYLLACEAE
Common Chickweed

See it at the right moment in bright sunlight and stellaria really does live up to its name with its tiny five-petalled white flowers giving the impression of twinkling stars. This small-leaved (and small-flowered) procumbent plant does indeed have many star qualities. These allow it to grow almost anywhere at almost any time of the year, to be the first to flower in the new year, to be nutritious to all birds and fowl (and to us if we choose to take advantage of it), to grow fast horizontally, to put down tenacious fibrous roots, to provide good winter ground cover and to produce record quantities of viable seed several times a year: the ideal requisites for an ultra-precocious annual weed.

Chickweed is in there with many of the adaptive advantages of the fast multiplying and high number-scoring annual weeds like the previous two and shepherd's purse, groundsel, the thistles and so many others. Its particular advantage is its capacity to survive or indeed thrive through winters. It is even reported to flower and set seed under snow cover. Hence one of its other common names is 'winterweed'. On cold winter afternoons it takes another curious protective measure: at dusk paired leaves apparently fold together to envelop tender new growth. Who first noticed that one wonders?

Its most damaging propensity is simply to smother ground with its mat-like growth and to smother whatever else is trying to grow there. An average plant is said to have 250 seed capsules each with an average of 10 seeds. Multiply this up by three generations in a year and there is, as Salisbury bizarrely calculated, enough potential plant matter to clothe

clothe an area three times the size of the Isle of Wight in a year. In any case, vegetable beds in the autumn, as more and more space becomes available, are where chickweed particularly makes a grab for it.

Beware! On this one's back are also aggressive viruses and fungi – notoriously cucumber mosaic virus, the scourge of courgettes and suchlike.

Chickweed, too, is resistant to standard herbicides. It is a much tougher cookie than its slight appearance suggests. Watch it carefully.

WHAT TO DO

- Hoe out as soon as it appears before it has time to secure its fibrous roots.
- Consider leaving it as a protective mat on the soil in the main part of the winter, especially if your area is now more prone to battering rain than to frost.
- Harvest for your chickens or for yourself. It is an acceptable spinach, so they say.
- Don't try tugging it out as all you will be doing is snatching off the top growth and leaving the tenacious roots.
- Dig in, in later winter especially.

LEFT A lettuce being enveloped by an edible weed – a choice of two salad plants to take back to the kitchen, or perhaps only one if things are left much longer.

Caryophyllales

27

Amaranthus retroflexus

AMARANTHACEAE
Pigweed

Pigweed is otherwise known as 'careless weed' because it betrays a slack gardener. This is a bit hard because it is easy to be caught out by the seedlings which at first have the neat look of promising garden plants. But these soon turn into a sprawling menace – alias common tumbleweed. Then it is conspicuous and quite easy (and gratifying) to remove. Furthermore, it is most delicious and highly nutritious to pigs. But note: whether 'careless', 'common tumble' or 'pig', we call it a weed every time.

Pigweed's nutritional value comes from its seeds which are produced on a mass of flowering finger-like spikes. One plant (which is said to be able to reach three metres in all directions) can produce a million seeds – beat that! In prehistoric times they were valued as a grain crop both in Europe and the Americas. Then better alternatives emerged and the plants found themselves downgraded to weed status.

The above comments are pretty well how we view amaranthus in genteel Western Europe. But go to the United States and hear the farmers rail against pigweeds for being the number one spoiler of their crops. Then see how 'weed scientists' put the same plants on the top of the list for their research papers and amaranthus takes on an entirely different story. Super fast off the mark, with record seed production and prolonged germination, prone to variation and to widespread hybridisation (leaving dock standing) and ingeniously adaptive to herbicides (indeed providing a chilling case-study on the hot topic of 'the evolution of herbicide resistance'), a selection of the 70 amaranthus species worldwide have the reputation of 'weed' propensity as no other. Quite naturally, then, the geneticists have been homing in on this genus to unravel genomes and even to plan genetic counter-attacks. Phew! What would Darwin have made of all this – the spirit of

ABOVE AND RIGHT *Amaranthus caudatus* (love-lies-bleeding), pigweed's more acceptable cousin, and Japanese knotweed as pictured and recommended by William Robinson in *The English Flower Garden*, 1883).

WEEDS, WEEDING (& DARWIN)

his work being carried forward with extraordinary creativity and pace? Needless to say, the pigweed menace is not just limited to the United States.

Before concluding, let us give a mention to our garden sort-of-friend, *Amaranthus caudatus*, most often known as 'Love-lies-bleeding'. With its deep-red tassels, it is an oddball plant which comes in and out of favour, as if teasing us on the delicate weed/non-weed divide. 'A very striking object when full grown but…', as William Robinson put it in 1883.

WHAT TO DO
- Get an eye in for its smart seedlings and hoe out asap.
- Otherwise hand pull (with gloves against itchy leaves) and dig out larger plants to make excellent compost (without the seeds, of course)
- Harvest young leaves for spinach or salads (a favoured ingredient for 'mixed leaf salad').
- Introduce its delightful cousin *Amaranthus caudatus,* known as love-lies-bleeding or tassel flower.

28

Fallopia japonica
POLYGONACEAE
Japanese Knotweed

Just as we may still be reeling from the challenges of dock and pigweed, now we have, in relatively close company, a character with an even more outrageous reputation and an 'alien' to boot on which to vent all our latent xenophobic spleen. 'Japweed', as we have now come contemptuously to refer to it, hits the popular press headlines with ever more horrific stories of breaking into our houses or of costing the taxpayer multiple millions (such us in the preparation of the London Olympic Park). It is the ultimate weed in the public consciousness. As always, there are other sides to the story.

Polygonum cuspidatum, as this plant was known when it was first introduced to Britain from Japan in 1825, was promoted then as a prized new find, a charming ornamental plant which also provided excellent cattle fodder. It was soon to gain eminent status in Victorian gardens. In 1879 *The Garden* (William Robinson's new magazine) described it as 'a plant of sterling merit, now becoming quite common ... and is undoubtably one of the finest herbaceous plants in cultivation'. It is still to be seen in a few older gardens: 'a beautiful sight in full bloom with its feathery masses of creamy white flowers and characteristic heart-shaped leaf', according to Edward Salisbury fifty years ago. Then it was simply referred to as 'Japanese knotgrass'. Sometimes bold gardeners will still find a fitting niche to show it off and challenge preconceptions. For example, it was given a place for a while by the entrance to Kew Gardens.

However, this former novelty had another reputation as 'a pioneer species' as it was the first to arrive in the Far East on volcanic lava, river gravels and managed pastures. It took a good century and more after its arrival in Britain for *Reynoutria japonica* (as its name became before settling down to *Fallopia japonica*) to start demonstrating its

pioneering spirit and slip out of gardens in earnest to find a home beside railway lines, waterways, roadsides and any available bits of wasteland. Damp south Wales particularly suited it, much to the horror of local residents who took time to wake up to the scale and sheer force of the invasion which swamped out swathes of local native vegetation, even bracken. Not only does its canopy blot out everything below, but when its leaves fall they create a dense impenetrable mulch which suppresses any other potential seedling.

What is extraordinary is that it is extremely rare for this plant to produce any viable seed. It has simply spread as one vast clone and has claims to be the largest single female in the world. Its source of strength lies underground in a massive and extremely tough rhizome system which takes saws to penetrate and break it up. Most herbicides fail to reach its furthest parts, though they can substantially stall its progress. In the meantime extended patches of sickly half-alive sprayed knotweed do nothing to lift the spirits.

So how has this seedless clone come to spread so far and wide? Well, our gardener forebears must take the prime responsibility for its initial major distribution. Old stocks of knotweed rhizomes must have remained in reserve all over the country and appear able to regenerate after many years of suppression. Rhizome fragments put through a garden shredder and then composted or sent elsewhere are quite happy to regenerate. Massive and extensive movement of topsoil from construction sites must also play its part, and so too has fly-tipping of garden waste. Waterways provide easy transport as is well evident. In all, there is a strong element of sheer brute force in the way this character has insistently put itself about and stayed put despite persistent attempts at eradication. No way now can it simply be sent home.

WHAT TO DO

- Remove or move (house). Such is the horticulturalist's forceful reaction to this one.
- Persistently, persistently, persistently cut or spray top growth over a year and more.
- Avoid importing topsoil which is not carefully sourced.
- Meanwhile wait for the experts to come up with an effective biological control (which is being investigated), in other words an appropriate pest, bearing in mind that native ones so far are being found inadequate for the job and imported ones bring the risk of themselves getting out of control.

LEFT *Fallopia japonica* elegantly arching over a pathway in Le Jardin des Sambucs in France.

Caryophyllales

29

Fallopia baldshuanica
POLYGONACEAE
Russian Vine

You want the new garden shed to be instantly clothed with a climbing plant? Then Russian vine is what first comes to mind. It will do the job fast and elegantly and all in one season. But three seasons later, if unattended, it will have spread at least three times further, and almost certainly into unwanted space. 'Mile-a-minute', its other adopted name, tells it all. 'Russian', too, stirs up xenophobic alarm yet again.

LEFT Russian vine planted to make a screen at the end of a garden now comes tumbling over the garden wall to begin obstructing the pavement for passers-by.

As with its close cousin, Japanese knotweed, *F. baldshuanica* was introduced to the United Kingdom as a welcome novelty from abroad, this time as an import from Tajikistan in 1883. The feathery white flowers are similar in both plants and likewise the red stems. Apart from its involvement in hybridising with its cousin, this one's invasive power is far less alarming and more controllable. But it is a forceful presence which needs watching and attending to before it climbs over and eventually pulls down every neighbouring shrub or tree – and even that shed.

WHAT TO DO
- Trim annually to keep within wanted bounds.
- Think about having an alternative fast-growing (but not quite so fast) climber such as *Clematis montana*, or the evergreen and beautifully spring-scented *Clematis armandii*.

30

Drosera rotundiflora
DROSERACEAE
Sundew

Given the appropriate circumstances (nitrogen-deficient and boggy ground) sundews can be most invasive and will not suffer competition from other plants apart from sphagnum moss and weak grasses. Dealing with this alien-looking specimen can take up excessive amounts of our time too. Perhaps these are stretching-it-a-bit reasons for letting this exotic insectivorous plant appear in our rogues' gallery of weeds. But let us look briefly at the sundew for a little relief, and for Darwin's sake, especially.

Darwin excitedly found 'thousands' of sundews in the Ashdown Forest, just fifteen miles down the road from Downe, on a short family holiday in the summer after the publication of the *Origin*. The repercussions of the publication had been pretty stressful and it seemed as if he alighted upon these intriguing curiosities as a most welcome

FIG. 4.
(*Drosera rotundifolia.*)
Leaf (enlarged) with all the tentacles closely inflected, from immersion in a solution of phosphate of ammonia (one part to 87,500 of water).

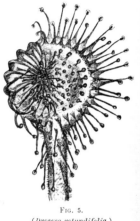

FIG. 5.
(*Drosera rotundifolia.*)
Leaf (enlarged) with the tentacles on one side inflected over a bit of meat placed on the disc.

LEFT Here are two sundews as drawn by Darwin's son, George, for his father's book. These are Darwin's captions: Fig 4. (*Drosera rotundifolia.*) Leaf (enlarged) with all the tentacles closely inflected, from immersion in a solution of phosphate of ammonia (one part to 87,500 of water). Fig 5. (*Drosera rotundifolia.*) Leaf (enlarged) with the tentacles on one side inflected over a bit of meat placed on the disc.

distraction, just like finding a new toy which could be played with endlessly. Specimens were brought back to his greenhouse where he teased them with all sorts of bits and pieces (assorted insects, drops of milk, olive oil, egg white, gelatin, tea, sherry, various chemicals, his urine, a hair from his wife, and so on) to try to find out how and what those sticky, hairy leaf pads entrapped and processed by way of 'food'.

Darwin became well and truly hooked by it all until the following February when he presented his findings to the Royal Society. Then fifteen years later (the same period of time from first draft to final completion of the *Origin*) he completed a whole book on insectivorous plants. By that point he had investigated many more examples of carnivorous plants sent to him from all over the world. They played a significant role in bringing to general attention the idea of 'convergent evolution', that is, why plants from so many entirely different families can converge on adapting to a changed environment in quite similar ways, like the process of foliar feeding on insects when all other sources of nutrients fail. Darwin clocked up 80 different carnivorous species and now we know nearly 500 from around the world from a wide spectrum of families.

In post-Victorian Britain, it is we who have become the invasive threat to sundews by taking over their natural habitats, drenching them with counter-productive fertilisers and developing drainage systems. It is hard to see that these marvels deserve this assault from us. In time, no doubt, a select few will find a way of re-adapting.

Caryophyllales

In early twenty-first century New Zealand some sundews are officially classified as weeds. These are the ones brought in from South Africa, *Drosera capensis*. They have become a serious threat to the native vegetation of a particular upland area.

There you are, we were right all along to have put Darwin's hungry playfellows on our list.

WHAT TO DO

- Feed and observe.
- Or treat as a weed and douse with nitrates – heaven forbid!

BELOW Sundews together with a butterwort (a fellow insectivorous plant) on a North Wales mountainside.

Caryophyllales

31

Opuntia stricta
CACTACEAE
Prickly Pear

Try taking a bite of a prickly pear, and never ever again! The fine prickles stay excruciatingly in your mouth for many days.

To conclude our round-up of this particularly eclectic group of plants, we must include the opuntias as our example from the cacti. Together they have to be among the most outrageously defensive, if not aggressive, of all plants. In Britain, as yet, opuntias are only to be found nurtured in a cactus house, apart from occasional appearances in the freak conditions of the far south west. Some of us are familiar with them from Mediterranean holidays and other foreign holidays. Perhaps they are something we can anticipate soon

on our southern shores as a consequence of posited climate change. That is an alarming prospect from what we know of opuntias elsewhere in the world.

Australia learned the bitter lesson with opuntia in the late nineteenth and early twentieth century. A native of Central America, it was introduced to Queensland as an effective, fast-growing hedging plant for the new ranching industry. It promised, in addition, its own sideline of cochineal food-dye production from the cochineal beetles that infested it. Whatever its promises, the new wonder plant rapidly became Australia's 'worst weed ever', submerging approximately 24 billion hectares of Queensland under a two-metre-deep impenetrable mat. But then there was an equally dramatic turnaround. In 1925 a South American moth, *Cactoblastis cactorum* (yes, really!), was introduced and its larvae systematically consumed and eradicated the cactus. It is an exemplary success story of biological control which has been hard to beat and which might give hope that a similar solution might be found for controlling Japanese knotweed.

Yet we are still left wondering how prickly pear comes to have such an imposing presence for us. Its piled-up pads of extra-toughened, spiny, thickly-succulent leaves-cum-jointed-stem say it all. They are an ultimate adaptation to hot drought conditions. Just as with sundews, cacti are not the only major plant group to find their convergent way to adopt the 'succulent' approach for surviving particular drought conditions.

Unsurprisingly, Darwin had his own pertinent say on the matter too. He found a particular species growing on the arid Patagonian plain and could not resist prodding it. It was, he noted, 'remarkable by the irritability of its stamens, when I inserted either a piece of stick or the end of my finger in the plant. The segments of the perianth also closed on the pistil, but more slowly than the stamens.' Of course, he was trying to simulate the touch of a pollinating insect. The said piece of opuntia was bottled in spirits of wine, sent back to England, named *Opuntia darwinii* by Henslow (Darwin's botany mentor) and preserved to this day in Cambridge. On his five-week stay by the Galapagos Islands he found a further species, *Opuntia galapagaeia*. With self-preservation defences, as demonstrated by Darwin and others, this is certainly not a plant to be messed around with.

WHAT TO DO

- Protect and savour as an exotic wonder.
- Dig up / literally eradicate.
- or simply introduce *Cactoblastis cactorum* to it.

LEFT Prickly pear nestled into a corner of a French garden, providing a touch of exotica – and a warning to stay clear.

Caryophyllales

Core Eudicots: Rosids and Asterids

Now for the two massive top branches. DNA sequencing confirms a decisive dividing of the ways right here between the rosids and the asterids (which, we can see, already have their own link with the caryophyllales). Our natural next step appears to be towards the rosids. But before we go there, let's just take a small peek across the way to the base of the asterids. It's too tantalising to wait any longer. We go straight to the primroses. Just why do we have to bring nature's prime beauties into the weeds picture?

32

Primula vulgare
PRIMULACEAE
Primrose

How can the '*prima rosa*', this pure spring beauty beloved in the countryside and by every gardener too (even attracting an RHS Award of Garden Merit), ever be unwanted anywhere? Well, think about it. A natural primrose can look rather odd and uncomfortable in many a modern spring bed filled, as it may well be, with the latest brightly-coloured primrose hybrids. Does it not then become a plant to be moved into a friendlier spot – say a grassy bank – rather than be left stranded as a weed-like odd-one-out? The exquisite perfection of this wild flower highlights how contrived and artificial our gardens can become when garish hybrid cousins steal the show. Of course to many purists it is these brash newcomers who are the unwanted ones and to be banished. So, primroses aptly remind us of our starting point: any plant can be a weed somewhere, sometime.

Weeds or not, primroses had Darwin totally captivated. 'I don't think anything in my scientific life has given me so much satisfaction as making out the meaning of these plants,' he confessed in his short autobiographical memoir. He was especially intrigued by primrose 'heterostyly', that is the plant's habit of having two flower forms with styles and stamens of different lengths and positional relation to each other.

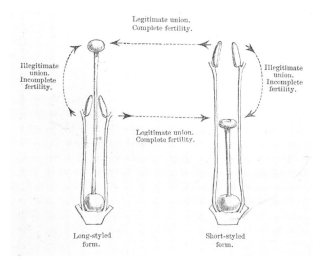

LEFT Darwin's illustration of the two forms of primrose with a photograph above of the two different flowers seen in cross-section.

Legitimate union.
Complete fertility.

Illegitimate
union.
Incomplete
fertility.

Illegitimate
union.
Incomplete
fertility.

Legitimate union.
Complete fertility.

Long-styled
form.

Short-styled
form.

While writing the *Origin*, Darwin found himself investigating primroses and became curious as to why these plants were divided into two kinds according to the relative positions of their sexual parts. Half had a style appearing in the centre of the flower with stamens hidden below (now popularly known as 'pin'), while the other half had their style hidden below the anthers which now appeared in the middle of the flower (a 'thrum'). Were

Ericales

these plants on the way to becoming dioecious (single-sexed), a state of existence we will be meeting shortly in the case of nettles and holly, for example? This was one of Darwin's suppositions, as he deduced that these differences favoured, if not guaranteed, cross-pollination. He backed this up by explaining how the antics of insects, particularly those of nocturnal moths with a long proboscis, ensured this more productive fertilisation.

The whole process absorbed Darwin for many years well after the publication of the *Origin.* He wrote it all up in some detail eighteen years later in his book *The Different Forms of Flowers on Plants of the Same Species.*

Unwittingly, Darwin touched upon another key element in weed success. He pursued the breeding mechanisms of primroses with such enthusiasm and all the scientific precision that was available to him because they appeared to demonstrate the extraordinary lengths that plants can go to assure cross-fertilisation and hence enriched reproductive resources (he had no knowledge of genes but was certainly reaching closely towards the basis of such a concept). Yes, primroses perform remarkable out-reaching fertilisation but, as Darwin eventually acknowledged, they could and would also fall back on themselves, quite literally, when 'thrum' pollen falls onto the stigma below it (while this obviously cannot happen with the 'pin' above the anthers). But, as he worked out over repeated tests, the end results of self-fertilisation were far less successful than those of cross-fertilisation. This dual capacity of primroses to self- and cross-pollinate (with far more elaborate subtleties that we have shown) with a distinctly better success rate from out-crossing exemplifies par excellence a key trait particular to weed success, as we have already seen emerging in previous candidates. Simple primroses win with such subtleties.

WHAT TO DO

- Relish and enjoy.
- Move to a grassy bank or any less formal part of the garden, even in partial shade.
- Look for the 'pins' and 'thrums' and see if they are fairly balanced.
- Use flowers and early leaves in salads, if they can be spared.
- But, really, feel challenged about the nature of your garden. How far do you wish to carry the artifice that is any garden? Think hard about integrating the old and the new, the domesticated and the undomesticated, and how best to let the *'prima rosa'* enchant, as it always will.

OPPOSITE BELOW Scarlet pimpernel seductively spreading its wings, as illustrated in Stephenson's *Medical Botany*, 1834.

33

Anagallis arvensis
PRIMULACEAE
Scarlet Pimpernel

Scarlet pimpernel, a cheeky weed from the fields is also from the primula family. As a freely-seeding annual (averaging 900 seeds per plant) it relishes disturbed ground, grabbing its space with prostrate growth. With its flashing red flowers (noted for the hairy stalks of their stamens) which open and close according to the weather or time of day, it is otherwise known as 'poor man's weatherglass'. It is poisonous if ingested by man, dog or horse and yet we call it 'anagallis' meaning 'to laugh aloud'!

WHAT TO DO
- Quietly remove from the garden.
- Try instead one of the beautiful anagallis cultivars; they are super on sunny days.

Ericales

NOW WE return to the rosids, to meet, first of all, the geraniums.

34

Geranium spp.

GERANIACEAE
Cranesbills

Geranium dissectum (Cut-leafed Cranesbill) is one of those annual plants which are frequently about on field and garden margins ready to make a move into newly disturbed soil. In fact its recorded frequency has increased during the last fifty years and it is a persistent major seed contaminant, especially of clover. As a distinctly weedy version of the many fine garden varieties there is no need for it all.

Geranium molle (Dove's-foot Cranesbill) – foot of a dove and bill of a crane, what an anatomical mix-up for a mere weed! A 'common <u>and garden</u>' specimen if ever there was one. An annual which will often over-winter as a distinctive rosette ready to spring into pink flower at the first opportunity and then explode out its 2,000-odd seeds to carry on the endless show. The seed also finds its way into other seed and again notoriously into clover.

Other regular garden visitors include *G. columbium, G. rotundifolium, G. pusillum* and *G. lucidum.*

WHAT TO DO

- Prise out with a fork.
- Introduce a good cultivar instead.

OPPOSITE ABOVE LEFT Cut-leafed cranesbill.

OPPOSITE ABOVE RIGHT Dove's-foot cranesbill.

OPPOSITE BELOW The ubiquitous pink garden cranesbill geranium – a good-old standby but one which can sometimes stand by a little too vigorously. A garden plant which definitely needs watching for its weed-invasive potential.

Geraniales

WEEDS, WEEDING (& DARWIN)

35

Oenothera biennis

ONAGRACEAE
Evening Primrose

Over to a nearby branch and we are with the myrtales for evening primrose, rosebay willowherb and purple loosetrife to raise their problematic heads. Evening primrose startles, and in several regards is startling. Most unusually its flowers first appear at the end of the day and, if you are lucky enough to be around, there is to be heard an astonishing rustle of buds springing open. Then too, early on a dewy morning, the shimmering beauty of the new soft-yellow blooms is simply breathtaking. But then again, do such wonders of nature really fit in with a garden?

As with the common primrose, this part namesake and fellow beauty of the wayside puts us in a gardening quandary. Is it a weed, a garden flower or just a wild flower? Of course, it is all three. *Oenothera biennis* appeared in mainland Europe from North America in the seventeenth century and started to make a presence in Britain in the early nineteenth century. Perhaps it was first savoured in our gardens as a relatively rare delight, but certainly that is no longer the case. Hovering around everywhere, it is questionably a bit too common for many garden niches. And certainly its capacity to proliferate all over the place puts it squarely in the realm of the weeds.

Edward Salisbury, that distinguished director of Kew Gardens, singled out this plant for exceptional seed production and claimed that 'a large garden plant of this species might well have over 33,000 potential offspring'. (This figure was diligently arrived at by counting seed capsules per plant, seeds per capsule, calculating averages and then taking into account average germination rates.) Even though he saw it as a garden plant, Salisbury was well aware that its progeny needed to be drastically weeded to manageable proportions. On top of this, further research has found the seed to have record viability, lasting to 80 years.

All this is sustained by the plant being a true biennial. It is not just an over-wintering annual but takes its time to build up a strong leafy rosette with a substantial tap-root food store in the first year, all ready to take off into erect flowering spikes the following year. For some reason the plants have a tendency to stand in straight lines. Appropriately one of its regional names is 'King Henry's Guard'.

Most startling of all is the shock that evening primroses happened to bring to the course of evolutionary science. Early in the twentieth century Hugo de Vries, a Dutch botanist at the University of Amsterdam, found himself using these plants for Mendelian

WEEDS, WEEDING (& DARWIN)

LEFT Evening primrose plants standing to attention in a back garden, producing new flowers every evening and thereby creating a superabundance of seeds to carry on the biennial show.

genetics research. In fact over a few years he managed to breed seven new varieties. He noticed that each new batch that he sowed came up with a few baffling surprises, plants varied considerably in size, in the colour and shape of leaves and of petals, stems and veins. He also found that they bred true if self-fertilised. Here, he thought, were 'new elementary species' created in a single generation through what he called 'mutation'.

De Vries and his followers, who named themselves 'saltationists' (from *saltus,* jump), believed they had struck a blow at Darwinian evolution which upheld gradualism as its central plank. In 1932 a prominent biologist, speaking for his discipline, wrote, 'All of Darwin's "particular views" have gone down wind: variation, survival of the fittest, natural selection, sexual selection, and all the rest. Darwin is very nearly, if not quite ... outmoded.' However, it did not take long for the saltationists too to fall out of fashion and, as we shall see, for the Darwinian case to be reasserted with more convincing explanations of its subtleties.

WHAT TO DO
- Select ruthlessly. Decide where, if at all, evening primrose looks best.
- Dig out superfluous rosettes in the first year, if they were not hoed or hand weeded as seedlings. And jump to it!

Myrtales

36

Chamerion angustifolium
ONAGRACEAE
Rosebay Willowherb

Another major delight of waysides, a prime natural associate of woodland clearance and notorious 'fireweed' habitant of former bombsites, rosebay willowherb is just too much of the wild and too 'common' to be acceptable in any garden, other than in its wildest corners. But it is always there waiting to make an entry if given half a chance, sneaking under the fence with its perennial rhizomatous root system, or by delivering its prolific wind-born seeds (averaged at 80,000 per plant, Salisbury again) over the fence. Like its promiscuous cousin, the evening primrose, it appears to have New World ancestry and has only taken real hold around Britain during the last century, but this time allegedly as the result of increased heathland fires brought about by motorists, not to mention indirectly from enemy fire. Certainly the species is noticeably stimulated by extra-nitrates supplied by soot while at the same time having more tolerance of certain combustion by-products.

WHAT TO DO

- Fork out and apply suppressant mulch. It is usually easily recognised and dealt with.

Myrtales

WEEDS, WEEDING (& DARWIN)

37

Lythrum salicaria
LYTHRACEAE
Purple Loosestrife

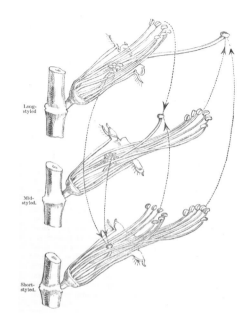

Long-
styled.

Mid-
styled.

Short-
styled.

After two plants which came from North America to Europe and then caused trouble, now we have one which went the other way and which has wrought far more havoc.

A European native, an occasional way-side plant and more particularly a waterside one, purple loosestrife is quite often to be found in British gardens. There it will blend discreetly into many a mixed bed and usefully fill that odd vacant space without causing a disruptive stir – an innocuous, mild-mannered character. Across the Atlantic where purple loosestrife evidently accompanied migrants in the early 1800s, there is quite a different story. In short, *Lythrum salicaria* now ranks as one of the worst weeds in a majority of the United States and is a cause of mega alarm. So how has this come about?

Firstly it is helpful to look back at a curious piece of Charles Darwin's post-*Origin* researches. Following on from his excitement with primroses and their flowers with two forms, this loosestrife came to his attention because it had three forms with different positioning of their flower sexual parts. His diagram showing the three forms is shown inset above. 'In the manner of their fertilisation', Darwin wrote, 'these plants offer a more remarkable case than can be found in any other plant or animal.... Nature has ordained a most complex marriage-arrangement, namely a triple union between three hermaphrodites, – each hermaphrodite being in its female organ quite distinct from the other two hermaphrodites and partially distinct in its male organs, and each furnished with two sets of males'.

OPPOSITE ABOVE Rosebay willowherb menacing with its fiery floral display.
OPPOSITE BELOW Later a seedy wisp of the willowherb proclaims it's still here and all set to procreate.
ABOVE Darwin's own diagram showing the three forms of purple loosestrife flower.

Myrtales

He scrupulously tested the relative fertility and sterility of all eighteen (3 x 6) possible unions of pollen and ovule and revealed an extraordinary reproductive power for plants in such a group situation where the three plant forms somehow maintain an even distribution, just as happens with the two forms of primrose. In effect a pack strategy takes hold, with, literally, the more, the merrier.

Can we therefore suppose that this botanical enigma has something do with why purple loosestrife ran so wild across North America? The standard first explanation for such 'alien invasions' is that these are a natural consequence of freeing a plant from the constraints of its home ecology. Whether purple loosestrife was intentionally imported or whether its seeds sneaked a ride in the sacks of soil used for ship ballast, the subsequent gathering momentum of its colonisation (essentially following and obstructing waterways as they were being constructed and developed with the progress of settlers) was epic. With classic weed opportunism, this was the plant most suited and most at the ready to follow in the settlers' tracks, occupying the newly disturbed ground and overwhelming the native flora. We assert that *Lythrum salicaria*'s unique capacity for a three-pronged 'pack' attack (as so deftly unravelled by Darwin) must have played a key role.

Of course there are additional explanations: notably, this plant's capacity to withstand the severe continental winters (being well-seasoned from Central Europe), its capacity to bulk out as a perennial with putative rhizomes and its seed production far outstripping that of virtually all annuals (up to three million seeds claimed per plant – putting even pigweed in the shade).

WHAT TO DO

In North America and Australasia:
- Outlaw! Follow the lead of many states in making purple loosestrife illegal. Can even the ingenuity of American lawyers make this work, one wonders?
- Shun the offers of nurseries who still offer enticing loosestrife cultivars.
- Apply biological control by introducing appropriate pests and pathogens, thereby redeveloping a constraining ecology. This appears to be the most realistic way forward. The biological control programmes for loosestrife are beginning to be cited as models to be emulated.

In the UK:
- Accept that loosestrife's pioneering capacity can be put to good advantage in helping to get a new garden going. It is a not-bad standby for filling up empty corners and for giving you time to think what might be a more desired planting.
- But then keep it under control and even be prepared to banish it totally once your other plant stock begins to really settle in.
- Amuse yourself examining the flowers to find the three types.

LEFT Purple loosestrife here acting up as a charmer beside the river Thames at Richmond. In North America and Australasia it is more often the dreaded invasive threat to the waterways themselves.

Myrtales

38

Viola spp.

VIOLACEAE
Wild Pansies / Heartsease

Viola arvensis and *Viola tricolor*, the two main wild pansies, which are both often just called heartsease, are cute and charming in their own way and in the garden they are likely to be evidence of former hybrids that have unravelled back to their beginnings. Fine in the cracks of paving or in wild-flower meadows but they have probably lost the right to stay on in main flower beds. Even so, one should not disregard the love potion potential as shown by Puck in *A Midsummer Night's Dream*,

> The juice of it on eyelids laid
> Will make or man or woman madly dote
> Upon the next live creature that it sees.

Darwin, himself was certainly wooed by these violas and sufficiently so to observe, experiment and then conclude that bumble bees were the only insects to visit and pollinate them – and

also red clover. Not only that, but also that their fortunes depended on mice and cats! He had found out that the number of bumble bees in a district depended on the number of resident field mice which destroy their combs and nests – and that the number of mice depended on the number of cats, which in turn depended on the number of households around and about. So violas are evidently more secure the nearer they are to us.

WHAT TO DO
• Relocate to the more suitable parts of the garden.

Viola odorata
Violet

In the same family, and of the same genus too, is the oh-so-sweet-scented violet. Sweet, really? 'What queer little flowers they are', exclaimed Darwin to Hooker. He was referring to the second flowering of violets in late summer, something which passes most of us by. No scent this time, and no bees or bumble bees to fertilise. Sex takes place behind closed doors. The tiny little flowers have scale-like petals which stay shut and produce just as many seed capsules as the sweetness-itself eponymous-coloured flowers. That's 'gleistogamy' (closed sexing) for you. Darwin played a big part in unravelling it with the help of his 'telescope' eyes.

For all this double performance, once at the beginning of the season and once at the end, we have to put up with a rather dull weed-like blanketing of uninteresting leaves all through the long summer – often somewhere on a shadier edge of a lawn. Is it worth it?

WHAT TO DO
• Accept with cautious moderation, as every garden should have just a few of those early-year welcoming sweeties. But beware there is a double lot of seeding going on as well as some vegetative spread.

OPPOSITE LEFT Heartsease (*Viola arvensis* in this instance) in its characteristic teasing mode.
OPPOSITE RIGHT Violets in full smothering leaf mode, as they persist through the summer following their early bloom.

Malpighiales

39

Euphorbia peplus
EUPHORBIACEAE
Petty Spurge

A prolific annual euphorbia: flowering, fruiting, seeding and germinating constantly over an eight-month season. Petty, in that seedlings can be quite pretty, but invariably out of place. Be warned, genuinely this time: spurge oil can purge drastically.

WHAT TO DO
• Hand weed (with gloves) or hoe.

40

Mercuriales perennis
EUPHORBIACEAE
Dog's Mercury

Poisonous and invasive, dog's mercury alarmed the Darwin family. It was quite possibly their most dreaded weed and certainly the cause of a rare family tiff. A young gardener's boy was dispatched each year to clear it from along the sandwalk, the path around a little wood where Darwin strolled almost every day. But on one occasion a new lad got it wrong, as Darwin's son Francis later recalled.

> As my father and mother reached the sandwalk they found bare earth, a great heap of wild ivy torn up by its roots and the abhorred dog's mercury flourishing alone. My father could not help laughing at her dismay ... and he used to say it was the only time she was ever cross with him.

RIGHT Dog's mercury here shown lifted out of the ground with its underground rhizomatous network.

Malpighiales

WEEDS, WEEDING (& DARWIN)

'There is not a more fatal plant native of our country than this', warned Culpepper in the seventeenth century, and he berated other herbals for not telling their readers about it too. A legendary reputation of lethal danger stuck to dog's mercury, and no doubt alerted the Darwins. But nowadays no big deal is made of it. One herbalist simply states 'edible qualities: none'. When dried, any toxic qualities are said to disappear. Even so, bruise the leaves and you will be met with the smell of rotting fish. And it is wise not to handle any euphorbia too much because the milky sap can be a nasty skin irritant, and stalks easily snap to release it.

Dog's mercury has two other adaptive advantages. Like nettle (Weed 46), it is dioecious with separate male and female plants (and evidently Darwin never allowed himself to look closely to pick up on this). Secondly it spreads vegetatively with shallow rhizomes pushing it along a metre or so a year and also has assured cross-pollination to produce healthy seedlings with a chance of being more widely distributed. And, like its woodland companion the bramble, it is polyploid, octoploid in fact, with 64 chromosomes apiece. So watch out for this one, a chancey customer indeed. Though be warned that Darwin's gardeners do not appear ever to have dealt with it effectively. Dog's mercury is still to be seen to this day on the corner of the sandwalk at the back of Down House.

WHAT TO DO

- Decide whether to oust or manage it. Dog's mercury is only likely to grow in shady woodland and make a temporary display in early spring.
- In either case wear gloves. Ease it out with a fork and, if you wish to be more successful than Darwin's boy, do so thoroughly and follow up with a dense mulch. But in woodland this may be difficult because of other roots. The weed wins out with adaptive opportunism yet again.

41

Hypericum perforatum
HYPERICACEAE
Perforate St John's Wort

An attractive wild flower with an erudite common name and a plant which all too freely breezes into gardens. Yes, it is distinguished by a peculiar perforated effect, the 'perforations' being translucent dots scattered over its leaves which are little oil sacs that

WEEDS, WEEDING (& DARWIN)

can give off a rosin-like odour if bruised. Its inflorescence, slightly oily too, also has an open perforated effect, immediately distinguishing it from the denser flowers of ragwort (*Senecio jacobaea*, Weed 94) with which it will sometimes cohabit. Well, there is a natural selective 'reason for everything', as Darwinists will insist. Quite what it is in this case is yet another subtle challenge to us. No doubt here is some unique defence against predation combined, perhaps, with some particularly effective and unique insect symbiosis.

As a perennial, perforate St John's wort securely roots itself, either deeply – down a metre if the soil will allow – or widely – with lateral roots near the surface if the soil is shallow. It is susceptible to drought and depends on the deeper roots to access water reserves. But if the main stems are cut or broken then the lateral shoots will bud.

This hypericum is also an exceptionally free seeder. Estimates of average number of seeds per plant vary from 26,000 to 34,000. One estimate even went as far as 150,000. Whatever, there are an amazing quantity ready to scatter on the slightest breeze. So no wonder seedlings spring up all over the place in our gardens.

Although it can be a merciful relief spotting this character and finding that it is not another ragwort, it, too, needs to be treated warily for potential toxicity. On the one hand it is apparently valued for having anti-depressant and anti-inflammatory qualities and on the other, grazing animals are said to acquire a disastrous craving for it, giving them photosensitivity and other debilitating conditions, even when it is dried in hay.

WHAT TO DO

- Just keep working the garden, for this weed 'cannot withstand cultivation' (Garden Organic). No slacking and you should easily be free of it.
- Don't just cut off (mow) or pull out flower shoots. This plant readily regenerates from its rhizomatous roots. And don't burn as this promotes seed germination.
- Note that gall midge and the flea beetle readily consume this plant.
- And remember, this oily fellow will always slip through the net again somehow.

Malpighiales

42

Oxalis spp.
OXALIDACEAE
Wood Sorrel

Oxalis debilis and *Oxalis corymbosa* are two plants about which botanists appear to be in some confusion as to whether they are distinctly different, one and the same, or – as is most usually asserted – one is a sub-species of the other. But, gardeners have no confusion about what a horrendous intrusion either can be. On first finding, wood sorrel may intrigue as an exotic novelty with its delicate pink or brick-red flowers – indeed, the plants originate from Hawaii – but don't be tempted to leave be, for in a year this newcomer will multiply profusely and be immensely challenging to eradicate.

The not-so-secret weapon of these plants is their capacity to reproduce vegetatively by growing quantities of bulbils, just like the lesser celandine (Weed 9). These are produced below ground around the top of a short swollen tap root. Once just one root is allowed to mature, the bulbils readily detach to generate a mighty second generation the following year. Then they become past masters at mingling and out-competing with whatever else is around. So, not surprisingly, there is more to be said about trying to control it than describing it in the first place.

LEFT The yellow sorrel (*Oxalis corniculata*) spreads along the ground, often looking quite attractive at first. But plants will soon be all over the place as the seed pods notoriously turn themselves inside out to eject their seeds up to nearly a metre.
RIGHT Wood sorrel – its weed armoury being, especially, that succulent root and those multiple bulbils.

WEEDS, WEEDING (& DARWIN)

WHAT TO DO

- Grow in a pot if you must. Oxalis barely produces viable seed to spread about.
- Get in early. Pick out – or rather gently prise out – the new shoots as soon as they appear in early summer. This is the only time the shoots come out quite easily with their yet undeveloped bulbil still attached. Finicky work, but realistically the only chance and needing daily attention over a good month. But be realistic – who can do that?
- Compromise. Do your best at the above in the early stages and then have lusty annuals inserted and at the ready to hide and partially suppress the oxalis with their cover. Of course, the oxalis will still be there in the autumn and you will be up for the same again next year.
- After any careful weeding in autumn, be sure to scrape up and burn any easily separated bulbils left on the soil surface.
- Resist using a weedkiller. It is difficult to apply without risking other plants and oxalis is said to be quite resistant anyway.
- Make drastic and total clearance of infected beds and follow by strong suppressant mulch for a whole year.
- Be wary of importing leaf mould from woodland (says he with bitter experience).

Oxalis corniculata
Creeping Wood Sorrel

The yellow-flowered variety with a normal but clinging root or series of roots and a prostrate spreading habit. One of the lawn invaders needing to be dealt with, but what a relief: no bulbils. There is a disarmingly attractive purple variety.

Oxalis pes-caprae
Bermuda Buttercup

Another dubious exotic. Say no more.

RIGHT So seductive! Is this how bramble gets away with it in our gardens? In this case it scrambles over a shrub with fellow runaway tendencies. Respectable *Cotoneaster horizontalis* also needs to be taken in hand from time to time, though it is nothing like the horror of bramble. And just to taunt us even more is a leaf of *Humulus lupulus* 'Aureus' cheekily exceeding its bounds too.

Oxalidales

WEEDS, WEEDING (& DARWIN)

43

Rubus fruticosus spp.

ROSACEAE
Bramble

Brambles are exasperating, both to botanists and to gardeners. Even Darwin snapped about 'the endless disputes whether or not some fifty species of British brambles are good species', as he wound up his argument in the concluding pages of the *Origin*. But that is nothing compared with this whole assemblage's confrontational stance with the everyday gardener.

Brambles appear to have all the advantages over us that any plant could want. Their roots and their shoots both have extraordinary capacities to spread and regenerate by themselves (resources of vegetative reproduction). And then the flowers also produce vast quantities of viable seeds – often, amazingly, through parthenogenesis (bypassing pollination altogether). These are all scattered far and wide through the consumption of their most tempting and delicious fruits.

At the core of these impressive powers of multiplication is 'polyploidy', a condition of having multiple chromosomes (sets of genes). Instead of having the standard two chromosomes, brambles can have double the amount, even treble, quadruple or more. Why and how they do this, and to what extent is not easily discernible (that is, why some fertilising cells fail to divide before fusion), but the net result is a measure of added strength, luxuriance and capacity for variation.

But let us not beat about this particular prickly bush. Brambles can present us with an almighty challenge. Abandon your home for a year or so and they may well have you locked out – as those with holiday homes in remote parts sometimes find to their dismay. More regularly, they can obstruct footpaths, send out 'trip-wire' shoots, and simply go on a rampage in extensive gardens that include some woodland whose margins they love to inhabit.

We tend to be aware, especially, of the shoots which arch up over their own thickets as well as over and into other shrubs. But, not so overtly visible, there are other stems which will shoot out in a straight line through grass at ground level, while branching too. Whether arching or ground hugging, both kinds of shoots can extend up to five metres or more in a season, eventually to insert their many growing tips into the ground where newly emerging 'adventitious roots' avidly seize their chance. Of course, most of these new plantlets can easily be removed, even pulled out or mown out, but inevitably there will be the odd devil which finds its way to the base of a tree or shrub and then inextricably entwines its roots into the established larger roots – a dastardly bit of survival selection.

Then there is underground action too. Roots will radiate from a tuberous core to spread branchingly both deep and wide, and if they have moved sufficiently from their base, they will send up an occasional sucker. Sometimes we see new shoots in a row, all arising from the same lateral root.

Sexual reproduction is more erratic, sporadic and can even be quite phoney. As we suggested at the beginning, some brambles get by without any fertilisation but with pollen simply stimulating the female parts to form an embryo seed on their own rather than fusing with them, a process known as 'pseudogamy'. But others can successfully carry out

WEEDS, WEEDING (& DARWIN)

Rosales

cross-pollination with the aid of insects, which, as we know, hover around blackberries in often distasteful profusion. Here is the potential for significant new variants to arise, while vegetative cloning then sustains the variations most suited to particular niches and so on. Altogether we have a richly rewarding process both in securing short-term garden advantage and in surviving longer-term extinction threats.

Meanwhile brambles display their own extraordinary range of variation. There are some 300 varieties/sub-species now known in the United Kingdom. There is a bramble for every time slot; a bramble for every type of soil, air, light, temperature or moisture condition; a bramble with every shade of flower, taste of fruit and slight difference of leaf shape; and further variation seemingly just for the hell of it. A minefield for botanists to categorise, let alone for gardeners to deal with.

And finally, just to think of it: Baron von Mueller, a contemporary of Darwin (and strong evolution refusenik) and 'arguably Australia's greatest botanist', according to Tim Low, went round Australia with a bag of blackberry seeds, scattering them wherever he went and declaring that poor people in time to come would bless him for his thoughtfulness. In fact, the folk of Victoria came to damn him for introducing their very worst weed.

WHAT TO DO

- In smaller gardens the occasional new seedling is easily pulled up and we can assume that any major endemic growth was cleared before the garden was started.
- In larger gardens, reserve a fine winter's day for a full-on clearance and it can be one of the most satisfying jobs of all. It will involve grubbing (with mattock), digging up (with spade) and prising out (with fork). Even just pulling (with gloves on) can often be quite effective. Whatever, it is especially satisfying to extract the tuberous core, even though a few weaker threads will inevitably remain to enable eventual regeneration. Then the reward: a crackling, warming bonfire … and a new, beautiful, clear space (well, just for a while).
- Harvest the fruit. Feast on blackberry and apple crumble, and make some bramble jelly.

Rosales

44

Aphanes (Alchemilla) arvensis
ROSACEAE
Parsley Piert

Strange that this gentle small tussock of a plant should be from the same family (the extended rose family) as bramble, but there we are – another resilient weed from the fields, equally adept as garden hanger-on and capable of defying its annual status by over-wintering over years. Cyclic seed dormancy is the special trick up this one's sleeve.

WHAT TO DO
- Don't be deceived by this character's pretence at being genuine lady's mantle or even of an incipient geranium. Hoe (shallow roots), or hand weed or fork out if you have left it too long.

45

Potentilla reptans
ROSACEAE
Creeping Cinquefoil

Cinquefoil, named from its stalks of five-toothed leaflets, radiates. Its radiating creep is itself outrageously creepy. The leaflets have a characteristic radiating form – a little bit akin to their family associate, the strawberry, whose similarly toothed leaflets radiate in threes, and this similarity can lead us to hesitate in dealing with them. But what is alarming is the fact that at the axil base of many of the cinquefoil leaf stalks prostrate stolon branches will spread out like the spikes of a wheel, putting down tough blackish tap roots from which arise satellite rosettes. The roots, penetrating down 30 or 40 cm, are notoriously difficult

WEEDS, WEEDING (& DARWIN)

Rosales

to extract, particularly because they seem to go for inserting themselves into paving or between stones in alpine beds. Cinquefoil has a tendency to insinuate itself as an alpine, its cute little yellow flower looking as if it should be there, but if you do not take action to remove it as soon as it appears, you will live to regret it bitterly.

Edward Salisbury, the renowned dispassionate commentator on weeds, had no hesitation in coming straight out with it. 'The cinquefoil is … one of the most troublesome weeds on account of the rapidity of its spread and the depth and vigour of its roots.' For Salisbury this is strong stuff, as if this one really had got under his skin by seriously affecting his own garden. He did his counting too. He saw up to fifteen shoots radiating from one rosette and found among them two 'runners' one of which ran to 186 cm, and the other to 198 cm. They 'bore tufts of leaves and roots at intervals, numbering 12 on the one and 16 in the other'. Then he added, 'It is therefore scarcely surprising that this weed can colonise at the rate of over 12 square yards in a single season!' Not satisfied, he goes on to calculate that by the end of the second year 784 new plants would have been generated from the original rosette from which fifteen branches had radiated.

BELOW Creeping cinquefoil asserting its right to creep along the edge of a path.

WHAT TO DO

- Learn from Salisbury's calculation. Act immediately should cinquefoil appear in your garden. This is one of the cases where an all-or-almost-nothing approach is required.
- Either dig up the whole invaded area, paving stones, brick, flower bed, alpine bed and all to remove every bit of vegetation before starting anew (and be sure to follow up by pulling out any weakened shoots which may reappear in the first month or so).
- Or accept that this could be one of the rarer cases where spot spraying of a glyphosate herbicide may be the best solution. A similar eagle-eyed follow-up (as above) will also be necessary.
- Or, resign yourself to living with it, but with periodic top-growth purges to reduce photosynthetic energy uptake.

46

Urtica dioica
URTICACEAE
Common Nettle

A real weed if ever there was one. Nettles like to hang around human habitation, particularly enjoying our nitrogenous waste, happy in uncompacted soil, enticed into piles of rubble, occupying scarce space, obstructing footpaths, and entrenching themselves hostilely in garden margins and on all those awkward spots. Can they ever be wanted? Much as we wish them banished whenever they obstruct or sting us, it would be a dull, anaemic world without them. Where would we be without their attractiveness to butterflies (Red Admiral, Peacock and Small Tortoiseshell); without their nutritional input for us and for grazing animals (appreciated more when dried in hay); without their manifold claimed health cures; without their many other bizarre attributes and uses and even without their characteristic stings.

How then do common nettles sustain their presumptuous presence around us? First to note is that they are 'dioecious', that is they are single sexed, existing only as female or as male plants. So, the differently sexed flowers ensure out-breeding with the aid of those butterflies and other insects. But each plant also spreads itself clonally, as we know well, with extending rhizomatous root systems and with surface stolons too. No wonder then that they are so vigorous, blooming in hairy health and bristling with vicious defences.

RIGHT Nettles all set to close in on a public footpath.

Rosales

And, those stings are merciless, an instant sharp pain turning into a persistent tingling itch if left untreated, a sure deterrent to so many predators besides us humans. Nicholas Harberd, whom we will meet shortly at Weed 53, eloquently described just what happened when he stepped (bare toed in sandals) into a nettle patch on a late July afternoon.

> The stinging hairs of nettles are single long cells, needles with bladders at their bases. The bladder is held within a clump of other smaller cells that rise above the surface of the leaf, and contains a cocktail of irritants. The hair itself is a capillary of the finest bore. Delicate, brittle as glass. The touch of my foot shattered a few of those fragile capillaries along lines of predetermined weakness. Exposing the sharp edges that then penetrated my skin. With my body pierced, the bladder's contents flowed into me. Molecules that attack, that generate the itch and sting. (*Seed to seed*, p.199/200)

A restrained account, considering that at the same moment the poor man also suffered a mosquito bite on his arm.

As for those yellow, sinewy, extended roots, that is another major challenge, especially as they will entwine into any other irremovable material, into brambles or tree roots. So tough and fibrous are they that their fibres have been used for weaving into coarse textiles (supposedly in Germany during the First World War). And, of course, the roots anchor the plants with devilish ultra security, while continually extending the clonal colonies and sending up dense clumps of those aforesaid hairy shoots.

WHAT TO DO

For this truly notorious weed, the options are multifold:

- 'Grasp' firmly to break the hairs before they manage to penetrate your skin. Even so, it is wiser to use gloves wherever possible, if you are manually trying to clear it.
- Watch out while hand-weeding especially with poor light or at dusk. Young seedlings appear to have extra venom.
- Soothe stings by rubbing with the traditional Dr Dock leaf (*Rumex* spp., Weed 23), bearing in mind that just washing with water will help. Calendula leaves are said to be even better.
- Suppress. Layers of old newspaper covered with other soil, woodchips or whatever, can do this quite effectively.
- Go for a complete dig out. Follow up with a continual pull out of any successive seedlings and regenerating root remnants.

Rosales

- Replace with something more wanted. Lush nettles indicate high fertility. Take advantage.
- Leave be and tend as a nature reserve or security barrier against unwanted intruders.
- Cultivate as an eco-friendlier alternative to cotton. Many hectares are currently being planted with common nettle from which stem fibres are being extracted and used as a cotton-like substitute (especially helped by being marketed in association with a designer label). Its evident all-round resistance makes it a promising competitor to the increasingly pest-ridden (and so pesticide-drenched) cotton.
- Treat yourself to some nettle soup or spinach in spring. 'It consumes the phlegmatic superfluities of man, that the coldness and moisture of winter has left behind', according to seventeenth-century Culpepper. Thus get yourself energised for some more gardening.

Urtica urens
Annual Nettle / Small Nettle

Beware of this lesser villain too. It comes and goes through a summer and autumn, each plant leaving behind another thousand and more seeds. It has a spikier effect with more sharply indented leaves, short and stumpy flowers (separate flowers of both sexes on the same plant this time). It is shorter and often more branched than its perennial cousin, and the lower leaf blades are shorter than their stalks which gives it a particular identifying feature.

Not to mention *Urica ferox* – the most ferocious nettle of all. It is a tree nettle in New Zealand which can grow up to five metres tall and which, on the lightest touch, can sting painfully hard for many days.

ABOVE The troublesome annual nettle, as if the common nettle were not enough!

Rosales

47

Soleiriolia soleiriolii

URTICACEAE

Mind-your-own-business / Mother-of-thousands

A strange family bedfellow of nettles, but you can see that this tiny-leaved, ground-hugging perennial has the same persistent invasive quality as its giant cousins. It, too, hovers just outside the house and anchors itself tightly into secure nooks and crannies, though all on a miniature scale. It is easy to be a bit deceived by it at first as a cute little green patch decorating a bit of boring brickwork, but it then insinuates its way in to become an annoying spreader and loses its charm becoming instead an indicator of out-of-control scruffiness.

WHAT TO DO

- Stamp on it, literally. Scratch/strim it down.
- Or accept and develop as a ground cover.

WEEDS, WEEDING (& DARWIN)

OPPOSITE Mind-your-own-business doing just that on some brick paving.
LEFT Pellitory of the wall firmly attached to a well-mortared garden boundary.

48

Parietaria judaica
URTICACEAE
Pellitory of the Wall

One of those plants that looks as if it could have promise with its red stems but never really gets beyond being an undistinguished, unkempt bit of nothing. It fixes itself into walls and tight corners from which it is almost impossible to dislodge.

WHAT TO DO
• Try to pull out – you'll be lucky! Appreciate, at least, its steadfastness and its zany name.

SO MUCH for urticaceae! The above four weed species from the nettle family happen to represent all the key members of that family. It is rare indeed for all members of a family to be such strong weed candidates.

Rosales

49

Trifolium repens

FABACEAE

White Clover

Clover is a mixed blessing, and especially white clover. Its fragrant bumble-bee-like flowers have charm, its shamrock leaves provide good nutritious grazing and its nitrogen-fixing roots fertilise the soil. But come a hot dry summer and it is very much an 'oh-no' of lawns, and an annoying opportunist into adjacent flower beds.

A procumbent perennial, white clover is yet another weed-inclined plant which takes full advantage of both clonal spreading and fertile flowers. Away push the stolons, through grass if necessary, rooting themselves repeatedly at short intervals while extending up to a metre each growing season. And the flowers buzz with bees – rolling

WEEDS, WEEDING (& DARWIN)

Fabales

children beware! – promoting cross-fertilisation and the abundant production of seeds which can ripen and germinate almost straightaway or hang on dormant in the soil seed bank for up to the standard five years or so. Grazing animals, of course, help in a widespread dispersal.

WHAT TO DO
- Respect clover's ecological niche: host to a range of insects feeding on its roots, leaves and seeds; good food for grazing animals (including slugs and snails), and good food for soil.
- Rake lawn before mowing so that growing shoots are lifted to get the chop.
- Mow less frequently to enable grass to get the upper hand.
- Observe for warnings of approaching storms! According to Pliny, 'the leaves tremble and stand upright against the coming of a tempest'.

Take note of two family cousins:

Trifolium dubium
Lesser Yellow Trefoil

Another closely-related lawn nuisance with smaller yellow to brown flowers and low-spreading shoots which do not root.

Medicago lupilina
Black Medick

Annual, similar to *T. dubium* but with distinctive black seed pods and sharp tipped leaves. Said to produce 2,350 seeds per plant – so mow with the grass box!

LEFT White clover – a dubious extra on lawns, and elsewhere.

Fabales

50

Ulex europaeus

FABACEAE

Common Gorse / Furze

And now for the utter brute of the pea family. Common gorse is that ferocious spine-covered beast which colonises common land all over southern Britain and will invade spacious wilder gardens too. Yellow flowers flicker tantalisingly against the dark green foliage, if you can call it foliage, through mild winters. Then in spring, a glorious yellow glow announces the real new year, an awesome sight. Carl Linnaeus famously 'fell on his knees and wept for joy' when he first spied the phenomenon on Putney Heath in 1736.

But don't touch, even with gloves on! The branches, which bush out with repeated sub-branching, bristle all over with sharp fine spikes. These are its leaves in a refined form, a sure defence, one would think, against hungry herbivores. In fact they are highly nutritious and are appreciated by grazers while young and tender and also after harvesting and storing. Their minimal surface area and shininess ensures low transpiration, as do the furrowed stems, so that bushes can withstand both hot dry summers and the blast of prevailing winds. The woody roots anchor all the top growth so securely as to make it almost irremovable by any kind of normal manhandling. And then all this vigorous growth is sustained by the extra food reserves stored in tubercles (modified lateral roots that contain *Rhizobium* bacteria), which is the unique pea family facility for extracting nitrogen from the air to 'fix' into the ground around the roots.

For sure, the strong colour of the flowers and their coconut-scented perfume is a major attraction to honey and bumble bees who insert their proboscises deep inside only to find themselves cheated of any nectar but covered in a good dusting of pollen which they go on to redistribute liberally. So seed pods eventually develop, until on a hot summer's day the air is crackling with the sound of the explosive ejecting of hard shiny seeds up to three metres away or more. Ants, apparently, then transport them even further. Then eventually – and dormancy capabilities can ensure that the eventuality can be staggered from a few weeks to anything up to thirty years – a new set of seedlings sets the next generation on its way.

Meanwhile the old generation still does very well for itself, sprouting an array of new shoots from its spreading roots. Here then is a classic example of an invasive plant entrenching itself both by vigorous vegetative extension and by prolific sexual reproduction. As to the new shoots: trampling, mowing, predation and grazing will knock out growing tips only to stimulate even more low lateral sprouting and resprouting. But the ultimate exasperation for us lies underground, where a combination of tap roots and spreading woody rhizomatous roots, all toughly sinuous, proves almost impossible to dislodge by hand.

WHAT TO DO
- Not easy, it has to be said.
- Sawing at the base of the stems is the only accessible action than can be taken with hand tools, followed by hacking at all regrowth.
- Otherwise it is a question of major grubbing out by heavy machinery, or maybe of some controlled burning.
- Biological control? There is indication that this has been successful in New Zealand from a native species giving a fight back.
- Meanwhile, enjoy the winter and spring show of flowers, and present a flowering shoot to your loved-one (apparently a folkloric symbol of enduring love).
- And remember, 'when the gorse is out of flower/kissing's out of season'.

LEFT Carl Linnaeus on his knees and weeping for joy on seeing gorse in abundant flower on Putney Heath in 1736.

Fabales

51

Pueraria lobata

FABACEAE
Kudzu Vine

A wonder weed, if ever there was one. And with a roller-coaster story to tell. It arrived in Philadelphia in 1876 as a stunning beauty sent from Japan for the United States first centennial celebrations. Then it

- turned runaway escapee by spreading twenty metres a year
- turned eco-saviour by helping to reclaim the dust bowls of the 1930s and 1940s
- turned eco-disaster by overrunning 7 million acres of the deep south – forests, farm land and all
- was declared a 'weed' by the U.S. Department of Agriculture in 1972
- became adapted to full-on herbicide resistance
- acquired a demon legend – 'shut your windows at night, or else it will be in!'
- but, it was found to provide fodder for goats (and us), to be excellent for basket-making and a source of miracle cures

All this from just another member of the pea family.

WHAT TO DO

- Enjoy the extended irony (assuming you are not directly afflicted).

RIGHT Kudzu vine – the ultimate tearaway member of the pea family, or so it seems in North America.
OPPOSITE Shepherd's purse flaunting its signature seedpods – all ready for their contents to be scattered back onto the vegetable bed.

Fabales

52

Capsella bursa pastoris
BRASSICACEAE
Shepherd's Purse

Shepherd's purse is everywhere, so ubiquitous and so slight that most of us barely notice it. A highly adaptable plant, this one thrives in all kinds of conditions and in huge numbers and with numerous other descriptive names too, 'pickpocket', 'witches' pouches', 'pepper and salt', 'mother's heart' and so on. Its telltale feature is, of course, that string of purse-like seed capsules held out quaintly from its flower stalk. The purses drop their small change of coin-like seeds in superabundance, and, as we well know, there is nothing like plentiful cash for making plenty more.

In the late twentieth century, a claim was made (see the Garden Organic website) that shepherd's purse was the second most common plant on earth. Just now it is said to be on the increase too. No doubt, as so often in the world of weeds, this is all somewhat of a wild exaggeration. Even so, there is more than enough shepherd's purse about for us gardeners, especially in the openly worked soil of kitchen gardens and annual beds. So how come?

Shepherd's purse plays all the tricks of a classic annual, and more. It can over-winter as a biennial and race away as an

'ephemeral' with repeated life cycles through the year. Shepherd's purse can complete a cycle within six weeks, though it takes a while for seed to ripen fully and break dormancy. Normally there are about three new generations in a year. But then consider that one plant produces many thousands of viable seeds (the counts vary from 1,000 to 90,000) and we are immediately in the realms of Malthusian population explosions. In their overcrowded struggle for existence, as Darwin realised, a few will win out.

And then shepherd's purse, along with many common annuals, has a further trump card: enclosed self-pollination. Its pollen is readily received by adjacent stigmas before the flower bud has even opened. Effective cross-pollination does not get a look in.

Without continued genetic shuffling, plants become set in their ways and, in fact, in many distinctly different ways or variations. And here we plunge straight into a dilemma that Darwin draws attention to right at beginning of his treatise. How do we distinguish between species and varieties? While noting the virtual impossibility of drawing clear lines, Darwin observed that common species have more variations than less common ones. Shepherd's purse certainly demonstrates the point and botanists now usually acknowledge it by classing this plant as an 'aggregate species' (*Capsella bursa pastoris* agg.).

Variations are expressed principally in different leaf shapes, fruit shapes and the number of seeds they contain and there are slight variations of flower colour too. These tend to be localised, each with its own favoured niche. Even so, more phenotypes (physically distinct varieties) are known to appear in frequently disturbed soils (gardens!). For a slight ubiquitous specimen, shepherd's purse is exceptionally resourceful.

So much more can be said about this amazingly adapted plant. Here is a summary:

- Shepherd's purse has its own fast foothold with its long, branching taproot.
- Its seed is slightly sticky, readily adhering to birds' feet and so going far and wide.
- In adverse conditions it produces fewer but larger seeds with higher germination rates.
- Its leaves are tasty in salads (peppery like rocket). It has decorative charm and is a cure for diarrhoea.
- Note that it is a host for brassicaceae pests and diseases, notably flea beetle and white-rust fungus.

WHAT TO DO

- Hoe/hand weed/dig in before seeding (within five weeks of seedling appearance).
- In effect, constantly cultivate to reduce build-up of shepherd's purse in the soil seed bank.

Brassicales

- Invite geese into your garden. Apparently they have a particular taste for shepherd's purse.
- Use young leaves to pep up a salad.

Note that from the same family also comes *Lunaria annua*, which for some curious reason we know as 'honesty'. Is this because the plant also displays its seed riches in transparent fruits like shepherd's purse, but this time dangling in those charming coil-like disks? A native plant which charms its way into gardens. So why not allow a little bit here and there to enhance that interlude before the big summer bloom takes over? Of course, it has the weedy tendency to proliferate all too freely. So watch out too.

53

Arabidopsis thaliana
BRASSICACEAE
Thale-cress

From the same family as shepherd's purse and sharing many characteristics, thale-cress is a sporadic garden visitor prone to colonising walls, gravel and well-drained stony ground in particular. It is generally of no real nuisance but it often finds itself dubbed a weed simply for being insufficiently interesting and superfluous to any of our everyday requirements. However it is of huge significance in our understanding of weeds and their ploys.

Thale-cress is small (rarely rising more than 22 cm), very quick (a potential four-week lifespan), highly adaptable, both self-pollinating (and so able to sustain variations – like shepherd's purse) and cross-pollinating (and so able to generate new variations) and notably tenacious as well. The perfect plant, in fact, for geneticists to work with and in the first year of this millennium, and for the first time for any plant, scientists triumphantly sequenced its genome – all 30,000 genes.

Fortunately for us lay followers, there is an enthralling account of the secret and not-so-secret life of thale-cress in *Seed to Seed* by Nicholas Harberd. He is a leading plant geneticist who was at the time directing research at the John Innes Centre, Norwich. We met him eight

Brassicales

weeds back among nettles. His account is in the form of a journal through a calendar year (2004) describing the development of laboratory research while he was also monitoring the progress of some thale-cress plants growing wild on a grave in a country churchyard. It is all acutely and most engagingly observed in true Darwin tradition and is a riveting read, as progress on both fronts is so precarious. We find ourselves in a delicious irony as we anxiously will the churchyard 'weeds' to survive through a succession of near wipeouts from slugs, rabbits, human interference, severe weather or whatever. Just one of the original small group hangs on to flower and shed seeds after virtually a whole year's struggle for existence and an extraordinary elongation of what would normally be a short life.

So, how do the 30,000 genes mastermind this extended survival? As Harberd explains, there is an intricate cross-networking of these genes which do far more than determine surface characteristics. Particularly intriguing seem to be the genes that encode proteins named DELLAs (one of a whole host of acronyms to just a few of which Harberd gently introduces us). DELLAs, which come in five different kinds, act to restrain plant growth and this restraint can only be relieved by hormones like, in this case, gibberellins. In effect, DELLAs enable the plants to respond to adverse conditions by putting their brakes on and not burning themselves out and wasting their energies in hopeless situations. Restraint and appropriate 'relief of restraint' are the key concepts behind all this, and they look to be the most important survival strategy of this plant, and indeed quite possibly of all plants. To attempt to sum up such detailed scientific research in one paragraph is glibly presumptuous, except to indicate that here is another tip-of-the-iceberg revelation, this time of a massive hidden realm of plant organisation.

Finally, a further ironic twist: as the prime plant used in the development of genetic engineering methodology, our little innocuous thale-cress has incidentally played a big part in the arrival of new 'superweeds'. One much cited product of this 'biotechnology' is a strain of oilseed rape modified for strong herbicide resistance. And then what happens? Well, as we rueful smug Darwinians can say with hindsight, the selecting out of a new generation of extra-resistant weeds is only to be expected (see chapter 4).

WHAT TO DO
- Apply restraint too. Pause and wonder before taking any action. Perhaps retain as a curiosity.
- If needs be, hoe, hand weed or carefully prise out of stony crevices before planting other flowers.
- Find out more. For a start, read *Seed to Seed* (Bloomsbury, 2006).

WEEDS, WEEDING (& DARWIN)

54

Cardamina hirsuta

BRASSICACEAE
Hairy Bittercress

This is the garden centre weed – the little number that readily tucks itself into any plant container. Buy a plant and get one of these free. Bittercress thrives in nurseries and garden centres for three good reasons. It particularly responds to continual watering and never being allowed to dry out. Its seed pods, produced within four or five weeks, all too readily explode open from the slightest disturbance, distributing seeds up to a metre away. And then the protected warmer conditions ensure an optimum seed ripening and germination.

Once imported into the garden, it is a persistent little pest, continually taunting us with its flagrant seediness. Each seedpod has about 20 seeds and each plant produces an average of 600 (30 pods' worth) in its average five week lifespan. And then there can be plants in fruit for over eight months of the year. Again, it is another regular ingredient of soil seed banks. Unpleasantly bitter in taste it is too, if you must try.

WHAT TO DO

- Snatch out of plant containers whenever seen.
- Hoe or hand weed <u>before</u> it seeds.
- Watch out for plants in pod as the slightest touch or attempt at weeding will cause a seed explosion. Maybe there's a case for leaving it alone – or that can be your excuse.

ABOVE Hairy bitterrcress seemingly all innocent and harmless, but actually all ready to explode.

Brassicales

55

Sinapis arvensis

BRASSICACEAE

Charlock

The resounding kick of that name, charlock (alias karlock, kedlock, kilk, shallock or hoardlock) has sent shivers of dread to arable farmers down the centuries. Autumn sowing of crops has helped to reduce its erratic prevalence but, strangely enough, in recent years charlock has become a problem with oilseed rape. There, of course, it is well camouflaged. It hovers around field edges and verges, even alongside pavements, and is an unwanted regular visitor of country and town gardens too.

Charlock's renown and the peculiar nature of its seeds had Darwin writing to the *Gardeners' Chronicle* again in 1855:

> *Vitality of Seeds.—*
> .... An arable field 15 years ago was laid down in pasture; nine years ago last spring, a portion was deeply ploughed up and planted with trees, and in the succeeding summer, as far as I can trust my memory, plenty of Charlock, which abounds in this neighbourhood, came up; but if my memory plays me false the case will prove so much the stronger. From being badly ploughed the whole of the land in the course of the year became covered with Grass and coarse weeds, and has remained so ever since, and the trees have now grown up. It is very improbable, from the well known habits of the Charlock, that it could have grown in the little wood after the first year or two; and though almost daily visiting it I have not noticed a plant. But this spring I had some Thorn bushes pulled up, and it was so done that not more than one or two (I speak after comparison) hand's breadth of earth was turned up. To my surprise in July I happened to observe on one of the little patches of earth no less than six dwarf Charlock plants in flower; on each of two other patches three plants; and on the fourth one plant. This made me on July 21st have three separate plots of ground, each 2 feet square, in different rather open parts of the wood, cleared of thick Grass and Weeds, and dug one spit deep. By August 1st many seedlings had come up, and several of them seemed to be cruciferous plants; so I marked with little sticks 11 of them on one of the beds; six on the second bed; and five on the third bed; two or three died, all the rest grew up and proved to be Charlock. I can state positively that no Charlock was growing near these beds; and I do not believe there was any within

WEEDS, WEEDING (& DARWIN)

Brassicales

a quarter of a mile, as the little wood is surrounded by Grass land. Now, to my mind, this seems good evidence that the Charlock seed had retained its vitality within a spit's depth of the surface during at least eight or nine years. In most cases, when plants spring up unexpectedly, as when a wood has been burnt down, it is not possible to feel sure (as has been remarked to me by Dr. Hooker) that the seeds had not been strewed about during the last year or two by birds or other means. Had the several Charlock plants come up on one spot alone, I should have thought that some accident had brought a pod there, and that I had overlooked during the previous years a few Charlock plants, but it seems to me improbable in the highest degree that on each of the 3 plots of ground, taken by simple hazard, several (in one of the cases 11) seeds should have been dropped by some unknown agency, having been brought from a quarter of a mile distance. But if when the land was ploughed, 9 years ago (or when arable, 15 years ago) the whole was, as I believe, almost covered by Charlock, the seed would have been scattered everywhere, ready to spring up at whatever point the land might subsequently be stirred up. I will only further remark that the power in seeds of retaining their vitality when buried in damp soil may well be an element in preserving the species, and, therefore, that seeds may be specially endowed with this capacity; whereas, the power of retaining vitality in a dry and artificial condition must be an indirect, and in one sense accidental, quality in seeds of little or no use to the species. *Charles Darwin, Down, Nov. 13.*

Four years after writing to the *Gardeners' Chronicle* Darwin cited charlock again in the *Origin*:

...One species of charlock has been known to supplant another species;... We can dimly see why the competition should be most severe between allied forms, which fill nearly the same place in the economy of nature; but probably in no one case could we precisely say why one species has been victorious over another in the great battle of life.

In both instances, painfully meticulous caution (so characteristic of Darwin) glimmers through in his attempted explanation as to why this weed is such a persistent winner. Its seeds lay buried in damp soil, biding their time, even waiting decades for farmers to switch from arable to grazing and back again to arable for those few seeds at last to germinate. Like the other annual brassicaceae, charlock produces viable seeds in superabundance and it only needs the minutest fraction to carry on the show.

After Darwin's time, charlock became a prime candidate for chemical control. At the beginning of the twentieth century solutions of copper sulphate and iron sulphate proved quite effective for a while. Then later ever more selective weedkillers were used including hormone based ones which have succeeded in reducing the population and its nuisance considerably. But, being a cross-pollinator, charlock has responded to selection pressure with a range of resistant varieties. More recently it has homed in quite intensively (and problematically) on organic systems.

Compared with the relatively more delicate shepherd's purse, bittercress and thale-cress, charlock is an unwelcome coarse beast, host to all the brassicaceae pests and diseases including the dreaded club root. Mercifully, when it arrives in a garden it is conspicuous, a salient reminder of its big part in human history, and is quite easily removed.

WHAT TO DO

- Hoe, pull out or dig out before flowering. Otherwise there is a strong chance of it reappearing at any time in the next ten years, or more.

WEEDS, WEEDING (& DARWIN)

56

Raphanus raphanistrus

BRASSICACEAE

Wild Radish / Runch

Wild radish is said to be 'as grievous a pest as Charlock', especially in non-calcareous soils. A classic example of a vigorous, coarse weed closely related to a valued food plant. Let your radishes go to seed and you have something not dissimilar to this wild variety and indeed the two can readily hybridise. Just like radishes too, they are speedy growers. Be alert!

It is an annual/occasional biennial again with a propensity to much variation with pale yellow, pale lilac or white flowers (sometimes purple-veined) all quite possible within a single population. Distinctive segmented seed pods, with each segmented seed breaking off independently, mark it out. The seeds release a toxic vapour which can harm other seeds stored in proximity.

WHAT TO DO

- Keep seeds and seeding out of it. Hoe/handweed whenever first noticed.
- Grow cultivar radishes instead – 'French Breakfast' or whatever.

OPPOSITE Charlock – the dreaded field weed which had Darwin writing to the paper. LEFT Wild radish – another brazen weed from the brassica family along with charlock and the next two weeds.

Brassicales

57

Alliaria petiolata
BRASSICACEAE
Garlic Mustard

Garlic mustard is a common plant of hedgerows and verges which will all too readily hop over into gardens. In some respects it appears as a white-flowered version of charlock yet with more luxuriant foliage (best seized as a tasty salad addition), making it a bit of a bully in suppressing other late-developing garden material. It is quite handsome in its early-summer flowering flush along a roadside, but a bit coarse and uncouth in the average garden. Its variability is highlighted in its range of seed size, both between plants and within the same plant. Smaller seeds germinate faster, and turn into slower seedlings but become taller plants in the end. Host to its own butterfly (green-veined white *Pieris napi*) and with seeds favoured by birds, it is integral to the entangled bank ecology, and certainly best left there.

WHAT TO DO
- Aim to take out, hoeing or hand weeding, at seedling stage. Fork out ones that have been missed.

LEFT Garlic mustard – weed of the early summer wayside, and best left there.

58

Armoracia rusticana
BRASSICACEAE
Horseradish

One of those plants we introduce to our gardens as a novel culinary idea and then two or three years down the line we are not so sure. It has become an ugly brute, virtually impossible to dislodge, its prized young roots descending deep and rapidly turning tough and woody. 'Rank' it is, absolutely epitomising that word as the last and coarsest of our cabbage-related weed representatives. It becomes infested with caterpillars chewing ragged holes. Not a pretty sight – the cabbage family at its toughest and crudest, though the source of a piquant condiment.

WHAT TO DO
- Think twice about introducing to a small garden.
- Grate harvested roots, savour in moderation.

RIGHT ABOVE Horseradish displaying promising luxuriance in early summer.
RIGHT BELOW Horseradish, as is customary, later in an unsightly state from caterpillar infestation.

Brassicales

59

Acer pseudoplatanus

SAPINDACEAE

Sycamore

A tree! And a tree at the top of a tree!

The sycamore, alias 'plane tree' (Scotland) or 'sycamore maple' and 'great maple' (USA), has an uncomfortable reputation both among arboriculturists and around gardens. There it will stand at the end of many a garden or neighbour's garden, substantial and even majestic in form, but a relative dullard of a tree, blocking the view, casting shade, showering its double-winged seeds to make carpets of vigorous seedlings, oozing sticky leaf secretions, casting out successions of hungry aphids and being generously endowed with dubious assorted fungi. Invariably neither suitably positioned nor really wanted as a first choice anywhere in our immediate vicinity, sycamore has the dubious honour of being a prime tree weed suspect.

In its defence, the sycamore is an accomplished coloniser of barren land and exposed terrains (so no wonder it arrives on bits we expose while making our gardens). Ecologically, it may well have a valuable role in the wild, preparing the ground for the more standard natives like oaks and ashes. A significant reason for this capacity is that sycamore has 'endomycorrhizal' status, meaning that it hosts fungi within its root cells. These fungi generate nutrients so that the tree is not dependent on an already fungal rich soil which most of the other temperate forest trees require.

What it comes down to is that the sycamore is not quite a fully accepted British native (well, not quite yet). For a long time it was thought to be an alien which arrived from central Europe supposedly in about the fifteenth century and later migrated to the New World. More often than not, we see it as a scattered loner, but notoriously the northernmost forest in mainland Britain is a fine sycamore plantation in Caithness.

In a bid to reassert its status, an intriguing alternative scenario has been proposed. Essentially, this claims that the sycamore could well be a British old timer which has come and all but gone several times due to its susceptibilities to drought. Its pollen has not been traced back in archaeological remains like the other natives but this is now explained by it having been found not to have the same duration capacity as other tree pollens, and also by it being virtually indistinguishable from other maple pollens. Perhaps this tree has weathered many long centuries in Britain with natural selection ensuring that just enough of its northern toughies survive each climate crisis to be able to stage an ever

WEEDS, WEEDING (& DARWIN)

ABOVE Sycamore straying into a yew hedge in the garden of Down House.

more resilient comeback when conditions became more favourable. Such speculations have to be plausible, but accepted with the supreme caution that Darwin himself always observed when evidence was slim (see Ted Green, 'Is there a case for the Celtic Maple or the Scots Plane?' *British Wildlife*, 2005).

Linnaeus perhaps got the best measure of this oddity by naming it *Acer pseudoplatanus*, translated as 'false-plane maple'. And whoever came up with 'sycamore', a biblical name for a mulberry-like fig tree, only added to the confusion. There we go: a tree sent to try us.

Sapindales

WHAT TO DO

- Watch for those seedlings and pull out as soon as seen.
- Be bold in regard to the full-grown monster that almost certainly planted itself. Weigh up the pros and cons for retaining it and don't feel guilty about felling to provide a new space.
- Respect sycamore as a valued host of wildlife, notably fungi, invertebrates, lichens and mosses, but perhaps not in one's own garden.
- Or why not introduce *Acer pseudoplatanus* 'Brilliantissimum', a slow-growing hybrid with salmon-pink young leaves turning yellow and then dark green, and reaching to about six metres? Or, for a more substantial size, the glossier leaved Norway maple (*Acer platanoides*)?

Fraxinus excelsior (ash) is often associated with sycamore (and oak) and so we give it a little mention here though this is not in its true place.

Ash (formerly in the same grouping as the sycamore but now staying with the santalales) is the other tearaway tree of which gardeners have to be wary. Sometimes riding on the back of the sycamore, as was suggested above, ash is an even more notorious opportunist. Its single-winged seeds hang in prominent clusters through most of the bare-wood winter ready to be scattered far and wide when the wind eventually so deems. Its seedlings are the curse and, as with the sycamores, they are easily tugged out in the first year but past that stage they become a problem and, all too soon, plausible young trees.

Curiously, it has been noticed that ash tends to alternate with sycamore in woodlands, perhaps as a co-evolutionary strategy, if not as a consequence of human interference by removal and felling. (Saville et al., 1995, 'Ecology of Sycamore in Britain', *Institute of Foresters Conference*). Whatever, both trees and their seedlings need watching most carefully.

Now, at the time of going to press, there is widespread alarm that ash is in serious trouble countrywide from an air-borne fungal infection resulting in 'die-back'. It might be asked whether there is any chance that the exceptional weed-like resilience of this tree will allow for resistant strains to come to the fore. If ever a tree demonstrated superlative powers of comeback it has to be this one. In any case, it would be a long haul of Darwinian selection.

60

Malva neglecta
MALVACEAE
Common Mallow / Dwarf Mallow

Finally we arrive at our last branch of the rosids. A common wayside pinkish-purple wild flower and garden visitor of late summer, the common mallow is the tough nut of the mallow family and strikingly so as an annual having a semi-prostrate habit and able to overtake and suppress its neighbours. It develops a stout, long, branching taproot which reinforces its assertive stance while giving it sufficient resources to survive a mild winter. *Neglecta*? Neglect it in the garden at your peril! It will be an uncharming bully of a weed that needs to be ousted while at the same time still appreciated as one of the regulars on the wayside, where it should stay firmly in residence.

WHAT TO DO
• Prise out with a fork.

RIGHT Common mallow – a prominent feature of late-summer roadsides and a strong would-be invader of gardens if given a chance.

Malvales

Core Eudicots: Asterids

Here we have a massive major branch of 80,000 species. This prime section of eudicots distinguishes itself with several unique characteristics, like having fused petals, their own particular ovule structure, the containing of unique chemical compounds, as well DNA sequences in common. What's more, 39 of our 100 named weeds appear here.

First we join the ericales where we had a brief preview to greet the primroses way back at Weed 32. Strange indeed that primroses emerged together with rhododendrons and balsams, but there we are, they are all imposing characters.

61

Rhododendron ponticum
ERICACEAE
'Ponticum'

The year 1763 is when it all started in Britain. That was when *Rhododendron ponticum* arrived as a delightful oriental novelty from Pontus in Turkey when it was presumably on its way to the New World. Yes, when first seen, it is a delightful blousy purple-flowered shrub, but the attraction wears off when you realise that it is also the brazen flag of acidic terrain and that in such terrain it often seems to spread everywhere.

In Victorian Britain a new wave of far superior and still highly regarded rhododendrons arrived from the Himalayas, thanks especially to the explorations of Joseph Hooker, Darwin's close associate from Kew. The status of *R. ponticum* plummeted but not before the genie was well and truly out of the bottle and ensconced in the wild. But *R. ponticum* retained its hold in the garden because nurserymen depended on its rootstock for grafting the Himalayan newcomers because they were relatively weak and needed that extra *ponticum* vigour. So, ensconced in this way, *R. ponticum* suckers are always poised to make a break for it, and they often do so while pushing out the classier, but weaker, Himalayans.

WHAT TO DO

- Obey the order posted on this gate in North Wales – as if control could be so straightforward.

LEFT The flower of the 'Ponticum' rhododendron is irrefutably magnificent in its prime but, as most gardeners agree, it is not a patch on all the other rhododendrons. It is also set apart for being one of the most rampantly invasive of all shrubs, especially in the wild.

Ericales

62

Impatiens glandulifera
ERICACEAE
Himalayan Balsam

Hard on the heels of the rhododendrons was this other oriental invader, Himalayan balsam, an annual arriving in Britain in 1839 from the Indian mountains. As so often with foreign novelties brought back by avid colonial plant hunters, 60 years later it was described as 'another terrible weed'. And terrible it is still:

- terrible for having a revolting odour
- terrible for out-competing other vegetation and reducing species diversity
- terrible for growing and putting itself about phenomenally fast. (One statistic claims its spread to be 645 square kilometres per year in the United Kingdom. A figure no doubt helped by rivers dispersing seeds long distances, and by boots and tyres picking up and distributing sticky seed-laden mud)
- terrible for taking over river banks and obstructing watercourses
- and terrible for being a seductive charmer while showing off exotic prowess

Nicknamed 'policeman's helmet' (its large pale purple or white flowers are just like an old bobby's headgear on its side), *Impatiens glandulifera* is now as good as native throughout the United Kingdom, being adaptable to a wide range of conditions, including shady areas. It has distinctive reddish succulent stems, bearing leaves in twos and threes, and sometimes reaches up to three metres in height, which puts it in competition to be the tallest British annual.

'Touch-me-not', this balsam's other nickname, gives warning of its notorious exploding seed pods. Just lightly brush against the plants when mature – say while strolling along a tow path – and seeds will be ejected up to seven metres. And a moderate-sized plant has 800 viable seeds to expel.

When all is done at the end of the season, a considerable bulk of material dies down leaving bare ground exposed to winter weathering and erosion, and making perfect conditions for next year's seedlings.

WHAT TO DO

- Pull out – quite easy as roots are shallow. Then plant up straightaway with something more desirable so as not to leave the space vacant for a comeback.
- Cut down or mow especially at the end of June, late enough for new shoots not to make it to flowering. Or graze with animals.
- Be grateful (or maybe not) for this close cousin (and part progenitor) of the ubiquitous standby bedding plant, 'Busy Lizzie'.
- Use this plant's leaves to sooth your nerves, which may be exacerbated by it in the first place. They can be distilled into an oily remedy for irritability – supposedly.

LEFT Himalayan balsam – the initial charmer.
BELOW The same Himalayan balsam – the takeover scourge of waterways.

Ericales

63

Galium aparine

RUBIACEAE

Cleavers / Goosegrass / Bedstraw

Cleavers, as one might expect from such a name, clings, whether together in a clump, to other plants or notoriously to ourselves and clothes. Once the plant has matured it literally clings on by a thread, or rather a thin threadlike stalk into which the base of the plant withers. What a cunning ruse this seems to be; any attempt to remove the plants will always leave the root behind to regenerate.

Clinging to this plant, too, are an astonishing number of common names: sticky willy, kisses, sweethearts, stick-a-back, cling rascal, gripgrass, goose bumps, hairiff, claggy meggies, robin-on-the-hedge, to mention just a fraction of its telltale labels. And yes, geese are most partial to a bit of goosegrass and we can appreciate how its cushion-like mass might momentarily appeal as bedstraw.

Classed among Britain's ten most common annual weeds by Garden Organic, this multi-named scoundrel, unlike the other nine top troublemakers, cannot boast exceptional seed production (a mere 300–400 per sizeable plant), nor lengthy dormant durability (only up to two to three years), nor easy germination (inhibited by light and temperatures over 15 degrees centigrade). However, this latter restraint prompts cleavers to take on a partial biennial habit with seedlings emerging as the temperature drops in autumn. These will hold on and toughen up through a severe winter to have a head start the following year. Then, as likely as not, there is the back-up of a second set of seeds waiting to germinate in the spring in true annual style.

The new little plants slowly gather strength and size during the early part of the year and then suddenly make a break with a dramatic summer growth spurt, extending shoots up to a metre and half in a tangled clinging mass. The seeds' germination requirement of cool cover may also partly explain why plants tend to emerge in shady or semi-shady areas and why, too, they are regarded as an indicator of loamy soil. It is

RIGHT *Galium aparine* as collected by Darwin in Patagonia in 1832 and sent back to Cambridge. To have 34 plantlets set out on one herbarium sheet grossly breaks the general custom of presenting a single specimen. Evidently Darwin was struck by its weed-like profusion. Patches of small plants like this are how we gardeners often experience this plant – all too ominously as they lie in wait for their early-summer take-off.

Gentianales

WEEDS, WEEDING (& DARWIN)

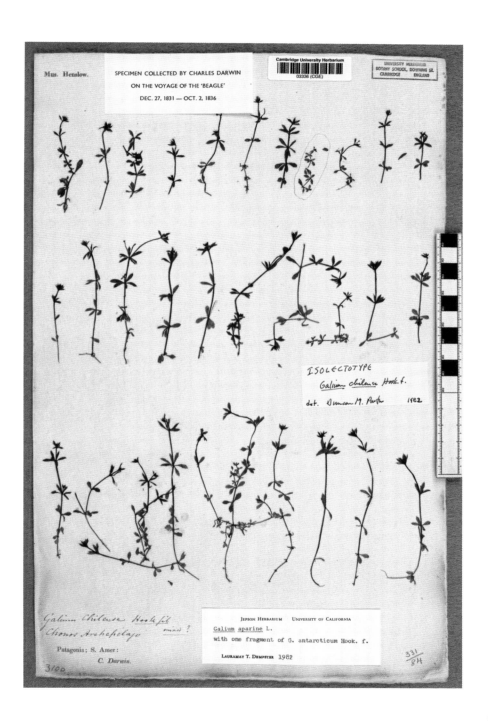

ISOLECTOTYPE

Galium chilense Hook. f.

det. Duncan M. Porter   1982

JEPSON HERBARIUM   UNIVERSITY OF CALIFORNIA

Galium aparine L.

with one fragment of G. antarcticum Hook. f.

LAURAMAY T. DEMPSTER 1982

Galium chilense Hook. fil.

Chonos Archipelago

Patagonia; S. Amer:

C. Darwin.

3100

331/8H

Gentianales

these areas which we tend to take our eye off when the rest of the garden is bursting into bloom, so clumps of cleavers often catch us unaware.

The infamous clinging act of this otherwise flimsy plant is all due to its being covered – stalks, leaves and fruits – by soft hook-like bristles. When the moment comes for it to take off, away it scampers and climbs as if drunk on discovering this proclivity. Strangely, Darwin missed out on this one in his thorough round-up of climbing mechanisms, even though he had sent back that herbarium sheet of samples from South America, perhaps because it all too readily just sticks to itself and makes a relatively fleeting appearance. Nevertheless, cleavers is the scourge of certain crops like oilseed rape, which it will smother just as that seed is setting. In the garden, it makes its own sudden shaming appearance, usually attempting to obliterate our more subtle specimens kept in more obscure corners. Oh dear!

And who is primarily to blame for putting this character about? We are of course, usually as a result of wading in to remove the weed by the armful. There we are – boots, socks, legs or trousers, arms or sleeves – covered in the sticky, petit-pois-sized fruits. Our fellow creatures play their part too. Fruits stick all too readily onto their body parts and the seeds, passing easily through the guts of cattle, horses, pigs, goats and birds are all the more fortified from coats of excreta.

WHAT TO DO

- First let's acknowledge how easy and gratifying it is to extract cleavers, coming out as it does in satisfying bundles when in full growth (though leaving roots behind). Gloves are advised for those with sensitive skin.
- Obviously the wise and thorough gardener will hoe it earlier, and later when the autumn seedlings arise. But it's not a drastic deal either way, it has to be said.

Gentianales

64

Symphytum officinale
BORAGINACEAE
Common Comfrey / Borage

With regard to comfrey (formerly more often called borage), Gerard, while not even giving cleavers a mention, was ecstatic: 'the leaves and flowers of borage put into wine make men and women glad and merry, driving away sadnesse, dullnesse and melancholy.' Was he on a high when he went on to eulogise it for providing the ultimate cure-all drug and pick-me-up tonic? Is it addictive, one might wonder? Well, once introduced into a garden it will not give up easily – be warned. It can be a bullying thug and 'thug' has stuck with it as another common name, yet at the same time it has beguiling charm.

Comfrey certainly seduced the founders of the organic movement in Britain, Henry Doubleday in the nineteenth century and Lawrence D. Hills in the twentieth. They homed in on its fertilising qualities besides its medicinal values, discovering that its leaves are rich in potassium and other nutrients due to the unique capacity of its deep lush roots to retrieve such riches from the subsoil. They developed a particular strain (Bocking 14) which was said to be the gardener's wonder standby. And, whether through that strain or others, it unfailingly stands by. If it is any consolation to those of us affected by this

menace, the poor gardeners at Ryton Organic Gardens now also curse comfrey as one of their worst weeds. This legacy of their forebears is certainly not all good news for them.

And of course it is these penetrating roots, distinctive with their dusty black outer covering and white fleshy interior – and so easily breakable – which hang on in there come what may, whether extremes of weather or all our efforts at digging. And like all such demons, comfrey takes refuge by intermingling its roots with the root systems of other precious perennials like asparagus and fruit bushes.

Common comfrey looks the part of a standard herb with its greyish green leaves, whose colour is enhanced by tiny hairs which can be a skin irritant. From broad basal leaves, stalks emerge with narrower leaves ending in a little unfurling coil of flowers, pinkish at first in opening bud form and then glowing a most beautiful blue, all at that early time of year when drifts of blue enchant and predominate. There we are, a curse again that a plant should put us into such a love–hate predicament.

And, aha, this plant had Darwin a-buzzing too, observing that it was more frequented by bees than almost any plant he observed. Furthermore, he noticed that should the bees fail to appear, comfrey (he knew it too as *Borago officinalis*) was capable of self-pollination, though yielding only a quarter of the amount of seeds. Not that this would inhibit such a tough perennial hanger-on.

WHAT TO DO

- If given the choice, resist introducing comfrey into your garden in the first place.
- Live and let live, while digging out as much as possible and trying to contain the rest in one area by not moving its soil around.
- Apply a glyphosate weedkiller – not so easy once it has moved in among valued perennials.
- Treat the herbalists with healthy scepticism, and amusement.
- But, by all means, make use of the leaves to stew up a potassium-rich cocktail to help get good tomatoes on their way.

Boraginaceae

OPPOSITE ABOVE Forget-me-not seedlings at different stages of growth competing to be the survivors of an overcrowded garden space in late summer.
OPPOSITE BELOW The select few forget-me-not survivors triumphantly flowering the following late spring, soon to scatter a new mass of seed as one of the most daring of weeds.

65

Myosotis spp.
BORAGINACEAE
Forget-me-not

Unsurprisingly with such a name, forget-me-not is the subject of much speculative folklore. In truth, as an average kind of plant growing in the average garden, *Myosotis* is at once unforgettable and forgettable. It is not a high status annual-cum-biennial but somehow, true to annual form, it reappears each year, as often as not to be selectively welcomed.

At one time, seeds of a standard cultivar will have been deliberately sown in a garden, giving rise to an everlasting dynasty of plants which can fill that early vacant space with a delightful soft blue so good for setting off tulips, and so much more innocent and easy to deal with than its thug of a cousin. Gradually the intensity of the blue washes out as the hybrid gradually fades back to its base as the field weed *Myosotis arvensis*.

Let one plant flower and there could be up to 3,000 seeds subsequently thrown out. But there is nothing to notice when you pull out the spent plant and forget-me-nots belie their name by becoming totally out of sight and out of mind for the rest of the summer. Then into autumn and catching us by surprise will be crowded patches of *Myosotis* seedlings, classically competing in their own overcrowded

'struggle for existence' (see chapter 4) and in far greater quantities than we can possibly accommodate. Here is a late-in-the-year weed invasion, just when we are letting down our guard, and we are obliged to step in.

Is there a sting in the tail? Yes, no, well almost so, for the flower stems will finish with a downward curl in the shape of a scorpion's tail. Hence one of the subspecies where this feature is especially emphasised: *Myosotis scorpioides*, a true 'forget-me-not'.

WHAT TO DO
- Ruthlessly select from the seedlings in late autumn or early spring, arrange and space out to look as if you have engineered some perfect planting.
- From time to time sow some new quality cultivars to intensify the blue colouring.

66

Calystegia sepium
CONVOLVULACEAE
Hedge Bindweed / Greater Bindweed

Convolvulus arvensis
CONVOLVULACEAE
Field Bindweed / Lesser Bindweed

'Bindweed is one despicable weed', says one despairing complainant from North America, and no doubt most of us are nodding our heads at such damning of a truly challenging plant. In fact, bindweed makes for a double bind, two distinctly different species, both most troublesome, to say the least.

Calystegia sepium, the runaway climber over hedges, shrubs, trees or whatever is available for twisting around, somehow 'gets' to our sensitivities and brings out the worst expletives. And what is worse, more often than not it succeeds in outwitting us by still hanging on to make repeated fightbacks. The only consolation is that it appears in the very best of gardens – RHS Wisley included. Vigilance always helps but localised extinction tends to be elusive. One despicable so-and-so, indeed.

RIGHT Hedge bindweed classically posed in Stephenson's *Medical Botany*, 1834, where it was labelled *Convolvulus sepium*. It is still commonly, though incorrectly, called convolvulus.

Solanales

WEEDS, WEEDING (& DARWIN)

ABOVE The same 'hedge bindweed' smothering a golden philadelphus and much else too in a mixed border in late summer. Shame on the gardener!

The antics of climbing plants also got to Charles Darwin, albeit from a rather different perspective. In fact, he became well and truly hooked. 'The more I look at plants', he wrote to his friend Joseph Hooker, 'the higher they rise in my mind; really the tendril bearers are higher organised, as far as adaptive sensitivity goes, than the lower animals.' He evidently uttered this with some feeling, maybe recalling his prolonged seven-year

WEEDS, WEEDING (& DARWIN)

study of barnacles, but perhaps more from finding entertaining relief in observing some potted climbers in his study while he was struggling with a severe bout of his recurring sickness. Watching, measuring and timing the plants twisting and rising almost before his very eyes had him gripped. The speed and distance a plant would range astonished him. He recorded a cucumber making a circle in 1½ to 2 hours.

Darwin went on to examine over one hundred climbing plants, and wrote a twice published (Linnean Society, 1865; Murray, 1875) eminent book on them covering ones with tendril handles, ones just twining (some clockwise, some anti-clockwise), ones, like ivy, gripping with centipede-like feet (aerial roots) and others, like brambles, using grappling thorn-hooks. But strangely, while he felt strongly about his chosen examples, our chief weed bugbear bindweed did not catch his attention – a clear demonstration that he was no hands-on gardener himself. But it should not be forgotten that bindweed's close cousin, morning glory, did engage him when he was investigating hybridisation.

Hedge bindweed is a scheming devil if ever there was one. A perennial, it lies in wait through the winter with little nests of clumsily zigzagging white rhizomes. These usually hover at 30 cm depth and are quite brittle enough to let fragments break off and remain behind when the bulk is forked out. The remaining rhizomes send up both shoots, ready to start twining, and stolons, which, in the relative obscurity at the base of higher undergrowth and shrubs, zoom along the soil surface in a straight bid for freedom capable of extending several metres at a go. When the stolons hit an obstacle, a fence (chain-linked ones, a favourite), a supportive cane or a stem of another substantial plant, they push down to set a new root system while sending a shoot up the new-found climbing opportunity. Then a second, a third, and possibly a good succession of other shoots may well twist around the same assemblage plaiting an impressive rope. Ropeweed is another of its common names. At home in the hedgerow, hedge bindweed also loves climbing up and all over garden shrubs and fruit bushes, seeming to strangulate branches and then smother out higher growth at the backs of borders. Allow it to continue unchecked on its natural course and it will easily do for many of your larger, prized garden exhibits in a season.

WHAT TO DO (Hedge bindweed)
- Remove all above ground growth at every opportunity, the earliest chance being the best. Sweeping your arm around the base of shrubs to catch any sneaking stolon or rising shoot can be quite rewarding to oneself and debilitating to the bindweed whose underground reserves can be seriously weakened by the reduction if not elimination of over ground growth. But the devils will always find a way for a comeback.

Solanales

- Use winter clearance time to dig out rhizomes as much as possible. It will often be surprising where they have got to and, unfortunately, this will include penetrating into other root systems, especially right under climbing opportunities.
- Apply a systemic herbicide. This bindweed is cited as a desired candidate for the glove treatment: that is dipping your rubber-gloved hands in a container of glyphosate solution and then stroking a significant stretch of leaves – quite a delicate operation if damage to other plants is to be avoided.
- Take consolation. This bindweed appears in the best of gardens and with average intermittent attention can be kept in reasonable control with an occasional herbicide blitz of the intertwining culprits.
- Grow morning glory and enjoy this cousin's breathtaking early greeting of late summer days.

Convolvulus arvensis is 'pernicious', so says the mild mannered Garden Organic. Whereas 'despicable' hedge bindweed favours climbing, 'pernicious' field bindweed scrambles over the more open areas of arable fields and, notoriously, over allotments. It, too, has a challenging root system. This time one that descends to inaccessible depths, apparently reaching down as far as five metres, as well as flaunting a spreading, twining, climbing and smothering top growth.

As with all of the more challenging weeds, field bindweed can beguile too, just for a moment, with its morning bloom of soft pink flowers, washed-out versions of morning glory. And these flowers do certainly do their job. Self incompatibility and a four-month flowering period see to it that a large number of flowers are cross-pollinated by assorted insects. Each flower capsule comes up with 1–4 seeds and the average annual seed production per new plant can mount up to 600 over a season. Their hard impermeable coats ensure a long, staggered dormancy. But if we try to remove the plants when they have just flowered, the disturbance easily fractures the protective shell to break dormancy and hasten the appearance of new seedlings. If we leave them alone, we are no better off. Late spring is the prime germination time. That is when we need to be most alert.

As to its perennial perniciousness, here's where the extending rhizomatous roots have it so well organised for themselves. A seedling sends a vertical taproot down about 3 cm, from which lateral roots reach out as far as 75 cm before turning down again to form secondary vertical roots from which horizontal laterals spread out once more, and so on to repeat the performance ever downwards and outwards. The root system descends in successive tiers reaching 1.2 metres deep in a year and 4 metres in just two and half years. The brittleness of the upper roots, in particular, becomes especially challenging, as fragments get left behind when being forked out. These rapidly regenerate with extra vigour, sometimes disturbingly spiralling up in close coils, presumably gathering up extra underground food reserves. Lower down, the rhizomes become much tougher, firmly resisting any attempts to pull them out.

In hot dry summers, when other plants are struggling and we might begin to relax on the weeding, this bindweed is thriving, always able to find a drink and, with its smaller leaves (which may shrink further), less vulnerable to transpiration stress. 'A pernicious perennial weed', oh yes!

WHAT TO DO (Field bindweed)

- Hoe persistently, both to knock out seedlings before they have a chance to establish (generally in late spring and early summer) and to deprive the older plants of their photosynthesis-generated food supply. Older established plants will eventually give up if life above ground is made impossible for long enough.
- But be prepared for a comeback. Seeds can lie dormant for at least twenty years. Moving soil around can easily reintroduce root fragments eager to take their chance.

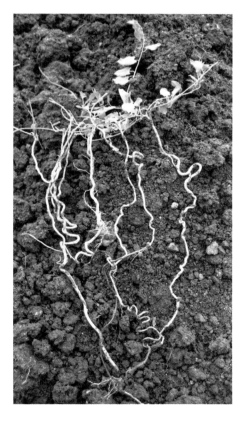

RIGHT ABOVE Field bindweed in temptress mode.
RIGHT BELOW Field bindweed with some of its deep penetrating rhizomes dug out of the ground.

Solanales

67

Solanum nigrum
SOLANACEAE
Black Nightshade

Just the name, black nightshade, sends a sinister shiver. In fact, it is barely toxic and especially when its berries turn black. In parts of India these are appreciated as a nutritious delicacy. Here in Europe, its apparent native home, we mainly know it as a nuisance invader of arable land and, of course, vegetable plots, daring to claim its place alongside its potato and tomato cousins and conspicuously maturing just when these do. Its flowers and fruits are a smaller edition of those of the potato, but it produces no tubers. In the seeding record stakes, a large plant is said to produce 153,000 seeds, with a top rate of germination. It has shown resistance to herbicides. Hence its ongoing pushy assertiveness.

Atropa belladonna or 'deadly nightshade' is said to be one of the most toxic plants to be found in the western hemisphere. Mercifully, unlike black nightshade, it is not a common garden invader.

RIGHT Black nightshade with some perpetual spinach, as if very much at home on an allotment.
OPPOSITE An overgrown Irish potato patch as photographed for a book on weeds in 1913.

Solanales

WHAT TO DO

- Of course, the seedlings should be hoed out in their early stages but black nightshade becomes much more imposing, and therefore recognisable, when mature with its black berries. Then it is still easily removed with a hefty tug.
- While with the potato family, give a thought to the original spud plant, *Solanum tuberosum*, which can itself act up as a weed – a 'volunteer', as they say. Once potatoes have been grown for a season, stray leftover tubers will ensure that the plant comes back in the same area to haunt us for a season or two and get in the way of the next rotation crop.
- But, you may be thinking, potatoes are known to be a pioneer crop and good for breaking into uncultivated weed-infested ground. So a productive way of doing some serious weed control can be to plant your potatoes in rows into roughly dug soil. Then, when the shoots first come through with a new crop of weeds, cover the whole lot by drawing earth over the row to make a little mound. Repeat the earthing up every week or two while suppressing each new set of weeds until the potato plants themselves are covering all the open ground. But beware! If good cultivation is not sustained the weeds will easily win again, as evidenced above.

Solanales

68

Datura stramonium
SOLANACEAE
Thorn Apple

Unlike black nightshade, thorn apple is alarmingly poisonous – to humans, horses, cattle, sheep, pigs, mules and chickens. It pops up quite frequently, usually individually and quite unpredictably. The two explanations for this are that seed can have an exceptional dormancy and that it can be an ingredient of mixed birdseed. It displays exotic showiness with its large trumpet-like flowers producing the sizeable prickly fruit by which it is named. It has the look of a newly-come outsider, yet apparently it was abundant in and around eighteenth-century London. Now in Britain its appearance is somewhat more sporadic, but enough to make us cautious, and to want it out.

WHAT TO DO
- Simply remove as soon as identified.
- Maybe go for one of its spectacular cultivars instead, like angels' trumpets, often grown in pots to impress the neighbours.

69

Mentha spp.
LAMIACEAE
Mint

Now meet the large lamiaceae family, formerly the labiatae. They are the ones which stick out their characteristic lower-petal tongues at us and are the family of many of our culinary herbs, like the many mints which are forever extending their varieties through a readiness for hybridisation. In gardening books virtually all of them come with a warning of 'invasive'. We draw attention to two in particular:

WEEDS, WEEDING (& DARWIN)

Mentha spicata
Spearmint

This is the kitchen standby and its spring growth is a much appreciated signal of the new season. The 'but' about spearmint is that, whatever you do, its rhizomatous roots make a dash for it and put up new shoots all over the place. And there is little more to be said.

WHAT TO DO
- Grow this mint in a container. It is unlikely to escape then but neither will it look too happy being a prisoner. Perhaps have a backup of successionally planted mint tubs.
- Or keep it in a small bed and use your regular cropping to keep bringing it back to one corner. The impressive rhizomes lift out quite easily and satisfyingly. Harvesting takes the role of weeding, for the watchful, at least.
- Relish fresh new mint as the ultimate accompaniment for new potatoes and peas, with salads and drinks, toothpaste, and to cure stomachache.

Mentha aquatica
Water Mint

Quite charming as an idea and on first appearances, but …

WHAT TO DO
- Don't be tempted. If you decide to give water mint a chance as a marginal plant in your new pond you are being totally unfair to everything else. Extracting it from a pond is far more difficult than from a bed, and, other than doing a total clear-out of everything, you are likely to become engaged in a never-ending battle.

RIGHT Aquatic mint charmingly set to take over a pond.

Lamiales

70

Lamium purpureum
LAMIACEAE
Red Dead Nettle

There is something rather reassuring about the concept of a dead nettle – a nettle lookalike without that sting.

Lamium purpureum, despite its 'red' epithet, definitely has purple flowers arising out of procumbent foliage which partly takes on a nettle-like form. It is an early riser, so to speak, as it will be among the first flowers to greet one in early spring, and then it will flower more or less continuously until October. It is self and insect-pollinating with abundant seed production over its long season. An annual with strong perennial hanging-on tendencies (or vice versa), it is a self-rooting creeper along the ground, happy in all soils, sun or shade and tolerant of extremes of temperature and moisture. There could hardly be a better collection of appropriate attributes for an opportunist coloniser of available open ground. Quite pretty on a verge, it is not special enough to warrant a place

Lamiales

in the garden where it will regularly present itself. It is no monstrous invader but rather a constant reminder of plants that should give way to more rewarding specimens. 'Badman' has been another of its adopted names, alongside 'purple archangel'. Make of it what you will, but probably not in the garden.

WHAT TO DO

- Remove seedlings with regular hoeing. It is also easily suppressed with mulch – for a while, that is.
- Replace with an upgraded cultivar such as *Lamium maculatum* 'Album'. Its variegated leaves and white flowers do much to brighten an otherwise dull shady space, and most especially as a herald of spring.

We should also note White Dead Nettle (*Lamium album*), the close cousin of the above, and the one with much more alarming nettle-likeness, on first glance. On a second glance, a beguiling charm takes over. White flowers peep through fresh green nettly leaves making up a sprightly little clump and much neater than the sprawling *L. purpureum*. Even so, it's a tease, and essentially of the wayside.

OPPOSITE Red dead nettle brightening up dark bare soil early in the year but its appeal soon fades as it untidily spreads.
LEFT White dead nettle in alliance with cleavers. Fair enough for the wayside but not for the garden.

Lamiales

71

Glechoma hederacea
LAMIACEAE
Ground Ivy

Formerly *Nepeta glechoma,* ground ivy is closely related to the catmints. With its creeping habit, it is perhaps the most persistent garden intruder of any in this family group. It looks innocent enough with a hint of a promising mallow, but don't be deceived. Its collection of other common names – creeping charlie, gill-over-the-ground, catsfoot, alehoof and run-away-robin – gives the game away.

Ground ivy gets away with it because it is happy in the shadier areas which we often overlook and, most especially, because it is a nifty little creeper along the ground. Not to worry then that it is pretty hopeless at viable seed production. With stolons (extended stems) reaching up to 70 cm and putting down roots at nodal points, it sneaks across garden edges or beside walls and paths, making a dash for it, if it can, onto enfeebled lawns. It is a good over-winterer, shrinking back into two leafed shoots or rosettes of 8 to 10 leaves, ready to make an early start in the new year.

LEFT ABOVE Ground ivy leaves rapidly covering the ground in the early year.
LEFT BELOW Ground ivy asking to be forgiven when later in flower.

This plant looks deceptively at home wherever it goes, which is hardly surprising since, being allelopathic, it secretes toxins and so inhibits potential competition. But, apart from a flush of early summer flowering (two-lipped purplish flowers on short spikes arising from leaf axils), it has nothing particularly interesting to offer, other than being quite an effective ground cover. Though before hops were found to be the business its pungent leaves were used in brewing beer.

WHAT TO DO

- Grub out by whatever means. It's not too difficult to pull or lift out, but of course it will still get the better of us by locking its roots under paving and brickwork, and the smallest remnant will all too easily regenerate. Persist and it will cease to resist – well, for a while.
- Take its presence as a warning to attend to your lawn. Encroaching ground ivy is essentially a reproach to a neglected sward. So, see to the lawn's light requirements, fertility, scarification, aeration, drainage, top dressing and regular mowing!
- Otherwise incorporate into a natural meadow effect – much harder to manage than it might at first seem.

72

Prunella vulgaris
LAMIACEAE
Self-heal

As its name suggests, this one has a reputation of old as an all-round wonder drug.

Hardly surprising then that it has hung around human habitations from way back, nor that it can be bit of an invasive nuisance as well, more especially into pastureland and lawns. In some respects,

RIGHT Self-heal – the season's successor to ground ivy with an even more striking flower.

notably in its flower form, it looks like a more filled-out version of the previous customer. In fact, it comes into flower in mid summer when ground ivy flowers ease off. It will be more showy while lasting well into the autumn.

Self-heal has small rhizomes but it reproduces most successfully by seeds – a mean number of 850 per plant. Curiously, due to apparent genetic control, some plants produce only flowering shoots, a few have vegetative shoots and others have both. And then there are both annual and perennial races among them as well. Therefore it has its own unique powerhouse to be an aggressive weed and a strong law unto its 'Self'.

WHAT TO DO

- Respect! If you like the flower, go for the more luxurious version, *Prunella grandiflora*.
- Apply good lawn care, as suggested above.
- Treat its claimed many medicinal properties (mouthwash, sore throat gargle, wound healer, antidote to food poisoning and too much fried foods, anti-inflamatory agent, etc.) with due caution.

73

Plantago major
PLANTAGINACEAE
Greater Plantain

Plantago lanceolata
Ribwort / Black Plantain

What is it about plantain? Why is this plant such an irritation and so often right there under our feet? One simple explanation for the latter is that our two plantains are exceptionally enduring perennials but also perform like fast multiplying annuals by producing and scattering vast quantities of enduring seeds. These are covered in a sticky mucilaginous substance, making them easily adhere to the soles of our shoes and whence they are taken wherever we tread.

WEEDS, WEEDING (& DARWIN)

LEFT Greater plantain as portrayed here by a woodcut in Gerard's *Herbal* has the air of a dapper little plant worthy of our attention. In reality it is notorious for the attention it pays us.
ABOVE This ribwort plantain betrays the more usual character of the plantains – rarely pert or tidy, and always around our feet.

Two distinctly different plantain species are apt to bother us as weeds: the round-leafed greater plantain and the ribbed narrow-leafed ribwort plantain. The former is more generally the lawn spoiler and the latter more often the occupier of other nooks and crannies. But that said, they are both found under our feet and all over the place.

Plantains, in fact, have stuck close to us since earliest times. Seeds were found in the stomachs of ancient Danes disinterred from the peat bogs. In Denmark, too, the discovery of plantain pollen grains in a layer of peat covering a bed of charcoal – itself evidently the result of forest burning – is thought to indicate deliberate creation of pasture land and the beginnings of Neolithic farming.

A little more recently, plantain made a name for itself when it crossed the Atlantic – never mind whether this was an intended import or an accidental one – with the early

Lamiales

settlers from Europe. The native Americans appropriately dubbed it 'white man's foot' as it rapidly spread across the continent on the heels of the new immigrants. The plants can survive almost anywhere, withstanding the extremes of hot arid summers, floods, compacted ground and long icy winters. Now growing in every continent bar Antarctica, plantain was rated by Edward Salisbury as 'one of the very hardiest weeds in the world … and likely to be with us forever'.

So what's wrong with it? Plantain is no great displacer of native vegetation, nor is it that detrimental to a garden – that is if you discount some lawns seen in late summer. If you are not a green sward perfectionist, you can tolerate and even enjoy the extra contribution of a few daisies followed by buttercups, then white clover buzzing with bees, but when next it is the turn of plantain to enlarge itself and flower, enough can be enough. The flowering shoots have less charm and take obtrusiveness one step too far. Then is the time to run for the weedkillers or whatever.

The trouble with both plantains in lawns is that the leaves form wide rosettes, adapting (with sufficient leaves lying flat against the ground) to the mower, and not the slightest bit harmed by trampling. Seizing the opportunity when grass growth generally slows down, the lingering rosettes suppress the grass underneath, look unsightly and leave a bare patch when the leaves later die back (if they do). And, even between weekly mowings, there's time for those annoying flowering shoots to spring up two centimetres or more, enough for its special propensity for wind-borne pollen distribution to take effect, as Darwin even commented upon in an aside. In effect, plantain plants make their own footprints over the grass, and, if left alone, these will remain and multiply, with unwitting assistance from our feet, over years.

Throughout history, therefore, we have kept this plant hanging around us as an irritant and to no great avail. Yes, plantain provides harmless grazing in and among grass, but the traditional herbalists, who tried hard to attribute useful properties to every plant, seem to have struggled with this one. Gerard scornfully dismissed its supposed attributes in the late sixteenth century: 'That three roots will cure one griefe, four another disease, six hanged around the necke are good for another malady &c. all of which are but ridiculous toyes.' Ironically, one of the healing properties still claimed for it today is for sore feet.

WHAT TO DO
- Humph! Your choice.

74

Veronica persica
PLANTAGINACEAE
Common Field Speedwell

Speedwell and forget-me-not both have catchy daredevil names and cheeky little blue-eyed flowers. Their similarity goes little further though they are both on that same larger asterid branch near the top of the evolutionary tree. Speedwell has drawn attention to itself recently by being wrenched from the scrophulaceae family to be placed footsore among the plantains by the new wave of molecular botanists. Like plantain, it seems to be under our feet wherever we go.

BELOW Speedwell, now known to be from the plantain family, will present a twinkling blue-eyed charm. But rarely will it earn a garden place – as its name, in effect, warns.

Lamiales

Barely known in Gerard's time and not mentioned by him, veronica is a relative newcomer to Britain. There is a record of *Veronica persica* in 1825 as an exotic novelty introduced from Persia. Seven years later Darwin sent back a specimen of *Veronica peregrina* from South America. Evidently it was a seasoned wanderer deemed originally to have set off from North America. Other close species like wall speedwell, spiked speedwell, heath speedwell and water speedwell tell of adaptation to a wide variety of niches, all in quite recent times and well earning the plant its familiar name. Meanwhile in 1870, our specimen, *Veronica persica*, was said to frequent England and fifty years later it was not only the most common speedwell but one of the most common of all annual weeds.

Common field speedwell is a typical annual opportunist, flowering all through the year, insect and self-pollinated, producing up to 7,000 seeds per plant and often with two generations a year. No wonder it has become one of the most classic little bits of nothing-very-much around.

Yet the flowers give off a teasing twinkle. They are charming as a wild flower and even possibly charming for a moment in a small area of the lawn, but somehow never quite up to the mark to earn a place in a garden these days. More irritating to the gardener is the fact that speedwell anchors itself rather too firmly (certainly resistant to a normal hand-weeding tug) by means of a taproot with a mop of tenacious side shoots.

WHAT TO DO

- Respond in kind – speedily.
- Hoe out seedlings (easily identified with their telltale scalloped leaves) before they put down their full anchors.
- Fork out plants that have got away and established themselves.
- Mow lawns with blades not too low, so allowing the grass to outgrow the speedwell.

RIGHT A speedwell seedling already displaying its scalloped leaf.

WEEDS, WEEDING (& DARWIN)

75

Digitalis purpurea
PLANTAGINACEAE
Foxglove

Foxgloves look so inviting – to little fingers, to bees and to gardens. Where such plants thrive naturally they will be everywhere and most certainly taking their chances in gardens. In parts of North Wales this is most certainly so, and that is where Darwin found himself in the summer of 1869, his sixty-first year. He had taken a bad fall from his much loved horse, Tommy, and, to recuperate, a family holiday was thought to be a good idea. So off they all went to stay in a house near Barmouth through June and July, and what else would he do there but get involved in observing the pollination of the foxgloves? He described his experiment seven years later in his book *The Effects of Cross- and Self-Fertilisation in the Vegetable Kingdom* (1876).

> I covered a plant growing in its native soil in North Wales with a net, and fertilised six flowers each with its own pollen, and six others with pollen from a distinct plant growing within the distance of a few feet. The covered plant was occasionally shaken with violence, so as to imitate the effects of a gale of wind, and thus to facilitate as far as possible self-fertilisation.

He made meticulous recordings of the consequent effects of self-fertilisation and insect (essentially bumble bee) cross-pollination, while collecting resultant seed capsules and taking them home to be grown on in his greenhouse. In short, cross-fertilisation won hands down with the production of distinctly more seeds and better plants all round. He repeated such experiments and went on to do more with so many other plants including our next example, verbascum (with similar results), as if he could never gather enough evidence; evidence which surely also indicates why these plants also succeed so well as garden weeds.

But this was not half of the evidence Darwin gathered in regard to foxglove success. With his own observations and referring to the recorded observations and deductions of fellow botanists, he outlined the seeming ingenuity of foxgloves in avoiding self-fertilisation when left to their own resources. For example, he noted that the pollen on the outer anthers close to the stigma matured early and dropped away before the stigma was advanced enough to make use of it. And then, as he wrote, 'the lower and inner side of the mouth of the corolla is thickly clothed with hairs, and these collect so much of

Lamiales

the pollen that I have seen the under surface of a humble-bee thickly dusted with it; but this can never be applied to the stigma, as the bees in retreating do not turn their under surfaces upwards'. Sharp observation indeed of some apparently extraordinary tactics of a plant to keep ahead of the game.

WHAT TO DO

- If foxgloves like to come into your garden, either find a semi-wild wooded space for them or else go for the cultivars. *D. purpurea* 'White' and 'Apricot' are good old-time cottage garden favourites.

Note that *Linaria vulgaris* (Common Toadflax and also in the plantain family) was yet another example Darwin used to build his case for the advantage of cross- over self-pollination. He sowed two beds, one with seed produced from self and one from cross-fertilised plants. He was gleeful to report yet again that the offspring of self-fertilised plants were distinctly less vigorous than the others. Most gardeners are gleeful not to have it around at all.

76

Verbascum thapsus
SCROPHULACEAE
Mullein

Mullein stands out. A statuesque touchy-feely plant, sometimes as tall or even taller than us, it is there to be noticed and admired – or not. A robust biennial plant of the wild, it frequently finds itself in gardens and puts us on the spot: should we greet and keep it as an old friend, or send it packing as an unwelcome intruder?

Outstanding, above all, are verbascum seeds. A dedicated botanist, Mr WJ Beale from Michigan, USA, set up an experiment in 1879 to test how long the seeds of twenty common weeds would remain viable. One hundred years later just the verbascum seed was found to be viable, and very much so. As the soil bank's most senior occupant, it reserves the right to lie low for long years and then, as if on a whim, to make an appearance seemingly

LEFT Foxgloves enjoying the shelter of a dry stone wall near Barmouth in North Wales where Darwin lit upon these plants with particularly keen interest.

Lamiales

out of nowhere. It far outstrips the secrecy of charlock (Weed 54) which we saw Darwin reporting earlier. Not only that but once established in the second year of a biennial cycle it will withstand storm battering, drought and moth predation, hanging on bedraggled and bent double, though still characterfully statuesque, with a long succession of flowers and the showering of another 150,000 or so seeds, and set to survive the next 100 years.

'Singular' is how Darwin described verbascum in the *Origin* chapter on hybridism where he states that individual plants of certain species of lobelia, verbascum and passiflora, could easily be fertilised by pollen of a distinct species, but not by pollen of the same plant, though this pollen could be proved to be perfectly sound by fertilising other plants or species. A few pages later he excitedly writes of a case

> far more remarkable ... at first incredible; the result of an astonishing number of experiments made during many years on nine species of Verbascum, by so good an observer and so hostile a witness as Gartner: namely that the yellow and white varieties when crossed produce less seed than similarly coloured varieties of the same species.

Darwin goes on to spell out the anomalies of the various verbascum crosses, building up to his crux explanation for the emergence of new species, where this frustrating blunt instrument of sterility (or partial sterility) plays a key role in eventually securing stable new differences. The role of sterility dogged Darwin from way back, as we saw in the case of his double-petalled buttercups (Weed 15).

Verbascum came to Darwin's attention again seventeen years later, in the book in which he wrote up his foxglove experiments. He followed similar procedures of netting some plants and not others to compare self and cross-fertilisation, and even repeating the process into a second generation. This time he had to admit that 'two of the self-fertilised plants exceed in height their crossed opponents' though on averaging the six examples of each the crossed plants were distinctly higher. His honesty in recording such results, even though they did not always support his case 100 per cent, is impressive.

WHAT TO DO

• Go on, allow yourself the odd verbascum visitor, especially as its seed may have waited many many years in your garden to take its turn to germintate. Explore, too, the many most rewarding different species.

RIGHT Mullein almost bent double from over-flowering and with moth-eaten leaves.

WEEDS, WEEDING (& DARWIN)

77

Buddleja davidii
SCROPHULACEAE
Butterfly Bush

Buddleja has changed families several times, or rather botanists have repeatedly reallocated it. Now, with DNA evidence it has settled onto the scruffy scrophulaceae just as other former members of this family have been shifted away, mainly to the plantains. Perhaps it is a bit unfair to cast scrophulaceae as scruffy, but both our weed candidates from this family can have a somewhat dishevelled, greying look.

LEFT Buddleja by the railway – now one of the most favoured haunts of this relative newcomer and resulting in escalating clearance costs for rail companies.
OPPOSITE Holly, on the other hand is an old-timer which barely strays. Even so, it can be a prickly character, and in several ways.

Strange to think that Darwin could not have known this extremely common shrub, but it has found its way into his garden now, cheekily sticking out of the wall the other side of the kitchen garden. It was only introduced to Britain from China in the 1890s by way of the famous French missionary and plant collector Père David. Subsequently grown and loved by gardeners, it has garnered a reputation as the outstanding attractor of butterflies. Nowadays it is simply everywhere and notoriously a coloniser of derelict urban sites. It is the plant that grows out of concrete (a lover of lime and an indicator of soil alkalinity) and offers testimony to the resilience of the plant kingdom and its capacity to survive and come back from the severest obliteration. It is the curse of railway companies who have to spend huge sums each year to prevent it encroaching onto tracks.

An invasive plant worldwide and in so short a time. Could it be anything to do with its hermaphrodite flowers, their stated three million seeds per 'average plant', or its profound seed dormancy (just like its verbascum cousins)? Even so it remains a fine shrub with a well-deserved place in the garden.

WHAT TO DO

- Enjoy in your garden – there is a good range of associated fine species to choose from.
- Prune hard in spring and trim after flowering. Watch out for seedlings to be removed.
- Respect what an extraordinary Chinese takeover it represents.

78

Ilex aquifolium
AQUIFOLIACEAE
Holly

Why pick on holly – the all-year garden performer? Evergreen and ever shining dark green at that, it peaks, if we are lucky, with that glorious show of bright red berries – the icon of Christmas cheer.

We love holly for many other reasons too. It offers wonderful variety with a fine range of trees and bushes of all different forms and sizes and has leaves of every configuration,

WEEDS, WEEDING (& DARWIN)

complexion and variegation. We admire it, too, for its powers of endurance. The angular *aquifolium* leaves withstand extremes of temperature (allowing minimal transpiration) and fend off any would-be grazers. And, to be a little more prosaic, we value this plant as a useful standby, especially for taking care of those shadier, more problematic corners.

But, as we also know, sometimes this shrub of so much promise can disappoint:

- those berries will not always appear, nor necessarily for that long
- unwanted seedlings may spring up all over the garden, sprouting from seeds excreted from birds who have feasted on the berries
- some seedlings may get away to establish new shrubs, putting us in a quandary as to whether we want them in these self-chosen spots
- older hollies may turn ungainly, far outgrowing their original allotted space
- and then there's all that hostility from the spiny leaves. Gardeners keep clear!

This prickly customer turns out to be rather more complex than is evident at first. Admirable as holly is in so many ways, its troublesome tendencies are quite enough to push it onto this list, assisted, it has to be admitted, by Darwin, who, in character, went straight to looking at what the plant was really about.

Hollies thrived around Darwin's Kentish home. His family enjoyed the popular tradition of bringing in sprays to put around the hearth at Christmas. In spring his curiosity was repeatedly aroused by watching bees fly from the flowers of one holly to those of another, even if they were spaced quite far apart. When he set up his sandwalk, that little looping footpath just beyond his kitchen garden, he had one whole side planted with a holly hedge, and so allowed himself thereafter to be constantly reminded of its own peculiar ways. Sad to say, you can see it would have been the aggressive holly which rapidly made the path impassable following Darwin's death.

What interests us now is that Darwin happened to choose holly as his prime plant example to explain how Natural Selection might work. In the key fourth chapter of *Origin* he has a section on 'Illustrations of the Action of Natural Selection'. He begins by speculating about wolf slimness being a survival advantage when a pack of wolves find themselves with no other food option but to be chasing after ever more agile deer. He then turns to holly for his illustration of how a plant might stumble upon reproductive advantages for itself, and muses on the idea that some insects originally might have acquired a taste for sugar by licking the sticky underside of laurel leaves, and then that a sugar craving might have

LEFT The trimmed holly hedge still lining Darwin's sandwalk in Kent.

Aquifoliales

led them to search for sweets elsewhere, like the insides of flowers. The rest is history, so to speak, with flowers and insects finding themselves hooked into a mutually advantageous partnership which they were to refine forever after as changing circumstances required.

Darwin also chose to light on holly as his example because it went one step further in its reproductive strategies. It was dioecious (remember nettles, Weed 42 and dog's mercury, Weed 37) and had separate female plants (with berried fruits) and male plants (without berries and so accounting for some of the disappointment likely to be encountered by seasonal gatherers of berried branches). He speculates as to why this separation of the sexes might have paid off and so become fully established. The whole discussion takes two and half pages (to which readers are strongly encouraged to turn). Even in summary, we see that the armoury which holly has gathered in order to survive is pretty impressive. Alert gardeners certainly know this too.

There are three piquant postscripts to this holly exposé:

First, while emphasising again that holly comes in many varieties, subspecies and species, we should note that exact status in this regard is sometimes uncertain and throws another little wobbly into just what defines a species.

Second, we see that DNA analysis now points to the Canaries and Azores as the likely place of origin for holly. Darwin passed through these islands on his outward voyage but was unable to stop because of a suspected cholera outbreak on board. He missed out on discovering an outstanding display of plant diversification in what is now described as the 'Galapagos of botany'. Still thriving in the oceanic conditions of this archipelago is a wide range of hollies, and of ivies (which we come to next).

Third, quite late in his life, on 3 January 1877, Darwin was writing yet again to the *Gardeners' Chronicle*, contributing to a correspondence on why there seemed to be so few berries on the holly trees at the end of the previous year. Of course he had the answer. He wrote a lucid and detailed account of his observations through that year, concluding with characteristic frankness: 'Therefore, as I believe, we cannot decorate our Christmas hearths with the scarlet berries of the Holly, because bees were rare during the spring; but what caused their rarity I do not in the least know.'

WHAT TO DO

- Pull or grub out random seedlings and don't be hoodwinked by a single red berry into thinking they should stay.
- Prune annually just before Christmas – for the decorative bonus.
- Take a look at those 'Illustrations of the Action of Natural Selection' in the fourth chapter of the *Origin*.

Aquifoliales

SHIFTING ACROSS a secondary branch we now join the apiales, represented here by the two families: araliaceae (with ivy) and apiaceae, historically well known as the umbellifera or the carrot family. This latter family really is historic, being the first group of plants to be subjected to systematic (classification) study, way back in 1672 by a certain Robert Morrison. That was the relatively straightforward bit. Much more problematic right to this day has been deciding just where this family fits in with all the others. Suffice to say that just in the last few years they were spotted as out of place by the DNA analysts and moved across a whole major branch from the rosids to the asterids. There they are now, near the top of our tree, with their little flowers arrayed in their distinctive umbrella forms. Both families are known to have many members which are said to be 'promiscuous', that is their openly displayed flowers can be pollinated by a wide variety of organisms.

79

Hedera helix
ARALIACEAE
Ivy

Ivy, with softer foliage than holly, also has its garden place, especially as a groundcover of difficult shady patches and as an acceptable climber with characterful autumn flowering.

But, even more so than with holly, this plant just will not stay put. If not watchfully curtailed, *Hedera helix* readily spreads itself about, shooting into flower beds and seemingly crawling up walls and trees with its tightly gripping caterpillar-like rootlets. If left, it can weaken and then overwhelm its supports until, after one mighty storm too many, all comes

RIGHT Ivy earning its keep in the autumn with a pleasing and unusual floral display.

tumbling down. Well, that's the drastic picture, and pretty much as Darwin's grandfather, Erasmus Darwin, saw it too:

> Yes! Smiling Flora drives her armed car
> Through the thick ranks of vegetable war;
> Herb, shrub, and tree, with strong emotions rise
> For light and air, and battle in the skies;
> Whose roots diverging with opposing toil
> Contend below for moisture and for soil;
> Round the tall Elm the flattering Ivies bend,
> And strangle, as they clasp, their struggling friend.
> (from *The Temple of Nature*, 1803, an epic poem by Erasmus Darwin)

Erasmus trumpets the struggles of nature and the grand succession of life. He was well ahead of his times, like his grandson was to be, and unknowingly prepared the ground for him.

In Rodmell churchyard ivy has won the battle, sitting proudly over the stump of an old elm. Outside the churchyard quite close by, elm hangs on. Despite attacks of Dutch Elm Disease, and probably in part as a reaction to this onslaught on older trees, elm suckers are spreading alongside a path in a weed-like rampage.

WHAT TO DO

- Have periodic purges of excessive ivy growth, more vigilantly so when it is covering walls and assaulting fruit trees.
- Recognise that ivy can have a reasonably balanced symbiotic relationship with trees and that together they can provide a sustained rich wildlife habitat which sometimes, at least, should be allowed to follow its natural course.

80

Anthriscus sylvestris
APIACEAE
Cow Parsley

The annual display of *Anthriscus sylvestris* alongside country lanes is an exotic extravaganza like no other. What a greeting for the arrival of early summer! For an all-too brief week or two we can wallow in showers of lacy froth – simple umbel upon umbel beautifully adorning that extended marginal space. *Anthriscus sylvestris*, the botanical name, somehow conjures up the magic too, whereas mundane 'cow parsley' is only more appropriate when the soft foliage is emerging ahead of the flowering.

LEFT Ivy taking over a tree stump in a churchyard.
RIGHT Cow parsley taking over a verge in early summer.

Its abundance and its temporary swamping of all other undergrowth is immensely impressive. Hardly surprising, then, that this luxuriant plant finds its way into gardens too, where its more mundane 'cow-parsley' image invariably puts it out of place, and where it can persist and come back again and again in awkward-to-get-at niches.

'*Sylvestris*' indicates that its natural habitat is around woodland and its margins. More widespread cultivation of available land has led these plants into retreating to the protection to be found beside roadside hedgerows where it is generally closer to gardens. The 'cow' epithet, on the other hand, acknowledges that it is eagerly grazed by cattle if they can get at it, even though it is of low nutritional value.

Strangely enough, while the multiple umbels display the flowers to enable the easiest open-access insect pollination, which leads to the extraordinary successful seed production of up to 10,000 seeds per plant, vegetative reproduction remains the plant's strongest means for pushing itself about, and as good as literally so too. Cow parsley perennates, as they say, by buds in the axils of the basal leaves, which develop into new plants once the old flowers die. Hence those dense clusters of plants along roadsides. But in gardens where the ground is regularly disturbed, seeds and seedlings stand more chance of progressing through their two-year cycle.

WHAT TO DO

- Look out for telltale seedlings, which, as always, provide the best chance of eradication.
- Otherwise, just slicing through the plant base will always help to allay the intrusion as a significant bulk of material can often be removed with some satisfaction. There will invariably be a comeback but this will be reduced if you can get in early to cut off immature flowering stems. Apparently this will stimulate axillary buds to have another go at producing flowers and in so doing will deplete food reserves in the roots. This reduces vegetative reproduction and so plant numbers decline. But cutting at the base once the plants have fully flowered stimulates vegetative growth and reproduction.
- If you have the space, lush conditions and the inclination, there are variously coloured anthriscus cultivars worth trying. They can certainly be grandly atmospheric at that burgeoning new-season time of year.

OPPOSITE ABOVE A dreaded charmless patch like this simply makes the heart sink. Ground elder demonstrates the total triumph of a weed over fine former garden plants.
OPPOSITE BELOW The tangling rhizomes of ground elder off which little roots are constantly sprouting.

Apiales

WEEDS, WEEDING (& DARWIN)

81

Aegopodium podagaria
APIACEAE
Ground Elder / Goutweed

For many British gardeners ground elder is the ultimate enemy, the supreme perennial weed and the most dreaded invader of the perennial bed. It puts cow parsley totally into the shade as a garden nuisance, tiresome as that can be at times. And, putting into the shade is exactly what ground elder does. It suppresses other plants with a simple blanket effect.

Yet in parts of North America, goutweed, as it is known there (and especially its less vigorous variegated form), is a valued garden plant, being decorative and offering good salad leaves in early summer. It is thought that in hotter drier summers ground elder loses the capacity to be as invasive as it is in the cooler and semi-shaded parts of Western Europe. And even here it hovers around the edges of woody areas as if innocently playing a minor ecological role quite unlike its aggressive takeover bids in gardens.

In the domesticated situation, the plant's underground network comes into forceful play. It consists of multiple strands of entangling rhizome. These are extending buried stems which do not descend into inaccessible depths like field bindweed, bracken and horsetail, but instead vigorously push out horizontally while constantly branching in a tangle to penetrate every other root system around.

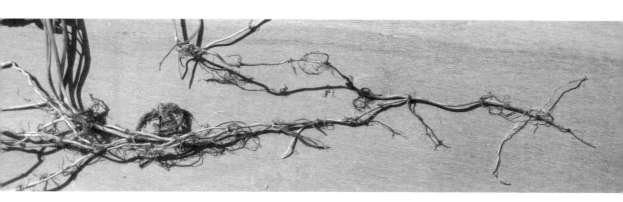

Botany textbooks cite these below-ground horizontal tendencies – sometimes bending up a bit and then bending down again, and sometimes turning its underside up before settling on a more level course – as a unique and puzzling phenomenon. Auxins play a part, but there is lot more to it.

It's salutary to examine one such extending stem (which we gardeners will often quite naturally but mistakenly assume to be a section of root). At intervals of 4 to 5 centimetres the stem bears short scale leaves. In the angle between each scale leaf and the rhizome there is an axillary bud which has the potential to sprout a new branch. Root fibres will also adventitiously develop from these points, as well as basal leaves making a break for it, especially at the growing tips. In a single season one rhizome may extend up to a metre in length. Then at certain points multiple branching takes place and the joint thickens into a rosette-like crown which is resilient enough to send up flowering shoots.

And for a brief mid-summer spell there can be a moment when it is difficult not to be charmed as delicate lace-like white flowers break through, setting off everything around them, the more informal, the better.

WEEDS, WEEDING (& DARWIN)

You might for a moment say all is forgiven, if it were not for the alarm of an imminent shower of seeds. But, by all accounts, the seeds are the least of our problems. Seedlings barely get a look-in. It is those rhizomes which remain the dominant reproductive powerhouse.

Finally we have to admit to a disconcerting special relationship. It is assumed that ground elder is one of the plants which came to Britain with the Romans (and more latterly found its way to the New World), quite possibly as a medicinal asset. Whatever is the case, ground elder invariably appears to grow not far from human habitation. Although we have drawn attention to some of its intensely-felt nuisance qualities we must acknowledge that many non-gardeners are blissfully unbothered.

WHAT TO DO

- Make a clean break of it. Dig out the whole offending bed, removing all plants including every visible root fragment. Replant with new stock taking the opportunity for a completely new flower bed. Perhaps use annuals for the first year. Watch out and immediately remove any ground elder sprouting from the tiniest root remains. In the first few days these will pull out easily.
- Mow. Ground elder succumbs to constant mowing at normal lawn lengths. If there is plenty of lawn, island beds are sometimes shifted around to deal with severe perennial weed invasions.
- Otherwise apply constant vigilance, especially watching areas which are slightly shaded and which you are most likely to forget. If you can't undertake the drastic actions suggested in the first two options, it is always advisable to remove all growth that you can see and access, and as often as you can. That, of course, is much more easily said than done. But at least pull out the new season's top growth as it appears so as to allow the prized garden perennials to get the upper hand in the first competitive bid to cover the ground.
- Don't rule out carefully targeted use of a glyphosate weedkiller to deal with a small invasion in an awkward spot, but this is difficult without affecting surrounding plants.
- Scrutinise the root ball of any plant given to you by well-meaning friends. Even quarantine such plants. They can quite often provide a sly route of ground elder entry.
- Curse it, curse it, curse it and so sustain solidarity with fellow gardeners.

Apiales

82

Daucus carota

APIACEAE

Queen Anne's Lace / Wild Carrot / Bird's Nest

Now, for a change, let's be genuinely charmed by the exquisite Queen Anne's lace effect of the wild carrot. This plant also seduces a fine range of insects, often to further charming effect for us.

The laciness of the umbellifera flower heads reaches near perfection with this one, and with a frilly fringe too.

But watch out! It can dance all over your garden. In the semi-wild Jardin des Sambucs in the French Cévennes it does just that, and shows itself as a wily seducer. And among the plant's hosts is the dreaded carrot fly – the scourge of our garden carrots. It's a good idea to keep it well away from vegetable plots, along with all other carrot-fly-hosting members of the wider carrot family.

That said, this (or to be precise, a subspecies of this one) is *the* carrot from which all the domesticated varieties have been bred and the one that has stood the test of time. So there it is, in reserve for breeders to use to back cross renewed resilience – disease and pest resistance especially – into the swollen roots on which we have come so much to depend.

WHAT TO DO

• Keep well away from vegetable gardens, at the very least.

RIGHT Queen Anne's lace in exquisite lacy floral mode, exquisite too to insects who help to secure its successive generations.
OPPOSITE Fool's parsley and its poisons challenging the gardener not to be taken in.

Apiales

WEEDS, WEEDING (& DARWIN)

83

Aethusa cynapium
APIACEAE
Fool's Parsley

Not immediately that different from the entry opposite, and with branching carrotty foliage impersonating a valued herb too. And a regular garden intruder taboot. But don't be fooled for one moment! Its other common names – 'dog poison' and 'lesser hemlock' tell the tale.

WHAT TO DO
- Keep well at bay from any part of the garden, though it will have no problem in forcing an entry.

Apiales

84

Conium maculatum

APIACEAE
Hemlock

Which brings us to one of the most lethal of all plants and one of which Socrates was made to take a fusion when found guilty of impiety in Ancient Greece. At first glance it is not that different from the previous two weeds, nor indeed from cow parsley. So, if ever in doubt, the clarity of this detailed nineteenth-century print should help. But note it can be up to 2.5 metres tall, its stem smooth and usually spotted or streaked with red and purple in its lower half, and its leaves distinctly triangular and smelling of mice. It thrives in damp areas, flowering in spring, and is found all over the place and is declared 'invasive' in twelve of the United States, including California.

BELOW Hemlock stems looking appealingly exotic in a brief roadside show.
RIGHT Hemlock, a plant to identify for safety's sake – with the help here of Stephenson's *Medical Botany*, 1834.

WEEDS, WEEDING (& DARWIN)

Apiales

Apiales

WHAT TO DO

- Take the trouble to search out and identify this one, if only to feel more confident that you won't ever mistake it for something less harmful in the future. Coming into full flower a week or two after cow parsley fades away, it can make quite an impression, what with its height, finer leaves, shiny blotchy stem and mousy odour. Once knowlingly experienced in early summer, it is then not easily forgotten.

85

Heracleum sphondylium
APIACEAE
Hogweed

Heracleum mantegazzianum
Giant Hogweed

They call themselves weeds, but these ones are unlikely just to slip into a garden unnoticed because they are so conspicuously large. They have no problem, however, in pushing themselves onto this list. For a start, hogweeds themselves and their white umbels will adorn roadside verges as the later-summer counterpart of cow parsley, and we know all too well what such positioning usually leads to. Also the plants tend to reach a little higher than their predecessors and grow in a more spread out and less densely clumped way. Their large decorative seed heads at the same time have an air of mega-proliferation menace, with hundreds of winged seeds to each umbel and a stated average of 5,013 per plant.

Giant hogweed is an absolute terror if handled. A photo-sensitive sap is released even on just brushing against plant hairs and it can be a severe skin irritant as soon as exposed to the sun, sending people rushing to hospital. Yet it is a veritably awesome specimen, indeed a handsome one with claims of reaching higher (up to four metres) than any other herbaceous plant in Western Europe. It can take up to four years to flower and it will then keel over. It was yet another prized, menace-to-be plant introduced to Britain in the early nineteenth century when it was brought back from the Caucasus by excited plant collectors to become the next 'must-have' piece of foreign exotica for big gardens and, presumably, quite soon to fall out of fashion and make its way into the wild.

Be aware that the two hogweeds can be quite variable in size and form, and indeed that they can hybridise.

Apiales

WEEDS, WEEDING (& DARWIN)

WHAT TO DO

• A bold gardener with a sizeable garden might just find the right space for giant hogweed as those Victorian gardeners must have done. Nicholas Brückin at the Jardin des Sambucs has done just that by introducing three or four plants in a damp hollow of his steep mountainside so that you can look down on the remarkable wide flower heads from a balcony above.

BELOW It's devilishly hard not to be captivated by such a sight. But we know all too well what will happen with those dripping seeds.

86

Centranthus ruber
CAPRIFOLIACEAE
Red Valerian / Valerian

Like its Roman namesake, the Emperor Valerian (AD253–60), this valerian (not to be confused with another one of the same name, *Valeriana officinalis* of stress-relief renown) began its life by the Mediterranean, from where it went on to colonise most of Europe and then later spread across the New World. And somehow, away from its original home base, it tends to stand out for not quite fitting in with its surroundings – depending on our visual sensibilities.

It is absolutely in character that red valerian will install itself by the garden gate, seemingly not making up its mind whether it really wants to come in or stay outside. It appears to have a bit of a history of wandering in and out of the garden: from naturalising in the wild, to settling into gardens and then retreating back as a garden escape.

Part of its awkwardness for us too may be associated with its colouring which can be a pleasing strong red, but will usually fade and stand out as a jarring orangey pink. Here, anyway, is yet another weed candidate with an exceptional capacity for variation.

WHAT TO DO
- Perhaps resign yourself that this plant is probably best left hovering around the margins of your garden where, aptly, it links domesticated and undomesticated space.

RIGHT Valerian characteristically ensconced by a front garden wall.
OPPOSITE Teasel telling us it cannot be ignored. Whether or not it should sometimes be invited into the garden can be a difficult dilemma.

Dipsacales

WEEDS, WEEDING (& DARWIN)

87

Dipsacus fullonum
CAPRIFOLIACEAE
Teasel / Fuller's Teasel

We have to say it: for gardeners this biennial can be a bit of a tease. It will hover around gardens and leave us unsure about what is to be done. Florists are drawn to it, but does that oblige us to have it in the garden?

Teasel's weed status results from the fact that it is a redundant cultivated plant. Up until nearly the end of the nineteenth century it was grown in fields and sometimes in gardens to provide disposable 'fulling' tools for the wool industry. The seed heads were used to comb out impurities and to 'tease' out the fibres. But by the twentieth century, teasel seed heads were replaced by metal cards, leaving the plants to wander around commons and verges, as well as continuing to hang around gardens.

There is a little irony about the removal of 'impurities', as teasel is notoriously infested with maggots in the seed heads (Gerard fulminated about this way back) and in the little basins which form at the leaf axils. Studies on two sites on Wimbledon Common suggest that teasel could have carnivorous tendencies, just like the sundews.

WHAT TO DO
- This depends on your style of gardening. Obviously teasels are not appropriate in formal beds, but in more informal gardens they can sometimes add that little risqué dash of the wild, the distinctive seed heads providing fine forms to linger from autumn into winter, setting off cosmos rather nicely, for example, and providing material for flower arrangers when few other suitable garden flowers remain.
- But beware of seed profusion, as this will lead on to much weeding, though giving you the opportunity to select – or not – the few which might give the garden that extra touch next year. Selection is of the essence.

Dipsacales

AT LAST, we perch on our final bit of branch, the asterales, around the top of the evolutionary tree of plants, and a top-heavy kind of tree this turns out to be and especially in regard to its weed members. For this order is far larger than all the rest, having nearly 25,000 species among twelve families, of which we now meet the campanulas and the vast daisy family (the compositae). All the families share special chemical properties, the same number of chromosomes and similar stamens which form a tube around the stile.

88

Campanula spp.
CAMPANULACEAE
Campanulas

To find campanulas alongside the compositae may seem a little puzzling at first. Delicate little bells look so unlike those mop-like flower heads but there they are, sharing special chemical properties, same chromosome numbers and similar stamens which at first are joined together as a tube around the style to enable sophisticated 'secondary pollination'.

In this campanula flower, the style pushes its way through the tube of stamens gathering their pollen grains and hoisting them up for even greater exposure to passing insects to be carried away and passed on elsewhere. With this extra assistance in their reproductive armoury, no wonder campanulas (and members of the daisy family) are so ahead of the game.

For us, those little blue bells are a strong draw and hard to resist, especially the many exquisite alpine species. And there the risks ensue. Just one or two of them can be incredibly invasive and rapidly displace everything around, especially those truly pretty examples. Maintaining a diverse balance of plants in an alpine garden without one or two species rapidly overtaking the rest is always a challenge.

ABOVE A campanula flower projecting its pollen-clad style for the insect world to pass around.
RIGHT A common campanula plant tenaciously attached to a flint wall while systematically spreading itself – often much more than the gardener wants.

Asterales

WEEDS, WEEDING (& DARWIN)

Edward Salisbury cites the aggression of the 'beautiful Creeping Bell-flower (*Campanula rapunculoides*), a plant well-nigh ineradicable when once established, except by the most drastic treatment'. A plant, in other words, to be admired in any other domain but one's own. Not in my back yard, in effect, which is a telling admission of the way we so often designate plants as weeds.

Campanula garganica, here locked into a flint wall, is promoted by the Royal Horticultural Society as 'a spreading perennial' which 'makes an excellent wall or bank plant'. Too true. Spreading it can certainly be, digging its tough rhizomatous roots into the tiniest cracks and pushing on and on. Yes, it is an absolute delight in full flower, but do we want it simply everywhere and virtually impossible to remove?

WHAT TO DO
- Choose your campanulas cautiously, perhaps avoiding the above two.

Asterales

NOW FINALLY, let's meet our last (and vast) family, the compositae (now asteraceae). Such a phenomenon they are that they merit their own special introduction.

The compositae, comprising ten per cent of all plant species, has strong claims to be the largest of all plant families and most certainly it leads among the eudicots. And it is alarming for us to realise that this family, commonly known as the daisy family (alias sunflower family), contains a much higher proportion of members with weedy and invasive tendencies than any other. Or to put it more grandly – and blandly – compositae have a well-above-average number of pioneers.

The name tells it all. The defining characteristic of compositae is that the flowers are themselves composites of tiny flowers – often hundreds of 'florets' – closely bunched together on a single capitulum (flower head). So explicit is this old-time name that it has generally remained in everyday botanical parlance despite asteraceae being the current official label. Nomenclature standardisation now requires all family names to be taken from the name of the species first to have been scientifically described in each family – the founding member, so to speak.

Another striking feature of the compositae is that they are exceptional chemists. They are a source of all kinds of herbal products as well as producing substances which act as natural fertilisers, pesticides and herbicides, and which therefore play a key part in the plants' own uninhibited growth.

As there are so many weed candidates in this group, we too take a composite approach by bunching many of them into cluster groups while, at the same time, giving due special attention to the more notorious individuals. Among the collections are quite a number of marginal examples, ones which are on the borderline between being good garden standbys, tiresome tearaways, or simply have the vice of being just too common. Their presence in a garden can create a disturbing frisson which itself can be a valued horticultural quality … or not. Edgy they are, on all counts.

Among the individual notorieties, the dandelion, especially, encapsulates the ultimate finesses, complexities and Darwinian 'fitness' of the compositae. It is a composite of all the compositae, dare we suggest, and is an example which warrants more detailed examination.

Asterales

89

Cirsium spp.

ASTERACEAE

Thistles

Prickly, noxious, injurious, invasive: thistles exude aggressive hostility, as Darwin himself found out only too forcefully early on in his formative voyage. Referring to the tamer thistle relative, the cardoon (*Cynara cardunculus*), he noted in his journal that near Rio,

> very many (probably several hundred) square miles are covered by one mass of these prickly plants, and are impenetrable by man and beast. Over the undulating plains, where these great beds occur, nothing else can now live. Before their introduction, however, the surface must have supported, as in other parts, a rank herbage. I doubt whether any case is on record of an invasion on so grand a scale of one plant over the aborigines.

RIGHT The cardoons here stand at the Victoria Gate entrance to Kew Gardens blocking the way ahead and telling us to pass along to the right.

Asterales

He observed, too, the invasive presence of 'giant thistles' (presumably the Scotch thistle, *Onopordum acanthium*, and that they reached into a lower latitude than the cardoons. Ahead of his times, Darwin all too astutely realised how this takeover of the landscape had come about. Yes, these assorted thistles had come with the first European settlers who, in effect, left this ecological havoc in their wake:

> Few countries have undergone more remarkable changes, since the year 1535, when the first colonist of La Plata landed with seventy-two horses. The countless herds of horses, cattle, and sheep, not only have altered the whole aspect of the vegetation, but they have almost banished the guanoco, deer and ostrich.

The above two examples can make characterful contributions towards the back of a mixed border, though the Scotch thistle will seed abundantly all over the place. They are cited here by way of a soft introduction to the prime thistle villains: creeping thistle and spear thistle.

Cirsium arvense
Creeping Thistle

An aggressive colonist, if ever there was one, creeping thistle is often to be found in patches, if not extensive drifts. This is because it occurs in clones in which formidable rhizomatous root systems link the plants and thereby spread them – sometimes twelve metres a year. As if to defy us, the principal root layer, from which sprout the flowering shoots, will often lie just below spade or plough reach. The roots are brittle and easily fragment when disturbed, only to regenerate their own sub-clones. Their enduring creeping capacity is truly impressive.

A neglected garden is prone to such a takeover but it has to be exceptionally neglected while still subject to some soil disturbance. More often, creeping thistle is troublesome to farmers in both arable crops and in pasture. Notoriously, over-grazing (especially by horses) can see a field scruffily devastated by such thistles. Unfortunately for us gardeners too, these thistles can adapt and thrive in all manner of soils and weather conditions, though thriving best in damp well-drained ground – as do our best garden plants.

RIGHT Creeping thistle generally grows to about 70 cm high in single stems. It is difficult to handle with its prickly stalk and leaves which end in slightly faded purple flowers and turn into an untidy fluffy assemblage of seeds waiting to be dispersed. Its appearance is known to be very variable.

Their forms, sizes and flower colourings are known to vary considerably due to genetic intricacies manifesting in 'phenotypic plasticity'.

Scruffy and defensively prickly as they may be, thistle colonies are usually complex networks. In one thistle patch there can be a number of separate clones and they will almost invariably be single sexed ('dioecious', like nettles, dog's mercury, holly et cetera). The distance between female and male clones, however, can be up to 50 metres (or supposedly even up to 390 metres) while still allowing cross-pollination.

Then an exceptionally high rate of seed viability (90 per cent after 16 days) occurs in quantities of anything from 20 to 200 per flower head, and up to 50,000 per plant. The mind may reel at such numbers but the few survivors out of these only really get a chance to multiply again if the ground is exposed – most probably by us gardeners.

So, one seedling appearing in our garden sends down a taproot from which rhizomes will radiate all over again. Thus the show goes on, unless we intervene, as indeed farmers are obliged to do by the 1959 Weeds Act, where this one is singled out for containment alongside its biennial associate, spear thistle (and together with ragwort and the two docks). Many North American states and other countries have it registered and even banned as 'noxious' too.

Asterales

WHAT TO DO

- Hoe out new shoots and seedlings in early summer. This is when the rhizome food reserves are said to be at their lowest and most vulnerable.
- Cut or hoe shoots in flower before they have a chance to go to seed, or snatch out with gloved hands.
- In essence, apply continual cultivation techniques.
- Reflect, if you wish, on how lucky you are not to depend on thistle seed fluff for pillow down or on thistle roots for flatulence-inducing food, as some of our forebears apparently did.
- And take heed from Darwin's experience in South America.

Cirsium vulgare
Spear Thistle

In essence, spear thistle is the biennial comrade-in-arms to perennial creeping thistle, quite often existing in partnership in similar terrain. But spear thistle may stand a little more apart, often in single more bush-like forms. It is altogether more tidy, even imposingly handsome. 'Spears' manifest themselves in the distinctly spiky ends of their leaves. You don't mess with spear thistles without your stoutest leather gloves.

Its biennial habit serves it most effectively. Being monocarpic, it is completely done for once it has flowered and set seeds. It disintegrates leaving a spare space where rosette seedlings can readily emerge again, as they will do elsewhere as well. Such rosettes may take their time, two or three years (extending the biennial period a bit) to gather strength before bursting into another full-blown flowering plant.

WHAT TO DO

- Look out for its early-stage rosettes and remove them.
- Respect and admire this plant in the wild, learning to distinguish it from its scruffier clonal cousin.

WEEDS, WEEDING (& DARWIN)

Asterales

90

Sonchus spp.

ASTERACEAE
Sow-thistles

Not from the immediate thistle clan but with milder thistly characteristics are the sow-thistles, beloved of swine and rabbits but not of gardeners. They happen to replicate thistles in the range of forms of their principal weed species: one tough resilient perennial and two ephemerals-cum-annuals-cum-biennials.

Sonchus oleraceus

Common Sow-thistle / Smooth Sow-thistle / milkweed / dindle / milky dickles / hare's lettuce

A commoner if ever there was one, and one which appears and reappears in and out of gardens throughout the full season. You can instantly see why it has no hope of attaining any kind of 'garden merit' when any possible attraction is so fleeting, its form is so ungainly and its greying leaves turn mildewy so soon.

OPPOSITE Spear thistle flower
– a smart one.
LEFT Common sow-thistle –
common even for a weed.

Asterales

RIGHT Prickly sow-thistle –
usually the more handsome
one.
BELOW Perennial sow-thistle
– the most aggressively
invasive one.

WEEDS, WEEDING (& DARWIN)

Sonchus asper
Prickly Sow-thistle

Standing out with fresher green colouring, prickly sow-thistle is definitely more thistle-like and so more resistant to manhandling. Together with its smooth sibling, it will often try its chances in our gardens arriving from parachuted seeds and then speedily ensconcing itself with a taproot which resists most tugging.

Sonchus arvensis
Field Sow-thistle / Corn Sow-thistle / Perennial Sow-thistle

This one is a tougher nut and considerably ups the stakes against attempted removal. Its leaves and stalks are stouter with even their surfaces bristling with suggestions of prickles. Like creeping thistle it has its vigorous spreading root system, in fact with considerably tougher roots which usually remain in the top 15 centimetres though radiating out a mere two to three metres a year. If your garden adjoins a field, beware lest it should sneak under a hedge and maybe even insinuate itself with a bit of rustic charm at first.

Weeds come and go. At the time and locality of writing this, perennial sow-thistle is one which is noticeably in the ascendant, dominating verges in late summer and right through the autumn. We gardeners are having to keep an eagle eye on it just now. It's the last thing we want slipping under the hedge.

WHAT TO DO
• Apply zero tolerance with all three. Take out the first two whenever they appear and feed to a pet rabbit, and maybe make yourself feel smart by observing the difference between the two invaders. Simply dig up the latter if ever it appears under the hedge as it just cannot match any garden plant.

Asterales

91

Arctium lappa
ASTERACEAE
Burdock

A robust perennial with large heart-shaped leaves and thistle-like flowers maturing into those notorious sticky burrs which were the inspiration for Velcro, this plant would seem to have alarming invasive potential. Mercifully it is of no serious threat to most gardens as it draws attention to itself so conspicuously with its gross foliage. And then the burrs, for all their clinging, cannot just pop over garden walls on their own.

Nevertheless, Richard Mabey observes that burdock finds its way into the paintings of at least a dozen of the old masters, from Claude Lorrain to Gainsborough and Stubbs, to the extent of being remarkably invasive, with those characterful leaves often acting as appropriate painterly groundcover for the foreground corners. For Stubbs, in particular, burdock can play an integral part in his whole composition. Mabey eloquently observes that in the painting of a lion devouring a horse (1769),

> Burdock leaves are picked out in high mortal detail. Their ribs are as contoured as the horse's. They are beginning to age, wilting at the edges, showing patches of brown rust. One is already dead, a tan husk drooping towards the ground. A weed, Stubbs seems to be suggesting, expresses stress and ageing like any other living thing.

WHAT TO DO
- Visit the National Gallery and enjoy spotting the burdock invasion of European landscape painting. That's as good a way as any of getting to know the handsome leaves and then dealing with them early if they appear in your garden. Otherwise they will go on to generate their all too catching burrs.

Asterales

WEEDS, WEEDING (& DARWIN)

92

Solidago canadensis et al.

ASTERACEAE
Golden Rod and suchlike

Here is a little bunch of compositae plants which taunt by being on the borderline between serviceable garden plants and mere weeds.

Take *Solidago canadensis*, poor old golden rod, much mocked for being 'common' in every sense and taking up space where something more classy might be. In fact, *Solidago canadensis* came to Britain in the mid-seventeeth century from North America and for a long time was prized by gardeners as an exotic novelty. But, as is often the case with newcomers, the novelty eventually wore thin. In 1883, for example, William Robinson had a quite different take on these plants. While singing the praises of the then relative newcomer, Japanese knotweed, Robinson was scathing about golden rod and even its praised variability, 'scarcely one of them is fitted for garden culture. In borders they merely serve to exterminate much more valuable plants, and to give a coarse and ragged appearance to gardens.' Now we hear of *Solidago canadensis* being a terrible

RIGHT One invasive garden plant after another. Golden rod sneakily intruding among some Japanese anemones to most beguiling effect.

invasive scourge of large swathes of China. Nevertheless, it still lingers around many European gardens as an old-time standby.

Take *Eupatorium cannabinum* or hemp agrimony. Call it by its Latin name in the garden or by its common name in the wild. That's one way of getting round something which is still acceptable in both camps.

Take *Ageratum* spp. (the ageratums). They have the same name both botanically and in common usage. But beware! There is *Ageratum microcarpum* which is a common (to the degree of being almost too common) bedding plant and there is *Ageratum conyzoides* which is an alarming weed of high toxicity.

Take *Centaurea scabiosa* (greater knapweed). This is a native wild flower which, as is sometimes claimed, can look even more at home in a border where it is appreciated for being one of those plants, like forget-me-not, whose flowering helps to bridge the spring/summer divide. And so on.

WHAT TO DO

- Allow yourself to dither about having such plants in your garden, unless you have immediately to hand something else distinctly more worthwhile.

BELOW LEFT Hemp agrimony (*Eupatorium cannabinum*) acting smart in the garden.
BELOW RIGHT Greater knapweed (*Centaurea scabiosa*) can also have its moment of playing a star horticultural role. With both hemp agrimony and this knapweed it somehow seems more appropriate to refer to them by their Latin names when they are invited into the garden.

Asterales

WEEDS, WEEDING (& DARWIN)

93

Senecio vulgaris
ASTERACEAE
Groundsel

The herbalist Gerard said it all back in 1597,

> Groundsel is called in Latine *Senecio*, because it waxeth old quickly…. The stalke of Groundsel is round, chamfered and divided into many branches. The leaves be green, long, and cut in the edges …. The floures be yellow, and turn to down, which is caried away with the wind. The root is full of strings and threds. These herbs are very common throughout England, and do grow almost everywhere. They flourish almost every moneth of the yeare.

Edward Salisbury in 1961 adds a hair-raising calculation. 'The average potential offspring from a single Groundsel plant is approximately 1000; and if all these survived and fruited and in their turn produced seedlings the entire population, by the end of the third generation in the autumn, could be of the order of 1000 million individuals.'

What more is there to be said of this absolutely classic come-and-come-again common 'ephemeral'? Only we should say that groundsel gets away with it by showing resistance to herbicides, as it happens, along with fellow ephemerals chickweed and fat-hen.

WHAT TO DO
• Hoe and hand weed persistently through the year.

RIGHT Groundsel as it ever was. The herbalist Gerard has it portrayed as quite a pretty specimen, as indeed it can be regarded if only we could forget for a moment that it is such an irritating and far too frequent intruder on allotments.

Asterales

94

Senecio jacobaea
ASTERACEAE
Common Ragwort

Ragwort, the biennial/perennial cousin of groundsel, is the one that really rings the alarm bells and especially in the farming community. Not only was it cited as one of the five 'injurious' villains in the 1959 Weeds Act but it was brought up again for special watchful attention in its own Ragwort Control Act in 2003. Yet it still proliferates in certain parts of the country with plague-like abundance. So it is hardly surprising that it sometimes arrives in gardens, especially in longer grass areas.

Asterales

The alarm arises from ragwort's toxicity to grazing cattle and horses who can suffer liver failure. Usually such animals will eschew it but the danger comes when they are suddenly let loose into a field when they are hungry, and more particularly when they consume it dried in hay. Within gardens it is of negligible health risk but it needs in any case to be ousted for its raggedness and lack of charm.

Yes, you may have guessed it by now: ragwort is a biennial which can hang on and on for years, as well as being a producer of abundant viable seeds out of its bunches of composite flowers. And those seeds are distributed far and wide on the breeze, like those of its annual-cum-ephemeral cousin. Cutting or grazing (less harmfully by sheep) of the foliage will only stimulate extended root growth. Likewise attempts at pulling roots will invariably leave fragments behind which will have no trouble in regenerating. On the other hand, in theory, once a plant has flowered it will keel over being monocarpic. But observation has shown that there will often be side shoots which last another year.

A persistent headache for farmers, ragwort is more of a manageable irritant to gardeners, who may be put off more by its illegal status and by the media hysteria sometimes generated, than by the reality.

Senecio squalidus
Oxford Ragwort

In fact, if anything, this is a slightly tidier version of the above. It came to the Oxford Botanic Gardens from Sicily in the late eighteenth century, whence it soon escaped, notoriously along the new railway lines of the next century.

WHAT TO DO
- Fork out carefully to avoid leaving fragments of root.
- Ragwort does pull out quite easily if the ground is moist and sometimes this can seem like a reasonable – and quicker – option.
- Take flower heads off young plants soon after they have flowered – and before the seeds are ready to fly – so letting it die naturally.
- Let sheep graze it (you should be so lucky!). That's what farmers sometimes do.
- Follow the advised Code of Practice set out by the 2003 Ragwort Control Act.
- Wait for severe weather conditions. Ragwort is susceptible to prolonged drought, flooding or extreme frosts.

Asterales

A footnote on coltsfoot (*Tussilago farfara*), another member of the senecio tribe. It charms exquisitely when its yellow dandelion-like flowers appear out of the ground in very early spring without any foliage. But then beware! Seeds quickly set and, once the distinctive colt's-foot-like leaves appear, the seeds are already dispersing. What's more, yet again we have a vigorous rhizome system capable of both pushing down and pushing out 'several feet' in a season. Advise no garden foothold for this otherwise beguiling curiosity – that is unless you have a chronic cough (*tussilago* is Latin for cough suppressant).

95

Bellis perennis
ASTERACEAE
Daisy

The *Bellis* flower, as its Latin name proclaims, is a beauty, and exquisitely so in its simplicity. And exquisite, too, is the performance of each flower. Every day, at an hour and half after sunrise, flowers will open with the outer frills – those rims of white-petalled florets – unfolding to reveal a yellow dome of tiny tubular flowers. Then at nightfall the white petals close back into a pinkish bud again. On overcast days flowers tend to act shy.

WEEDS, WEEDING (& DARWIN)

So there are two sets of florets within the one flower. The white marginal ones are female only and will only be responsive to insect-aided cross-pollination, whereas the inner yellow florets are hermaphrodite and get on with self-pollination – the principal lazy daisy way of fertilisation and reproduction.

The whole flower head becomes conical as an average of 125 fruits mature, all oval, flattened and sparsely covered with short hairs. As Edward Salisbury meticulously observed, each of these is around 1.5 to 2 mm in length with an average weight of 0.00015 gm. Seeds have a germination rate of up to 98 per cent and can mature in both spring and autumn. But without the parachutes of the dandelions and thistles they are not so readily distributed far from the parent plant, though birds, ants and boots will do their bit.

In one extended summer, a succession of thirty or more single flowering stems will emerge from a single plant. This consists of a prostrate rosette of leaves all culminating in a little rounded pad by which the plant claims its little space of about ten centimetres across, well secured by fibrous roots.

While we might readily cherish a few daisy blooms adding a little sparkle to our lawns or parts of them, the leafy plants themselves can stamp unseemly patches which become more prominent when grass growth slows right down in winter. Daisies are hardy perennial stayers after all, and what's more, can be vegetative spreaders (as well as plentiful seedling producers) sending out satellite rosettes and creating crowded little colonies while all the while suppressing more of the grass. So purges of those patches are called for from time to time.

WHAT TO DO

- Decide, if you can, where you stand on the dilemma (see caption below).
- If some controlling is in order, there are two equally practicable approaches: Apply a feed and weed nitrogen fertiliser which overpowers the broad-leaved weeds and promotes a spurt of the grass (needs rain or substantial watering after application to be effective).
- Or lift out with an appropriate fork or trowel and then reseed with grass.
- Note that mowing and flower picking only stimulates further flower production.
- Meanwhile enjoy the flowers that escape … and children's pleasure in making daisy chains.

LEFT A lawn adornment or a lawn spoiler? That's the daisy dilemma.

Asterales

Take note of the other principal daisy-like characters with weedy propensities:

- *Leucanthemum vulgare* (Ox-eye Daisy). The daisy which takes to the long grass (opposite).
- *Tanacetum parthenium* (Feverfew). Its pale yellow seedlings are good for brightening up a bed in the early part of the year but when the daisy-like flowers emerge it soon loses style and appeal (top left).
- *Erigeron annuus* (Fleabane). An attractive character within paving but its spreading needs to be watched (top right).
- *Galinsoga parviflora* (Galloping Soldier). An insignificant annual with tiny daisy-like flowers which was brought from Peru to Kew Gardens in the early nineteenth century and which was almost immediately galloping away down the street and all over London (above left).
- *Anthemis* spp. (Mayweeds). This mayweed is a standard late summer weed but other anthemis species and cultivars can be the most worthy of garden plants (above right).

Asterales

96

Helianthus annuus

ASTERACEAE
Sunflower

Sunflower a weed? 'Never!' I hear you shout. What a diabolical thought to slip in right now, just as we are reaching the end of this saga! But let's see where sunflowers come from: the present-day corn-belt region, out west in the USA, no less.

'In many of our western states one drives for hour after hour between long lines of wild sunflowers which, all untended, border the highways.' This is Edgar Anderson in the introduction to his seminal book, *Plants, Man and Life*, in 1952. Later he elaborates on the weedy presence of the sunflowers which are also to be found all around the towns, in railroad yards and hanging about any kind of wasteland. Whether or not sunflowers are quite so ubiquitous in that part of the world 60 years later, their position there as the old-time local commoners is still most revealing.

Bizarre as it seems to us at first, sunflowers do not produce good seed crops in their homeland, despite many attempts at their cultivation; nothing, that is, compared with their excellent productivity in Europe. Anderson suggests that the sunflowers in their original home are handicapped in cultivation by their endemic pests and diseases, whereas maize does really well, and much better away from its constraining origins in Mexico. What an exchange!

So, three cheers for allowing former weeds a second chance elsewhere. How heartening, too, to know that aliens don't always wreak ecological havoc. The 'sunflower' family (the 'daisy' family's other common name) can hold its head up high in respect of this most distinguished lead member.

RIGHT Sunflower as seen in Britain by Gerard in 1597.
OPPOSITE Yarrow foliage with its thousands of tiny leaves as good as winning the battle with some lawn grass.

Asterales

97

Achillea millefolium

ASTERACEAE

Yarrow

And then we have yarrow, the weed of a thousand leaves – '*mille folium*'. There they are, subdivided pinnately twice over to give them their characteristic moss-like appearance and all in a bid to take over the author's lawn.

The lawn, perhaps, is where the plant most commonly sneaks into a garden, aided maybe by not being that unattractive and providing a serviceable alternative green mat. Note the clover appearing also, and generating some welcome nitrogen. Grass, clover and yarrow all successfully adapt to the mower. The yarrow, unable to send up flowering shoots, puts all its energy into foliage production which, with the assistance of both rhizomes and stolons, is able to spread out steadily and barely noticed.

Elsewhere, on verges especially, yarrow is on the march with its seeding flowers. On casual first appearance and without looking closely, the inflorescences look just like those of the umbellifera family, white flat-topped umbels yet again. They are quite like wild carrots, though somewhat less refined. Well, don't be deceived. They are, of course, bunches of tiny all-white daisies assembled in umbel forms. Count all the compressed florets (the five outer

Asterales

petal-like ray ones surrounding the twenty or so tubular ones of the inner disc) of each tiny flower. There can be a few dozen at the head of each major stalk and there will be thousands of these all potentially producing their own seeds. There are an average of 6,000 per plant with 210 to 1,660 per stem say the dedicated counters.

Supporting those distinctive flower assemblages are equally distinctive stalks – furrowed, slightly woolly, often purplish and capable of rising well over half a metre – and very characteristic moss-like foliage which tends to hug around the base and proliferate out sideways, especially on lawns where it is given little other choice. Then the whole lot is supremely well anchored by a fibrous root system often reaching down a good twenty centimetres.

A tough cookie indeed. It appears to be able to hang on in almost everywhere (though especially in drier more alkaline grassland) and notably comes to more attention at the end of the season by outlasting many of its rivals. No surprise then that yarrow is an insistent garden visitor, taunting us too for being quite nice in moderation and even capable of being a comfortable foil to many garden plants.

Finally, we should mention that yarrow also displays exceptional plasticity. It has the capacity we have now seen many times in weeds to take on a lot of variation in shades of colour, form and size. And hardly surprising to find that it has a tendency to be resistant to herbicides. All this backed up by multiple chromosomes – strains of 36, 54 and 72 being recorded (Salisbury). No wonder it is such a temptress!

WHAT TO DO

- First accept it as a wake-up call to investigate and introduce some of the lovely garden varieties (not forgetting the old-time 'Golden Plate').
- Then apply your own subtle selection process, possibly to retain or remove to where it best suits your garden.
- Or damn it! Start again with something you really want.

RIGHT Yarrow flower revealing itself as a composite of composites and thereby one of the most enduring members of this amazing family and one which as often as not outlasts all the others to the very end of autumn.

WEEDS, WEEDING (& DARWIN)

Asterales

WEEDS, WEEDING (& DARWIN)

98

Taraxacum officinale
ASTERACEAE
Dandelion

The dandelion is simply extraordinary. So weed-like is this plant both in and out of gardens that it is all too easy to overlook its utter uniqueness. Rest your eyes on this common flower for a few moments and you will have to be an extremely hardened soul not to admit that here, just for a start, is a stunning beauty.

Remember the breathtaking charm of the 'primitive' five-petalled buttercup (Weed 15)? Now, it seems, a hundred million years or so after the emergence of the buttercup family, evolution arrives at a composition where, in effect, about two hundred buttercup-like flowers are compressed onto a single head. There it is, utterly alluring and especially to miniscule creatures, not to say to young children when the flower gives way to its filigree clock of blow-away seeds. The whole plant is, in fact, a streamlined operator like no other, perching as it does at one of the pinnacles of plant evolution. Hardly surprising, then, that it happens to be a runaway weed as well.

And dandelions torment us like no other garden troublemakers. Once they have parachuted in their seeds, plantlets are soon popping up everywhere. Mercifully most of them can be removed just as easily as they appear, except, that is, from all those awkward spots like between paving stones or among shrub roots, not to say in lawns. There they can entrench themselves for year after year. If ever a weed has the intelligence to size us up and outwit us where it really annoys – while exploiting to the full both annual and perennial capabilities – the dandelion has to be close to it. Or so it seems.

But, believe it or not, dandelions have their dedicated fans.

LEFT A dandelion plant with an enlarged single floret to its left as pictured in Stephenson's *Medical Botany*, 1834. The plant is renowned historically for its exceptional herbal properties. In this fine print the root has been unnaturally bent and shortened to fit the page.

Asterales

Welcome, then, to the world of taraxacology – the study of dandelions as pursued by an international coterie of dandelion geeks who are obsessed, as they readily admit, with the workings of this plant and identifying its seemingly infinite different manifestations. We are very fortunate that two such taraxacologists, Messrs AA Dudman and AJ Richards, have provided us with an excellent handbook to the dandelions of Great Britain and Ireland.

On the page opposite we see their diagrammatic breakdown of the plant with all its intricate details and scope for variation. As you see, there are so many aspects to be taken into account, but notice especially those toothed floret 'ligules', themselves capable of coming in so many different shades, shapes and sizes. Their five triangular teeth indicate the reduction of five petals into this one thin 'floret' form. The production of seeds, their dispersal distances and germination rates are in such record numbers that we begin to lose count by now. But what is totally disconcerting to note is that almost all their seeds are produced by 'apomixis', that is without any sexual pollination or even any 'pseudogamy' as we saw with brambles. Here is pure cloning – taking place on a phenomenal scale and at a phenomenal rate, and ensuring that the large number of variations are fixed in their particular modes.

To our left we get an idea of an extraordinary tap root below the rosette of those signature 'dents-de-lion' leaves, pictured here at about a third of its actual size. Such roots amass a formidable food store, as well as securing ultra-secure anchorage. Their defence is relative brittleness; fragments are easily left behind to regenerate if attempts are made to remove them. Essentially, it is these extended tap roots which give dandelions their perennial status – with a possible ten-year lifespan or more.

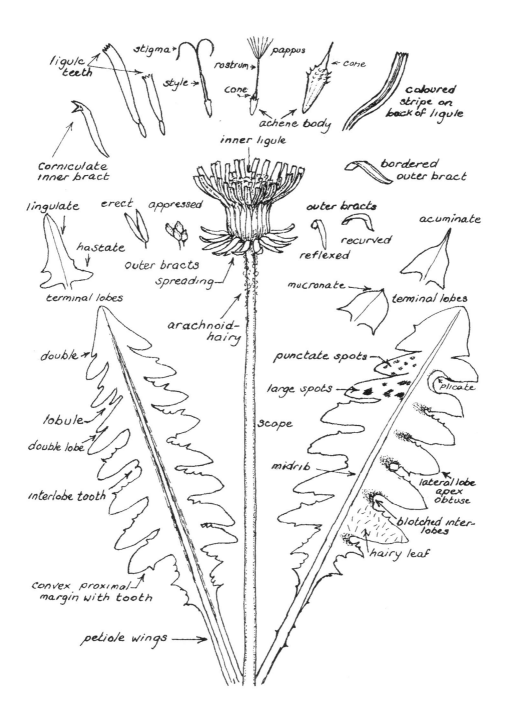

ligule
teeth

stigma

style

rostrum

pappus

cone

cone

achene body

coloured
stripe on
back of ligule

inner ligule

Corniculate
inner bract

bordered
outer bract

lingulate

erect   appressed

hastate

outer bracts

terminal lobes

outer bracts
spreading

arachnoid-
hairy

outer bracts

recurved

reflexed

mucronate

acuminate

terminal lobes

punctate spots

large spots

plicate

double

scape

lobule

double lobe

midrib

lateral lobe
apex
obtuse

interlobe tooth

blotched inter-
lobes

hairy leaf

convex proximal
margin with tooth

petiole wings

Asterales

Armed with such attention to detail, taraxacologists have identified close on 2,000 types of dandelion worldwide. In Britain and Ireland alone Dudman and Richards have noted 235 different 'species'. In their handbook they begin by teasing us with an illustration of two specimens which can hardly look more different.

Then they go on to tell us that these are actually two examples of one and the same 'species' – *Taraxacum eckmanii*. The one on the left is from a roadside verge in Northumberland and the one on the right from a damp meadow in Bohemia. Together they present a beautiful demonstration of 'phenotypic plasticity' which dandelions excel at – the capacity of single species to manifest themselves in contrasting forms. Yet such 'plasticity' is the mere beginning of how we account for a quite extraordinary range of persistent variations among dandelions.

As we have just suggested by mentioning 'species' in inverted commas, the question of determining so many different species amongst dandelions brings into question just what is meant by the term. In this case, at least, they may be referred to as 'micro-species' or 'aggregate species' under the umbrella of *Taraxacum officinale* agg., *Taraxacum officinale* being the first dandelion named by Linnaeus. Apomictic cloning ensures that the wide range of species remain in their separate identities which have virtually no chance of merging or diluting. Here are just four common species out of that huge crowd. Note that botanists look to record and identify separate species when the plants are in full bud, just before flowering.

WEEDS, WEEDING (& DARWIN)

ABOVE LEFT *Taraxacum alatum*
ABOVE RIGHT *Taraxacum undulatiflorum*
BELOW LEFT *Taraxacum faeroense*
BELOW RIGHT *Taraxacum laticordatum*

Asterales

WEEDS, WEEDING (& DARWIN)

Where, then, are these hundreds of different dandelions generally to be found? Apart from a select few which only thrive in specialist niches like sand dunes, cliff faces, high altitudes, marshland and so on, the vast majority, according to our taraxacologist friends, grow primarily on roadside verges – a key element of that entangled bank. In effect, it appears that these old-time 'flowers of the wayside' simply follow us on our travels. Draughts created by passing traffic ensure the continued dispersal of airborne seeds along highways and byways.

And then with a metaphorical overtone, we might ask where are all the dandelions heading? Sadly, their asexuality ensures that they are going nowhere. Only through mutations are they subject to change, so that 'logically', as Dudman and Richards admit, 'one might expect all lines would eventually acquire "bad" mutations' – that all asexual dandelions are 'doomed to extinction'.

The riposte might be 'but aren't we all so doomed eventually?' All of which leaves us to wonder which will see the other out – will it be ourselves or the dandelions? In the meantime, regardless of all their emphatic differences, for us everyday gardeners a dandelion remains a damned dandelion, one particular insolent garden weed which we all know too well. But for the relevance of Darwin's ideas this plant is highly provocative.

A species which finds itself in an apparent evolutionary dead-end and which has subdivided so arbitrarily throws the book back in Darwin's face, or rather at what we think we understand of his theory. Not surprisingly, a few modern evolutionist, who relish the challenge of unpicking and explaining apparent anomalies in Darwinian orthodoxy, home in on the dandelions with anguished determination, and consternation too.

LEFT The classic seedhead with hollowed pedicel (flower stem) extended for the take-off of seeds.
BELOW Dandelions at the base of a flint wall alongside a village lane – all set to travel.

Frogs, Flies and Dandelions is the catchy title of one such researcher's book. The Dutch author, Menno Schilthuizen, with the advantage of recent developments in genetics, came up with such statements that 'as soon as sex is abolished, the homogenised gene clusters shatter into myriads of better or worse 'frozen' gene combinations', though he added that 'without sex, biodiversity would not be partitioned into species, and the world would look entirely different'. 'A fuzzy sort of evolution', one of Schilthuizen's colleagues called this, but it is evolution nonetheless and one where natural selection continues to play its ruthless cards.

Darwin once mocked himself and made out he was so poor at naming wild flowers that he was 'unable to tell a daisy from a dandelion'. With hindsight we might say that perhaps it was just as well that he never got round to scrutinising this most extraordinary of all plants. He had more than enough on his plate without delving into the intricacies of this one.

WHAT TO DO

- First and foremost: step back and wonder at this little crowning glory of plant evolution; take your hat off to the taraxacologists and enjoy the late spring golden carpeting of roadside verges, for no doubt the dandelion is a beautiful composition.
- Harvest and make use of these nutritious, vitamin rich, health enhancing leaves and roots, though beware of their supposed '*pisse-en-lit*' diuretic effects.
- Lift out of open ground, gently prising with a fork, to make sure all the root comes out.
- Use a long narrow trowel if hand weeding.
- Mow lawns regularly with a low cut.
- Strim repeatedly over paving.
- Use a glyphosate herbicide for those other inaccessible locations.

Asterales

RIGHT Mouse-ear hawkweed, last but not least of our one hundred weeds to be pictorially identified and one which has far, far more to it than its name might suggest.

99

Hieraclium pilosella et al.

ASTERACEAE

Hawkweeds and other dandelion-like weeds

Legend has it that hawks hover over many of these dandelion lookalikes and that a bite of their flower heads does wonders for their formidable eyesight. Hence we have hawkweeds, hawk's beards, hawkbits and hawk goodness-knows-whats galore – and maybe these birds are scattering the seeds far and wide. Cats and mice also sneak in – nominally, at least. These plants, along with dandelions, all belong to the lettuce tribe (cichorieae).

- *Hieraclium pilosella* (Mouse-ear Hawkweed)
  You have reason to feel doubly humiliated on finding this one in your garden as it is described as 'a weed of degraded pastures, poor lawns and other sparse vegetation'. And, yes, this hawkweed is an all-too-common intruder and will degrade your lawn even further by secreting allelopathic toxins around its creeping plants. Even more alarming, this species is renowned for its own extensive variability – and hence adaptability – and the genus claims over 11,000 species worldwide. So hawkweeds are substantially more of a nightmare than even dandelions for botanists to figure out.

Asterales

- *Crepis capillaris* (Smooth Hawk's Beard)
  The leaf shape and rosette form are very dandelion-like on not-too-close observation. From each rosette rises a spray of dandelion-like flowers from branching unhollowed stems. Down below is a fleshy taproot which has to be eased out carefully. It only manages an annual life (though with a five-year seed life) but it has a distinctly tougher outward appearance than the dandelion.

- *Hypocheris radiata* (Cat's Ear)
  Yes, it does look as if there is a bit of an ears-to-the-ground cat-and-mouse chase with this range of plants. Cat's ear has a rosette of dandelion-shaped leaves which tend to curl up the tips, plausibly like the ears of an alert feline. Sometimes also referred to as long-rooted cat's ear, it makes itself a weed nuisance on drought-stricken lawns by tapping down into the deeper moisture while the shallower-rooted grass struggles.

- *Leontodon autumnalis* (Autumn Hawkbit)
  A late season opportunist, perhaps more watched over by conservationists than weeded by gardeners, and distinguished by its even more toothy ('*odon*') leaves. These, yet again, are in dandelion-rosette form and so not the best friends of lawns.

- *Lactuca virosa* and *Lactuca serriola* (Wild Lettuces)
  The wild lettuces, as one might expect, are a little more leafy and not so tied down by a ground-hugging rosette form, though they certainly don't heart up. Edward Salisbury notes that they made an invasive dash for it in Britain during the 1930s building of the arterial road system. Hitherto they tended to have been the specialist flora of areas like gravel pits, but then, literally, they took to the roads and roadsides (and hopped over garden hedges) and have never looked back, so to speak.
  More recently, their evolutionarily tried-and-tested resilience has been used by lettuce plant breeders who 'back cross' to improve the disease resistance of vulnerable modern hybrids. Weeds of the wild can sometimes offer key resources. Our own precarious livelihoods can depend on them.

WHAT TO DO
- Realise that by now we have had more than enough of meeting different kinds of weeds and that hawkweeds in their thousands are likely to elude us more than the rest of them. At the same time, take heart that by and large they are not forceful garden invaders. Indeed, a few of them make most desirable garden plants.

100

Siegesbeckia orientalis et cetera

ASTERACEAE
Weeds Anon

Never heard of these members of the compositae? That's totally excusable unless you are an historian of the eighteenth-century botanical world. *Siegesbeckia* is an insignificant wasteland weed, named by Carl Linneaus (flagrantly flouting the principles and propriety by which he set up his system) after a 'sticky' colleague whom he despised.

So that's it. We are left with just 'weeds', those remaining nonentities which will always reappear in our gardens, plants which might as well stay nameless as far as we everyday-gardeners are concerned. That's how it was for Darwin. He was not that hot on the names of common plants of the wild, as he readily admitted. In chapter four we will see how he set up a 'weed garden'. The identity of the particular plants which grew there was of no concern to him. They were just weeds.

Sorry! The '100 weeds' turn out to be a good many more, named and nameless. That's their way.

WHAT TO DO

- Allow yourself to curse dubious friends by naming your least favourite garden weeds after them.

3
Twenty ways to weed

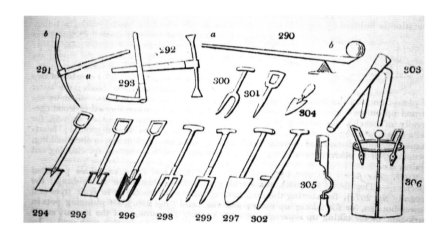

'Nothing is so interesting as weeding.' This is what Robert Louis Stevenson claimed in his later life, prefacing his remark with, 'I would rather do a good hour's weeding than write two pages of my best'. Stevenson was a near contemporary of Darwin (being forty years his junior but only living a further twelve years after his death) and like Darwin eagerly sought pleasurable relief from concentrated deskwork by getting out of the house as much as he could. Stevenson evidently found immense satisfaction from turning to a bit of weeding whereas Darwin would escape for a brisk stroll around the sandwalk, a circuit he had created just beyond his kitchen garden. Weeding was not for Darwin. He left that for his gardeners and we can assume that they were equipped with a fair number of the tools illustrated above. These are what were recommended in JC Loudon's *Encyclopaedia of Gardening*, the contemporary, much esteemed handbook treasured by the Darwin household.

ABOVE The principal tools of the trade available to Darwin's gardeners when they first came to work for him at Down House.
RIGHT Finding satisfaction hoeing between rows of young leeks.

Basic weeding remains the same to this day but the options open to us have much expanded since Darwin and Stevenson's day due to newer technologies and methodologies, extended scientific research and continual practical experiment. Weeding, therefore, is potentially more interesting than it has ever been, while at the same time it still brings us humbly down to earth. Even in its repetitive routines it can be both soothing and rewarding with its effects almost instantly enhancing a corner of the garden. So, in setting out to systematise the many wide-ranging What To Do strategies proposed in the previous chapter, here are twenty different approaches to this all-time horticultural challenge. You will see that, *yes*, each can be effective, *but* only up to a certain point where nature inevitably fights back with an incredible range of resourceful adaptive strategies.

The twenty approaches

1   Hoe
2   Dig in
3   Dig out
4   No dig
5   Prise out
6   Hand weed
7   Cover up
8   Select
9   Transplant
10 Leave be
11 Prune
12 Mow
13 Strim
14 Rotavate
15 Grub out
16 Burn
17 Infest
18 Poison
19 Manage
20 Know ourselves

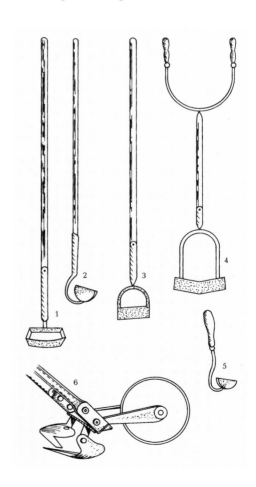

RIGHT Hoes come in many forms. The key ones for everyday use are the draw hoe (2) and the Dutch hoe (3).

1 HOE

Using a hoe and doing so repetitively (and in good humour) has to be our first step with weeding. Hoes are the chief tools designed specifically for weeding. They come in all shapes and sizes but essentially in two basic forms: 'Dutch hoes' which are pushed or 'draw hoes' which are pulled – and both are much more effective if their blades are kept relatively sharp, something which is so easy to overlook.

'Hoe, or weed immediately', hectored William Cobbett in 1829, 'and let me observe here, once and for all, that weeds never ought to be suffered to get to any size either in field or in garden, and especially in the latter.' This single sentence is the sole reference to weeds in Cobbett's 330-page book of instructions to gardeners, *The English Gardener*. This cursory admonishment is typical of the limited consideration given to weeds in almost every gardening manual ever since, where, as often as not, such plants are mentioned (if they are mentioned at all) in a dismissive way, almost as an unfortunate and slightly embarrassing afterthought regarding something that should never be there in the first place. Any reference to weeds will invariably come at the end of such books which often order their subjects alphabetically, and one suspects that authors are running out of steam by then.

All the same, Cobbett was dead right – well, up to a substantial point. Hoeing is a vital first step, and in many respects it has to be the beginning and end of it all, as we now see in a summary of five aspects of how best to go about it.

- Hoe to 'catch 'em young' – the way to knock out seedlings, especially those prolific annuals, before they have time to root too securely. Note that such hoeing works best in sunshine as the disturbed seedlings will rapidly solarise into disappearance, whereas damp conditions will give them a chance to re-root.

- Hoe just to cut off all top growth but leave roots. Done consistently this weakens roots and whole plants by preventing them from developing the ability to photosynthesise (draw energy sustenance from light) – the vital key to all plant life.

- Hoe before flowering – to prevent plants producing seeds and proliferating in that way. 'One year's seeding leads to seven years weeding', such is the durability of so many weed seeds.

- Hoe bare ground – to stop seedlings even appearing in the first place.

- Hoe the soil surface to create a valued tilth – in effect a dry dusty mulch which creates a better barrier against evaporation from below than does a crust (pan) brought on by heavy rain or watering. Moisture is conserved for the wanted plants. Also the looser tilth allows the next shower of rain to penetrate the soil and not rest in a puddle on the hardened surface ready to evaporate again in a drying wind or the next sunshine. Many old-hand gardeners swear by hoeing as a more worthwhile exercise than watering in a dry spell. All this particularly applies to kitchen gardens with plants grown in rows, which therefore need to be spaced a good hoe's width apart. Of course, it is also a good idea to keep a hoe's width clear where flower borders edge onto lawns.

But ...

Oh dear, there are quite as many cautions about hoeing as there are reasons for being stuck into it.

- A few weeds will still slip in, especially in tight proximity to the wanted plants.

- The seed bank within the soil is almost inexhaustible (see 'Dig in' opposite).

- Hoeing is indiscriminate. It risks knocking out slow-emerging wanted plants, and also reduces the option of taking advantage of desirable surprise visitors.

- Hoeing will only sever tap roots, which will usually then regenerate with extra vigour.

- Hoeing will often fail to reach and contain vegetatively spreading perennial weeds like ground elder and nettle.

- Inevitably, at some point you will lose your hoeing guard (a week or two away, maybe) and before you know where you are, the so-and-sos are back in embedded force.

- Not forgetting that each hoeing prepares a vacant space ready for the next batch of weeds to move in.

OPPOSITE Turning the soil over with a spade can bury the weeds in an instant, and to great satisfaction.

2 DIG IN

Traditional digging with a spade is a standard way of preparing a new bed and, in the process, burying all the surface weeds. It is made much easier by keeping a narrow trench into which to turn the next spadeful. To be really thorough, double-digging with a trench two spits deep can be done with quantities of manure being thrown in. These are practices especially associated with maintaining a vegetable plot. They can be immensely satisfying with a steady rhythmic activity steadily turning an untidy mess into a clean clear space, without, if done correctly, any undue back strain.

The question always arises as to when is the best time to do this. In heavy clay soils, for example, there can be short critical times in spring and autumn when the ground is midway between being rock hard and an impossible sticky substance. For a long time it was always thought best to make sure that the ground was turned over in the autumn, to expose the bugs and allow the clods to be weathered down by winter frosts. Many of us would see this as a satisfying late autumn activity for concluding the gardening year. But a succession of milder but wetter winters makes us think again. There is a strong case in such conditions to leave a weed cover on the ground over winter rather than let heavy rains batter the surface soil structure and leach out nutrients. Then the ground need only be thoroughly dug once in the early spring. As always, the choice may be more dependent on time, inclination or pressures of personal circumstance rather than on best cultivation practice.

But ...
- For sure, some of the buried material will eventually resurface with fresh shoots rising from the old roots.

- Regular turning-over of the soil helps to maintain a rich reserve of seeds at all levels – many experiments have been done to demonstrate the extent of a natural seed bank in soil. Darwin's observation in this regard is still quoted as one of the first to be recorded. In chapter thirteen of the *Origin* he suggests how birds might be responsible for the distribution of seeds.

> I do not believe that botanists are aware how charged the mud of ponds is with seeds; I have tried several little experiments, but will give only the most striking case: I took in February three table-spoonfuls of mud from three different points beneath water, on the edge of a little pond; this mud when dried weighed only 6¾ounces; I kept it in covered up in my study for six months, pulling up and counting each plant as it grew; the plants were of many kinds, and were altogether 537 in number; and yet the viscid mud was all contained in a breakfast cup! Considering these facts, I think it would be an inexplicable circumstance if water-birds did not transport the seeds of fresh-water plants to unstocked ponds and streams, situated at very distant points.

It is now known that a significant proportion of seeds, and especially weed seeds, have a potential dormancy of up to five or six years and will indeed benefit from a period of deeper burial followed by an abrupt raising to surface level. Annual digging serves them very well. So do we, by distributing them on our muddy boots – try cleaning them over a tray of sterile compost and see what new undergrowth emerges.

• The open surface of freshly dug soil is ideal for germinating any passing seeds, whether brought in unwittingly by us, by other creatures or just on the breeze.

3 DIG OUT

A garden fork is an ideal tool for extracting weeds, roots and all. The appropriate size of fork will depend on the space around the weed and the depth of the weed roots. Sometimes certain weeds are best eased out by using a fork to loosen the ground to allow the villains to be pulled out intact without undue disturbance of the ground and of their more valid neighbours.

But ...
The root systems of many weeds spread out, to penetrate other root systems, lodge under paving, extend beyond fork depth and easily break. They are therefore not removed easily without creating far greater ground and garden plant disturbance.

4 NO DIG

The 'perma-culture' and 'organic' approach to gardening which advocates no digging has a sound logic in regard to weed control as well. The less the ground is worked the less opportunities there are for weeds to move in and for the build-up of a seed bank.

But ...
Weeds are organic too and particularly thrive in naturally fertilised soil. They are needed as an important ingredient of garden compost, though there is always a dilemma as to when it is best to harvest them – early, when they are too small to be of any significance, or later, when they are bulky but laden with seed or with stronger roots.

5 PRISE OUT

There are now implements which will do just this. It takes the ingenuity of a direct Darwin descendant, great great grandson Philip Trevelyan, to devise and produce 'Lazy Dog' tools. These have a prong which is inserted under a plant and then the culprit is levered out of the ground root and all. Such a tool is particularly suitable for those brutes like dock, thistle and ragwort which frequent grazing fields – and gardens given half the chance.

But ...
The weeds need to be relatively mature to be gripped by the prong, and then there is a race to prise them out before they set seed.

6 HAND WEED

Here we come down to earth with a trowel or hand fork for real hands-on weeding, the most thorough and most satisfying of all weeding methods. This is time consuming but, for most of us who engage in it, this is time well consumed. We get down to the level of weeds, eye them up carefully and remove them with ease and ambidextrous precision. We saw at the beginning of the chapter how an author like Robert Louis Stevenson appreciated this activity, but not many gardening writers bother to discuss it. The late Christopher Lloyd was an eloquent exception, as he was about so many aspects of gardening practice:

The Pleasures of Hand-Weeding
Many gardeners will agree that hand-weeding is not the terrible drudgery that it is often made out to be. Some people find in it a kind of soothing monotony. It

leaves their minds free to develop the plot for their next novel or to perfect the brilliant repartee with which they should have countered a relative's latest example of unreasonableness.

Efficient hand-weeding requires that you should get down to the task on your knees: as comfortably as possible, with a soft rubber mat and a good sharp-pointed, sharp-edged, stainless-steel trowel.

You will observe that professional gardeners do all hand-weeding from a standing stooping position. They pull the weeds out (or break them off) by the hair and do not use a trowel. Their standards of weeding are mediocre, but they remain men, standing proudly, if not erect, at least on their two feet, whereas you and I become animals, even reptiles....

Weeding on your hands and knees means that your eyes are close to the ground – the scene of operations. They should always travel just ahead of the trowel point so that the unusual can be observed before it is destroyed. I never like to weed out anything that I can't identify. Not all seedlings are weeds. You may feel that life is too short to leave a seedling in till it's large enough to identify. My own feeling is that life's too interesting not to leave it there until you can identify it. Taking this view, you will very soon learn to recognise weed seedlings when they are no larger than a pair of seed leaves. The not so easily identified ones will then most probably turn out to be the progeny of some of your border plants or shrubs, and it may suit you to save and grow them on.

The practicalities of hand-weeding are open to a few more options than when Lloyd wrote this in his classic *The Well-Tempered Garden* over forty years ago. Knee pads and other forms of kneeling mat now abound. Also, we have more comfortable and flexible gloves, if we need to protect our hands from allergies or whatever, though there is something elementally magical about real hands-on weeding, even with the occasional prick and sting and resultant hardened, soil-ingrained hands.

Professional gardeners may still prefer to stoop rather than kneel, partly because they are likely to be in more of a hurry and also because they have a longer term concern for their knees (and for their trousers). Professional or amateur, no gardener can walk across a garden without also doing a bit of 'snatch and grab' of the odd weed which seems to have suddenly appeared. Hands, bare or gloved, available at any moment, are the best of all garden tools.

7 COVER UP

Now, having dealt with the main physical ways of removing weeds, let us pause to consider a preventative measure, especially as we keep giving warnings about opening up soil for the wretches to move into. Keeping the ground covered with anything is always better than nothing, as regards giving weeds the least opportunities. The choice of mulches or coverings is manifold:

Matting

Simply put down some matting. Either smart, purpose-made porous plastic-like material, or a piece of old carpeting (if it is genuinely porous).

Gravel

Fine gravel, usually referred to as grit, is the favoured natural solution for alpine beds. Beach pebbles, traditionally used for driveways, can also be extended elsewhere as the appropriate backdrop for front gardens around seaside areas.

Grass

What is a lawn but an excellent ground-cover? Grass cuttings also provide a useful temporary weed-suppressant covering under roses, or around potatoes, for example.

Other ground-covering plants

Ivy, periwinkle, stonecrop, *Ajuga reptans*, *Acaena*: we all have our standbys but they don't necessarily stay where we want them.

Dense planting

Keep your flower beds closely packed with garden plants and there will be less room for weeds to take over. Even so, ground elder and bindweed will still often make a bid for it in early summer. It can be worthwhile having a last tug at the top growth of such obnoxious brats at this critical competitive stage so as to give an illusion that they have gone away. This gives only a temporary break, as we well know, but that, unfortunately, is the case with virtually all weeding.

Newspaper

Andy Strachan, the head gardener at Garden Organic, swears by newspaper as one of the most effective mulching materials. Of course it should itself be covered by another material like sterile council-processed green waste, or gravel. Newspaper is particularly good at dealing with nettles. Lay down several layers and cover with leaf mould or anything more sightly. By the time it has done its job, it is beginning to decompose naturally.

Organic matter
Whether leaf mould, garden compost or rotted dung, organic matter can be usefully applied to the soil in winter not only to suppress the weeds below but also to be drawn into the topsoil by worms. Of course, much of it is likely to be seed rich, however careful you have been with what you put in your compost heap.

Paving
Excellent with bricks or slabs, but the weeds will always find the cracks from which they are most defiantly difficult to extract.

Decking
Another once-popular way of covering the ground, with significant gaps this time.

But ...
This last example gives the game away. Whatever covering is used, weeds will always slip through eventually. Covering up is as temporary as any weed control.

8 SELECT
Let us pause again from vigorous weeding or suppressing to think just what we are weeding. Not every plant which just appears unexpectedly is necessarily unwanted. Christopher Lloyd recounts that weeding in his own garden is like discovering a host of treasures – of course his garden in particular would be a treasure trove of delightful seedlings of all kinds. The unexpected beauty is what gives any garden that extra zip. Wise weeding has to have an element of selection – unnaturally taking out the majority of the seedlings to leave just a few to steal the show.

Then, let us step back again. Perhaps we should be giving more thought to selecting just what kind of garden we really want, especially with regard to its relationship with the plants outside. Looking into the nature of 'our own back gardens' is something we will come to in the last chapter with a brief round-up of alternative approaches.

9 TRANSPLANT

A plant is in the wrong place? Surely there is an obligation to consider moving it into a more acceptable place, if that is possible in one's garden? Into a wild flower corner?

10 LEAVE BE

What! Isn't that just throwing in the towel as a gardener? Not necessarily, as it could be a question of immediate practicality to leave one area untended while more urgent matters are undertaken. Prioritisation of tasks is essential in any garden. Besides, a little wild area can serve quite well to set off the rest. We can even claim it is just an experiment. Controlled conscious neglect can have its place, in moderation.

11 PRUNE

Pruning is not weeding, as we normally know it; that is obvious. However, garden plants have a tendency to outgrow the spaces which were allotted to them originally. Crowding of maturer specimens often means that a choice has to be made as to which should be weeded out to give the remainder enough space. Even whole trees and shrubs have to be weeded out at times. In the meantime, pruning helps to keep many a substantial plant within reasonable bounds, that is, keeping it out of the areas where it is not wanted.

But ...

As we all know, pruning usually stimulates new vigorous growth. That is the whole point of pruning roses hard every year. Pruning to contain plant size creates its own dilemma, one requiring ever more pruning. Better to be thoughtful about checking expected plant sizes before planting, and allowing more space between plants so that they do not force each other upwards in an etiolated condition while searching for light. Not at all easy when we love to pack our gardens with as much as we can.

12 MOW

To have a machine for cutting grass – for pruning it in fact – has to be one of the greatest steps forward for gardening that there has ever been. In Britain, it is hard to conceive how we might ever have managed without such a machine, or rather how there can ever be a garden without a mown lawn – although the advocates of the decking craze tried hard.

Mowing grass achieves far more than could have been anticipated when it was first being tried out. Lawn grasses – and lawns work best with a small mix of appropriate species – are ones that have evolved as a result of constant grazing over the last twenty million years or so. Today's naturally selected survivors have their growing points out of nibbling-reach at the very base of their leaves. Mowing, or grazing, stimulates the leaves to keep on growing from their lower end, in their natural but forever-thwarted bid to make flowers and seeds. Well that is no great advance in regard to weeding, you might say.

Aha, but mowing has the side benefit of weeding out other would-be intrusive plants – well, up to a point. As we all know only too well, there is a whole host of regular non-grass lawn invaders which manage to keep enough of their foliage sufficiently prostrate to be out of reach of the mower's blades. We have met them a good few times in the weeds list.

Then Darwin also discovered – indirectly from a little experiment which he carried out on his lawn – that mowing had other advantages. He marked off a patch of lawn 3 foot by 4 foot where he had no mowing done over two years. It became that predictable little wilderness – though what Darwin was interested to find was that the number of plant species in that area reduced substantially when left to their unmown competitive resources and the 'struggle for existence' took its toll. Darwin too had a canny new way of mowing introduced to his garden with a machine pulled by a donkey. We will meet this in the next chapter.

Mowing pays off all round it seems. Certainly, repeated mowing of any patch of relatively low-lying wilderness on relatively even terrain will lead to quite a reasonable turf – eliminating most of Dürer's weeds.

But ...

Mowing is an everlasting commitment, and perhaps even more so than straightforward weeding. Even so, a quick mow of the lawn, which machines now allow, and a trim of the lawn edges do wonders for an instant garden uplift. Leave the other weeding for another day – except in full season when we need the weeds to mix with the grass cuttings on the compost heap.

13 STRIM

The strimmer and its associate the brush-cutter are, in effect, long-armed mowing machines with a little more power and directional capacity. They are excellent for slicing off top growth, and making a lot of noise about it too. Once you have mown the lawn, the strimmer will take care of most of the odd corners where the mower could not quite complete the job. It comes in particularly handy for doing a temporary clean-up of weeds appearing in the cracks of paving and around the base of trees (but be very careful not to damage young bark) – that is, for creating an instant makeover effect.

But …

Be warned, only try this if there is no one else around, no vehicle about, your eyes and face are shielded and you are wearing trousers and solid footwear, as grit and pebbles go flying with the weed fragments. The strimmer cord also wears down fast in such circumstances. A strimmer is only an effective tool for the experienced gardener.

14 ROTAVATE

For many of us the idea of a machine to do all the hard digging in one fair swoop is attractive, especially when weeds instantly disappear as well. Repeated swoops at a week or two apart will help deal with the weeds more effectively in a kitchen garden.

But …

The 'buts' stack up. Fragments of perennial weeds will invariably try a comeback and the seed bank is nicely stirred up to get a new set of annuals on their way. Also the soil structure gets a destructive beating up. All said, the benefits of using a rotavator vary enormously according to particular circumstances and should not be dismissed outright.

15 GRUB OUT (with heavy machinery)

To bring a full-on digger into a garden is drastic. But for dealing with invasive alien shrubs – rhododendrons, gorse and suchlike – it has to be an option.

16 BURN

The idea of 'burn', for some of us at least, at first conjures up the image of dire 'slash and burn' operations destroying valued ancient forests – scorching the earth.

Hugely scaled down, 'flame weeders' can be the business in certain situations, such as along rows of vegetables at critical moments, and, of course, over gravelled areas. They use liquefied petroleum gas and therefore require considerable health and safety precautions, as well as a fair bit of setting up for their use in the first place. A local grower of organic vegetables finds a flame weeder mounted on the back of a tractor particularly useful in cleaning the ground around carrots (pre-emergence flaming) just a few days after they have been sown so that the up-and-coming veg seedlings can get a headstart over the opposition. With some vegetable species it is thought that flame weeding at the right moment will also aid germination. They do not disturb the soil and so do not stimulate a further flush of seedling emergence as hoeing will do. Flame weeders also have the advantage of being functional in all weather and soil conditions.

A basic flame weeder, with a fuel backpack and a flexible wand to direct the flame precisely where it is required, is available on the market for the everyday gardener. One more piece of kit for your armoury, if you wish. The *but* is the extra investment, the health and safety issues involved, and the evidence that certain weeds, like shepherd's purse and annual meadow grass, for instance, have flame tolerance.

17 INFEST (applying biological control)

Recall the prickly pear invasion of eastern Australia (Weed 31) in the previous chapter and *Cactoblastis* – the South American moth which was introduced to the cactus in order to nibble it back down to manageable proportions? This satisfactory solution is always the hope with biological control. It is much harder to organise on a garden scale, although we can fantasise all too readily about a slug genetically engineered to have an appetite for ground elder.

In the enclosed environment of a greenhouse, biological control is a little easier to organise, but then again, it is more effective when setting one bug onto another (as with dealing with aphids).

On a national and trans-national scale we can see that in longstanding native environments ecologies function with natural biological controls. *Fallopia japonica* is kept in rein in its Japanese homeland by local herbivores and other inhibitors. There are indications that European researchers are on the brink of finding a bug which could bring the Japanese knotweed under more control here. The challenge is full of risks that another invasive organism might be let loose and cause its own destructive damage. Wisely, the research is examining and trying to account for all such possibilities. Similar investigations are taking place for a biological control of purple loosestrife in North America. Increasingly, biological control is held as a way forward.

Another dimension to such an approach is being looked into in the United States for dealing with the massive explosion of pigweed. This weed's renowned capacity for both hybridisation and for resistance to herbicides has led researchers into trying to genetically modify a strong herbicide-susceptible variety and then let it loose to hybridise with the rest.

18 POISON (applying chemical control)

To poison weeds or not to poison them? Gardeners in Darwin's time started us on the slippery slope by using arsenic on the ground they wished to keep clear of weeds. Sad to say, it was twentieth-century warfare which set us on a path to dependence on weedkillers.

The case of 'The Lost Gardens of Heligan' in Cornwall is a telling one. The fourteen gardeners all went off to the Great War and not one of them returned. The garden vanished under a wilderness of ivy and bramble for the next eighty years. The national rural workforce, which up to that point had just about kept on top of the weeds, was decimated by the war. Dependence on the emerging chemicals industry became paramount.

Arable farming, in particular, found succour in the use of a varying range of chemical weed controls. Moving on from such non-selective compounds as dilute sulphuric acid and sodium chlorate with its attendant fire risks, the formulations became more refined and capable of selective use. In his 1961 book, *Weeds and Aliens*, Sir Edward Salisbury was riding on the crest of a wave which saw herbicides as the major breakthrough solution to the weeds problem. He even offered a specific prescription for dealing with each major weed. He listed twelve different compounds: BOV, DNOC, DNBP, MCPA, MCPB, MCPP, PCP, YCA, 2,4-D, 2,4-5-T, 2,4-DB and IPC, as they were known in their abbreviated forms.

Ten out of those twelve herbicides are now withdrawn from use by amateur gardeners for health and safety reasons, and most of them from all use whatsoever. The problem is not only that they have contaminating side effects, but also, as is to be expected from Darwinian selection, new resistant strains would be forever emerging. As if to cap it all, warfare in the second half of the twentieth century was to bring on the most shocking use of herbicide as a weapon of war itself – the use of 'agent orange' by the Americans in Vietnam. Seventy-five million litres sprayed over the rain forests in an attempt to flush out the Vietcong from their base caused health and environmental devastation that persists to this day.

There is a bitter irony that while the above lethal cocktail was being unleashed on hapless people abroad, at home in North America and Europe a new 'safe' herbicide was being developed using the active ingredient, glyphosate. It is used in many products and is best known to most of us by that household brand name 'Round-up', marketed as the safe 'systemic' herbicide which kills the plant without contaminating the soil or supposedly leaving any toxic residues. The organic movement, not surprisingly, has strong reservations even about this product, and the jury is still out about its longer term effects.

Most of us, as small-time amateur gardeners, feel left in the middle not sure what we should be doing in regard to the weedkiller options open to us. On the following page is a summary of the principal considerations that need to be weighed up.

Yes or No to using weedkillers

Yes! Certain weeds use poisons, so why shouldn't we use them too?
Buttercups and dandelions, for example, are both allelopathic, that is they secrete toxins to inhibit other plants from coming into their space. Giant hogweed, hemlock and the nightshades overtly display their strong if not lethal poisons.

No! Using any weedkiller flouts the principles of organic gardening.
Repeated use of chemicals, especially in one place, can lead to a build-up of toxicity with risks to food crops in miniscule but accumulating amounts.

Yes! Weedkillers using glyphosate, for example, are 'safe'.
Glyphosate is a substance permitted by government watchdogs and recommended by the RHS, for example. Once it has done its job of killing a targeted weed its toxic substances are said to become 'inactivated' and cause no soil contamination.

No! There are small health and safety risks from using glyphosate even so.
The Pesticide Incidents Appraisal Panel of the Health and Safety Executive record that glyphosate is the most frequent cause of complaints and poisoning incidents. Such reports, though, are extremely few.

Yes! Glyphosate can be spot on for those weeds in really awkward places.
It can be just the business for dealing with weeds whose roots become locked into those of a valued garden plant. Paint or dab the leaves of the culprit with this weedkiller in jelly form without touching the wanted plant. Tricky, but it works.

No! Too much of a fiddly bother for the busy gardener with a sizeable garden.
It takes considerable time, patience, planning, expense and calm dry weather conditions. Repeated cutting off of emergent shoots can help instead.

Yes! Weedkillers are good for keeping paths, patios and drives tidy.
Dealing with such circumstances, with the use of a sprayer in calm conditions involves the most straightforward application of a weedkiller.

No! Spraying a weedkiller has its own risks.
There are risks to other plants, animals, children and the user. Why not strim (13) instead? The weeds soon come back whatever, especially after a shower of rain.

Yes! Lawns benefit from applications of 'weed and feed' formulations.
This is especially so if you are aiming for a pure green sward.

No! This is choosing to eliminate buttercups, daisies and the like.
Also such applications depend upon being followed immediately by a good shower of rain or the lawn will become scorched.

Yes! Weedkillers can serve as a valuable last-resort standby.
They are useful when all else has failed, say with some nettles, brambles or persistent bindweed.

No! Even then, they may not be fully effective, especially in the longer term.
Such applications of weedkiller can be difficult and time-consuming to execute precisely. Also, glyphosate takes a few days to take effect. The first day or two the weeds may look even more thriving but then they go into a slow unsightly decline before withering away entirely.

Yes! Shouldn't we face the reality of how most of our food is produced?
Modern farming relies heavily on the use of herbicides. Isn't it humbug to pretend that we can all do without them just like that?

No! Shouldn't we also face the reality of natural selection at work?
Strains of herbicide-resistant weeds become selected out continuously to create ever more challenges to find new effective poisons. The herbicide battle with weeds can never be won once and for all. Rather, this battle merely generates ever more new battlefields – and ever more potent toxins around and about. Obviously there is a need for restraint in herbicide use to contain and reduce this vicious circle. Maybe in gardens we can do our little bit.

For all his promotion of weedkillers in 1961, Edward Salisbury still got the measure of their limited place. As he noted then: 'Herbicides should be regarded as a supplement to, not a substitute for, good husbandry – whether it be on the farm or in the garden.'

He could have added that using weedkillers correctly and effectively takes a lot of time, trouble and expense. It is rarely that once-and-for-all, oh-so-easy, quick fix which advertisers like to suggest. Ultimately 'good husbandry', with as much people-power as possible, has the extra edge.

19 MANAGE

The buck falls on us. As managing directors of our own gardens and allotments, we have overall responsibility for what is going on within our domains. Intimidated? This need not be so at all.

'Weed Management' is its own science and practice. There is even a complete guide called *Weed Management for Organic Farmers, Growers and Smallholders* (HDRA/Garden Organic, 2008). In essence, this is a reassuring volume which works on the assumption that as weeds are always with us it is best to work around them, diminishing their presence as much as possible around our crops (thinking of our own kitchen gardens in particular), while appreciating that they are not all bad and that together they are part and parcel of a larger ecology which we need to be sustaining.

Weed management, according to this guide, involves taking care of questions like:

Is weed control always needed?

How significantly do weeds affect crop yield? What is the long term effect of particular weed infestation? What may be their beneficial side effects? What is the likely balance between costs and benefits?

If control is needed, which method of control?

Cultural and preventative measures? Direct physical control? Biological control? Chemical control? The latter being totally out of the question for organic growers.

Where is control needed?

Spot targeted or a sweep through a whole bed? Inter-row or/and intra-row weeding? Will a patch-weeding approach suffice?

When is control needed?

The optimum moments to weed? The 'critical periods' of competition? The number of weeding operations needed?

No way, we realise, can management ever entertain a lazy, laissez-faire attitude.

20 KNOW OURSELVES

Managing, when it comes down to it, is a matter of coping as best we can. A modest aspiration, we might say, but a fine one. To cope well is to know our own physical strengths and weaknesses, to know our time limits, to be able to prioritise tasks, to operate within our own restricted material and financial resources, to know our own foibles, to know our families and friends well enough to have their full support, and, most especially, to know and understand our weed enemies. With such knowledge, the best possible weeding outcome undoubtedly will be achieved, and maybe, just maybe, 'a hundred battles won without a single loss'. Sun Tzu's maxim stands to this day.

BELOW To know yourself as a gardener is also to know when you can ease off from weeding. Once your vegetable crops have matured in the autumn, a few weeds can do them no harm. Then is the time to take a well-earned good month's rest from the treadmill.

4
Darwin in the garden

Darwin knew himself well, and certainly well enough to know that he was unlikely ever to stoop to do any gardening. He was only too aware, for a start, that he was unfit and prone to recurrent sickness which in any case prevented him from stooping to any significant extent. As was implied at the beginning of the last chapter, Darwin was from a social class which was likely to have fine gardens without having to tend them, so the idea of somebody from his family taking up gardening would never have arisen. More importantly, he knew he could not afford to be distracted at all from his scientific mission as a naturalist. All the same, he was never disdainful of what went on in a garden. On the contrary.

'When at Mr Case's school', as a nine-year-old, 'I was very fond of gardening', he later let on, while adding, 'I invented some great falsehoods about being able to colour crocuses as I liked'. 'I do not remember any mental pursuits except those of collecting stones and gardening', he also claimed. He might have mentioned what he got up to in his own back garden at his home in Shrewsbury. His childhood drawing (above) shows him in a tree house, with ropes and pulleys for sending messages. Gardens for him as a boy were places

RIGHT Charles, aged about seven, clutching a plant in a portrait with his sister, Catherine.

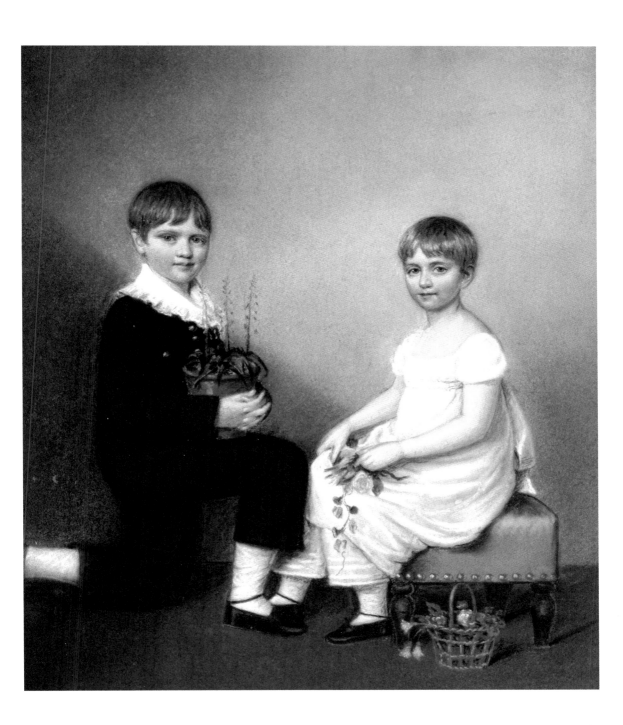

for fun, for taking risks, for trying out crazy ideas, and, of course, for a bit of mischief. The truth is that he never really grew out of his youthful habit of taking advantage of gardens in every possible way.

As soon as he arrived with his young family at Down House, Darwin was immediately out there, exploring the new garden and its surrounds. Within days he was noting those unusual double-flowered buttercups and planning bits of re-landscaping. Soon he was to have a new greenhouse, a place where he liked to potter and set up little experiments. Just outside this greenhouse, he took over a small section of the large kitchen garden to carry out his observations of primroses, cowslips, loosestrife, foxgloves and so on, with much use of netting to regulate insect activity. That was just enough for his gardeners to tolerate. His wife Emma, on the other hand, took more interest in the flower borders and played a guiding role with the planting there.

The lawn was a place for his children to play games, romp and roll around. On one occasion Darwin had his children lying on the grass spaced out at intervals in a line so that they could signal to their dad when and if particular bees flew past them. The grass was

ABOVE Henry Lettington and William Brooks, Darwin's gardeners, mow the lawn with a donkey.
RIGHT Darwin's greenhouse in Down House garden is still in use today.

no perfect weed-free sward, though, as we saw, his gardeners were proud of their mowing efforts. Family picnics and garden parties for villagers were all part of the constant use of the lawn in summer. For more tranquil summertime relaxation, Darwin tended to go a little further from the house to lie under a group of lime trees. Together the family lived to the full in the garden, enjoying and knowing all its many nooks and crannies.

For the patriarch, the garden was also every bit as much his workplace as his study was indoors. Indoors he had a microscope, outside he had what his brother called his telescope eyes. They did not miss a trick, especially at what bumble bees (which he called humble bees), honey bees or the tiniest insects were up to in and around plants, and the antics of the tiniest flowers like those of the second-time-round inflorescences of violets in late summer (Weed 32). Darwin had the shrewdest ideas of any one around about what really was going on with the manoeuvring of plant life at its most fundamental levels. To further his thoughts and mull over his ideas, he walked through the kitchen garden

BELOW Down House and its lawns where tennis and other games were played, watercolour by Albert Goodwin, *c*.1880.

every day on a regular midday constitutional to the sandwalk, where he would do several circuits, placing a flint on a pile each time he completed a lap.

So, what did Darwin's gardeners really make of his activities all around them? There was obviously a strong mutual respect but latterly Henry Lettington, his head gardener, let slip a telling remark. When a neighbour once inquired of Henry about his master's state of health, his reply was:

> Oh! My poor master has been very sadly. I often wish he had something to do. He moons about in the garden, and I have often seen him standing doing nothing before a flower for ten minutes at a time. If only he had a something to do I really believe he would be better.

'Something to do' for Lettington could only mean a physical task, like some proper gardening, as opposed to just getting in the way with observational experiments. Another member of the household staff who had just come from the Thackerays commented that it was a pity that Mr Darwin had not something to do like Mr Thackeray, after she had seen him watching an ant-heap for a whole hour. Emma, Charles's wife, had no such inhibitions about dirtying her hands. In fact, during one of her husband's severe downturns, she got stuck into a few days gardening to find relief from the household stress. She instinctively understood the value of gardening as therapy, even if her husband did not. Even so, all that 'mooning about' was, as we now know, extraordinarily fruitful.

Darwin was no gardener, it is clear, but he was absolutely the garden's all-presiding presence. To appreciate his unique role there, we need go no further than observe his decidedly eccentric interest in weeds. So far, and especially through chapter two, we have seen that Darwin had a brilliant forensic mind for uncovering the ingenious reproductive strategies of many of the plants which may present themselves to us as weeds. But as to their garden-nuisance propensities, he took no interest, nor showed any concern. Indeed, he once scoffed at his wife (much to her then brief fury) when she got worked up about a gardener's boy who, out of ignorance, had left some dog's mercury which he was asked to weed at the end of the sandwalk and removed some harmless ivy instead.

To Darwin, weeds were the incidental players, subjects of fun and mockery, if anything. He wrote teasingly to his American botanist friend, Asa Gray, on the subject,

> Does it not hurt your Yankee pride, that we thrash you so confoundedly? I'm sure Mrs Gray will stick up for your own weeds. Ask her whether they are not more honest, downright good sort of weeds.

Back came a reply that American weeds were 'modest, woodland, retiring things; and no match for the intrusive, pretentious, self-asserting foreigners'. (In fact, behind the jocularity, there was a strongly felt germ of a truth in there – which we have come across a number of times). The light-hearted self-mocking vein appears again, most significantly for us, when Darwin mentions in a letter to his friend Joseph Hooker, dated 21 March 1857, 'I am amusing myself with several little experiments; I have now got a little weed garden'. This 'little weed garden' was to play a star role. It provided a clinching detail (among many) in the third chapter of the *Origin,* the one on 'Struggle for Existence'. As he mentioned,

> ...on a piece of ground three feet long and two wide, dug and cleared, and where there could be no choking from other plants, I marked all the seedlings of our native weeds as they came up, and out of 357 no less than 295 were destroyed, chiefly by slugs and insects.

This snippet summarised a carefully planned and executed small experiment which Darwin carried out from January to August in 1857. He made light of it to Joseph Hooker but actually he kept his friend abreast of its progress, as if it was of incidental interest, in each of his almost monthly letters. Obviously it had prime significance which he consistently understated. Shown on the page opposite are the notes Darwin recorded on page 25 of his 'Experiment Book'. We see that he inserted a wire by each seedling as it emerged and removed it later if the plant failed to survive. On the opposite page (24) he totalled his monthly findings as transcribed in the inset on the right. Thus on 1 August there were just 62 marked plants left out of the 357 which all struggled for their existence on that plot.

		dead
March 31.		25
April 10		59
20		28
May 8		95
June 1		70
		277
June 1 Living		80/357
July 1		67/357 alive
Aug 1		62/357 alive

Of the marked plants
a few & very few new
ones have come up

Weed Garden

Mem. *Native* weeds.

(25)

but not my foul piece of weed

Piece of foul ~ground~ in Orchard, which had been ~shrubby & then for a year a tea~ strawberry bed — in size

36 inches by 24 inches (potato for large animals) — Dug in January & cleared of all perennials —

Early in March seed began to spring up: marked each daily.

March 31st about 55 marked, of which about 25 killed chiefly.

April 10. Pulled up 59 weeds making when seedlings before development

of true leaves had been damaged, I suppose of slugs, & may drawn out

by worms, & perhaps some beaten out by heavy rain. All, a nearly

all earliest seedlings thus destroyed. I think calluming grass seedlings

escape better than others. [no doubt they suffer more by being open

& exposed to weather & as few, so better chance of being damaged]

April 20. Pulled up 28 weeds, dead. — [I think dry weather in

beginning to tell against some]

May 8. Pulled up 95 weeds. — (I suspect still some seedlings

are killed by drought.)

June 1 Pulled up 70 weeds. —

— Left still 80 still living of several kinds most Ranunculus & Poa (i. nettle, some Compositae

(by tenacity few have come up during all May) Spergula, Lolium, Thistle

July 1 — 13 of the 80 are now dead, leaving 67 alive

a few more & but a few new seedlings have come up

now there are $\frac{67}{357}$ alive i.e. not one $\frac{1}{5}$ alive. Evidently

the final risk is in early state.

Aug. 1, 5 more of the 80 are dead — leaving 62 alive

30 $\frac{62}{6}$ $\frac{62}{8}$ — say between $\frac{1}{5}$ & $\frac{1}{6}$ perished last summer.
   $\frac{62}{372}$ $\frac{62}{310}$

old shrubbery & then strawberry neglected bed.

Today visitors to Down House see a replica of this experiment as one of the first curiosities to be observed as they approach the current public entrance to the house from the car park. No big deal is made of it. In fact, there is no sign to say what the little fenced-off space is doing just there. But there it is, Darwin's 1857 'weed garden', presented as an absolutely characteristic example of his early methodology – a 'dinky' little experiment (as an American blogger describes it), utterly straightforward and one that any of us could have set up but, in reality, only one that a genius with a crazy sense of practicality could have dreamed up and carried off.

The striking conclusion of the experiment is that 83 per cent of the original seedlings failed to survive to August. The head gardener at Down now repeats the experiment every year, and every year the failure rate comes in close to that 83 per cent. Or rather we should look to the survival rate of between one in five and one in six.

As weekend gardeners, we can relate strongly to aspects of the experiment – most especially to the devastation caused by slugs, and we even might wonder why Darwin's

BELOW The 'Weed Garden' just beside Down House, as it is demonstrated today.

slugs did not clean up on all the seedlings, as they so often do with our own lettuce seedlings. Recall the touch-and-go situation that Nicholas Harberd experienced with the survival (just) of his graveyard thale cress (Weed 53). The drama of his successive observations echoed that of Darwin's. Think too of our common experience of sowing lettuce seeds. The seed packets usually provide far more seeds than we are likely to need but they are there as a back-up (and because they happen to be plentiful too). We sow the seed quite densely to allow for non-viability, pest and disease damage and weed seedling competition but a little later usually find ourselves having to take out a large majority of the young seedlings to allow the rest sufficient space to bulk out to a desirable size. It is a lot of fiddly work to do what nature does far more crudely and wholeheartedly.

Rowan Blaik, Down House's current head gardener, reflected on Darwin's experiment in relation to his own experiences of repeating it a few times:

No matter how much a struggle a gardener's non-stop battle against weeds can be, at Down House, nature is helping out by killing off the least suitable 83% of weeds, often before we even get to them. Perhaps I should be proud in knowing that the weeds elsewhere in the garden, those that we end up hoeing down, those not lucky enough to be growing in the experiment plot, were descended from the best of the best. Possibly from an elite handful of weeds that once upon a time slipped by Darwin's own gardeners, Brooks and Lettington. A botanical rogues' gallery honed by generations of natural selection but not quite evolved enough at the moment, thank goodness, to make it past a well sharpened hoe.

Brooks' and Lettington's successor is quite right. What happened with weeds in the garden in Darwin's time and what has been happening to them ever since – surviving through their own struggles for existence, whether those be onslaughts from pests and diseases, weather extremes or competition among themselves and other plants, not to mention the destruction wreaked by zealous gardeners – does illustrate the basic processes of natural selection. That is what we posited tentatively at the beginning of this book by introducing weeds as nature's garden selection. But we delude ourselves if we imagine this is natural selection as Darwin saw it. His was the long view, the very long view.

In the 150 years since Darwin was playing with those weeds, despite all the interferences that the weeds in the whole garden have been subjected to by nature and by us, it is very doubtful that those free spirits will have changed visibly in any way. Even going back more than 400 years we see that Gerard's descriptions of these plants are still exactly as we observe them today. For Darwin, gardens were places for taking the long view and reflecting on what is happening over millions of years to enable the eventual appearance of all our beautiful garden plants, and of ourselves to tend them.

Natural Selection was, of course, Darwin's core concept for explaining how extraordinary, long-term changes might come about. His key fourth chapter of the *Origin* was originally titled just that and began by emphasising its 'power' as compared with that of selection carried out by ourselves.

Darwin borrowed the term 'selection' from the horticultural and agricultural trades, as he explained in his first chapter on 'Variation under Domestication'. He relayed how plant breeders cross-bred varieties of a particular plant and then picked out the most desirable offspring, from whose seeds they grew and refined their selection again, and so on repeatedly until an appealing and stable new cultivar was created and was ready to be marketed. The selection process involved the discarding and destruction of almost all the seedlings except the select few. He described how animal breeders (and notoriously pigeon fanciers) went through similar selection procedures for the domestication of farm stock. In effect, Darwin recognised that the selection undertaken by plant and animal breeders was happening by default all the time in the natural world but in an immeasurably more drawn out and precariously chance-ridden way. So he adopted the term 'Natural Selection' for the mechanism by which plants and all other living organisms gradually change naturally and how, over many millions of years, they may change out of all recognition.

Variation is what natural selection has to have to operate upon. Genes get shuffled, a new tint or an ever-so-slightly modified plant-part shape arrives for a moment, maybe a new plant acquires that extra bit of vigour (or the reverse) just for a while, and there is a gentle reminder that nothing ever stays quite the same. The plants with advantages to cope with more difficult times will be the ones self-selected to stay on. The gardening world (as we mentioned) is notorious for manipulating the tendency to variation and then parading the latest glamorous varieties. Change is just what we love in a garden, being always ready to find, try out and show off a new cultivar of a plant we know of old. In nature, though, the shuffling genes almost always ensure a tendency back to conformity – reversion to the norm, as they say. 'Almost always', of course, leaves the door open for rare dramatic deviations, possibly of major consequence.

But before going any further, it is worth putting on record again what was revealed about notorious variations among our one hundred weed examples. For a start, there was the double-flowered buttercup, which just turned up on Darwin's doorstep, and which was sterile, only to replicate itself insolently of its own accord. Then there were evening primroses which took to mutation, taking advantage of flaws in their self-copying mechanisms. And what about dandelions! They just went for it: a sexual start with occasional subsequent flings; erratic mutations; a lot of playing around with phenotypic plasticity; and a complete shutdown of all sexual activity whatsoever, all to allow for an almighty cloned seed production. Disturbing cases like these seem to be drawn to the world of weeds. They hang around defying gardeners and botanists alike. It is little consolation that in the longer evolutionary term they are destined to go nowhere.

Darwin would not allow himself to be diverted by such anomalies and aberrations, disturbed as he was at times by the dead-ends of sterility they often demonstrated. He worked out that this was par-for-the-course with much hybridisation, a useful break, if you like, to ensure that the more advantageous routes were followed. But he was fixated on variation appearing and then being sustained as vigorously as possible through normal reproductive processes; and he speculated on how modifications might arise – as from the effects of changed environmental conditions, on whether variations became used or disused, and so on. He recognised that varieties would establish themselves in 'communities of descent' and that sometimes freak 'monstrosities' would appear out of the blue and then exert their distorting influence on the local stock. Plants, it seemed, offered him by far the best opportunities for studying variation.

Some variations go on to become independent species whereas others linger as semi-permanent variations still in connection with their immediate heirs. Getting to the bottom of how variation worked bothered Darwin to the end, especially because variation had to be the stepping stone to speciation.

When he completed the *Origin* Darwin knew there was more work to be done on this and he set himself to write a follow-up volume just on variation. It was a laborious task and he managed to spin it out another nine years to 1868. *The Variation of Animals and Plants under Domestication* finally came out in two hefty volumes and is generally regarded as one of his more difficult works. The subject matter was followed up again in 1876 with *The Effects of Cross- and Self -Fertilisation in the Vegetable Kingdom* and the following year with *The Different Forms of Flowers on Plants of the Same Species*.

Species and the matter of how they come about was the crux of Darwin's investigations, as we all well know. But, first of all, we ourselves need to be more specific. How do we define the so-and-sos? Darwin had a tricky starting point as he admitted that, 'generally the term includes the unknown element of a distinct act of creation'. You can see why he felt compelled to challenge this flaky position. You can see, also, that he could only do so by working out more specifically how any species might originate. This challenge was for him, as he declared in the second sentence of his introduction to the *Origin*, to take on 'that mystery of mysteries'. It took him the whole book to unravel this puzzle as best he could, and almost twenty years to write it.

Looking through our list of one hundred weeds should give us confidence that we know a large number of plants as different discrete botanic entities – though we found uneasy situations with some of them, like the dandelions and brambles. We also have a comfortable common assumption that a species is a species because it has its own exclusive realm of inter-breeding – though at the same time, we know it does not always work out quite like that.

Darwin explained and summarised the last point rather more neatly: 'Hereafter we shall be compelled to acknowledge that the only distinction between species and well-marked varieties is, that the latter are known, or believed, to be connected at the present day by intermediate gradations whereas species were formerly thus connected.' To cut a long story a little shorter, we now have the tool of DNA sequencing to bring us closer to pinpointing the dividing lines between variations and species. That is all very well for the scientists in their laboratories, you might say, but not much help in working out a fine difference as met in a garden. We gardeners sometimes have that extra problem when certain weeds seem to camouflage themselves or nestle in with garden plants with not too dissimilar foliage, like ground elder amongst geraniums.

On top of trying to distinguish weed from weed, and weed from garden plant, there is that other elusive question we come up against: how do we distinguish between the appearances of species, subspecies, micro-species and aggregate species – not forgetting that there may also be multiple variations within these subgroupings? All these differentiations just represent branching twigs at the outer fringes of the whole evolutionary tree displaying the diversity of all life.

Diversity and diversification, Darwin found, were harder nuts to crack. In a brief autobiographical memoir, written for his family towards the end of his life, Darwin admitted that an explanation of diversification foxed him for some while, until one day, as he recollected:

RIGHT The author of *On the Origin of Species* stands by a climber-adorned pillar at the back of his house in the village of Downe. Before him is the splendid array of multitudinous species which filled his garden and which so absorbed him over the years, but at this moment, in about 1880, his eye is firmly fixed on the camera.

I can remember the very spot in the road, whilst in my carriage, when to my joy the solution occurred to me, and this was not long after I had come to Down. The solution, as I believe, is that the modified offspring of all dominant and increasing forms tend to become adapted* to many highly diversified places in the economy of nature.

*adapted, as we would now put it, to specialised ecological niches.

We can all identify with Darwin's eureka moment – coming quite out of the blue when sitting on a bus, or maybe when relaxing into a spot of weeding.

By diversification Darwin meant 'the tendency in organic beings descended from the same stock to diverge in character as they became modified'. 'That they have diverged greatly', he added, 'is obvious from the manner in which species of all kinds can be classed under genera, genera under families, families under sub-orders and so forth.'

Even so, according to Edward O. Wilson, who has played a major role in pushing the idea of the 'diversity of life' into the forefront of public consciousness in the last twenty years with his prize-winning book of that title, Darwin still did not quite get it. 'His thinking on diversity remained fuzzy,' claimed Wilson, 'he did not discover the process by which multiplication occurs. He understood in a general way the difference between vertical evolution and the splitting of species but he lacked a biological species concept based on reproductive isolation.' Darwin did not get it wrong, he simply was not to know the full story.

One hundred and fifty years on from Darwin's time, interest in ecology has exploded into public consciousness – with 'biodiversity' as the rallying cry of our times. No longer are we puzzling as to how an elaborate mixed-species scenario is attained in the first place, but rather we are worrying, if not panicking, as to how it can be sustained against all our unwitting efforts to undermine it. The longer-term self-interest of all of us depends on our not eroding biodiversity, weeds and all, into a position of irreversible meltdown.

Rebuked by his father as 'an idle sporting man', the young Charles made his own onslaught onto his natural surrounds as both an avid collector and shooter of all and sundry, even keeping tallies of the hundreds of birds he shot. He was unlikely to have been putting other species at risk, but such foolhardy actions could not be condoned these days. Naturalists of our times are stalwart conservationists. Priorities for them have dramatically changed from those of their forebears.

We should acknowledge that we meet, and usually skirt around, the biodiversity challenge in our own gardens every day. Traditionally we view these spaces as environments for particular collections of plants which we choose to the exclusion of all others (most of which we will then call weeds if they dare to intrude) as well as of other organisms which present a threat to their welfare. But concerns for biodiversity should incline us to be more inclusive of other life-forms, including, perhaps, being more open-minded about weeds. But how far should we go? This question is addressed briefly in the following chapter.

Evolution, the gentle step-by-step unfolding of change, is a comforting notion – who can possibly object to it? Evolution was around long before Darwin. It entered the English language in 1622, according to the *Oxford English Dictionary*. In fact, Darwin himself barely used the word. It did not appear at all in the first editions of the *Origin*; 'evolved' only came in as his very last word: 'endless forms most beautiful and most wonderful have been, and are being evolved'. He introduced the noun a couple of times in later editions, seemingly needing to get off his chest an exasperation which he had once endured with some of his colleagues.

> I formerly spoke to very many naturalists on the subject of evolution and never met any with sympathetic agreement. It is probable that some did then believe in evolution, but they were silent, or expressed themselves so ambiguously that it was not easy to understand their meaning. Now things are wholly changed and almost every naturalist admits the great principles of evolution.

Nowadays gardeners and naturalists alike appreciate gradual change. But Darwin looked to the very much larger timescale. *Natura non facit saltum* (Nature does not jump) was his assertion in the last chapter of the *Origin*. General acceptance of such evolutionary gradualism stands to this day, despite a flurry of interest in 'punctuated equilibrium' in the 1970s and, we might just add, despite our frustrated observation of certain weeds which appear to adapt to the onslaughts we inflict upon them.

Gradually, in the course of this book, we have come to see Darwin anew as the open-minded naturalist, with the crazy, far, far-sighted ideas, the man who was to be one of the most eminent scientists of all time. This is the guy who, late in life, had some earthworms serenaded by a cacophony of sounds – his grandson Bernard blowing a whistle, his son Francis playing the bassoon, his wife Emma playing the piano, and his daughter Elizabeth just shouting – all to find out whether the worms made any response (they did not). That was Charles Darwin, the endearing, rather eccentric family man, firmly grounded in his garden.

5
To round up

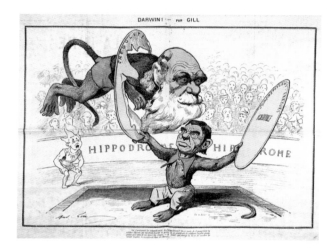

DARWIN! — par GILL

HIPPODROME

Weeds appear, right there in our gardens. We do our best to deal with them. And in doing so, we find ourselves, whether consciously or not, doing our best to prepare the way for their successors. For one of the defining characteristics of such plants is that they are proven opportunists and will seize their chance whenever freshly disturbed ground is to hand. If it is any consolation, we can think of them as nature's pioneers – the leading colonisers of vacant spaces. If nature is allowed to have its way for a good few years, more stable occupants will eventually follow in the pioneers' wake. But meanwhile in our gardens the cycle goes on: weeds followed by weeding, more weeds, more weeding, more weeds, and so on as if jumping through endless hoops.

The colonisers will have their own successions too – dandelions followed by docks, followed by nettles and brambles, maybe. The advance guard are often the 'ephemerals', those precocious little devils with two- or three-month life cycles. Their super-fast turnover

ABOVE A French cartoon commentating on the publication of Darwin's *The Descent of Man* in 1871.
RIGHT The Wild Garden as pictured by William Robinson in his 1870 book of that title.

269

puts the cycle into a crazy spin. Then annuals take a hold with their full season lifespans ending in their own ever greater showers of seeds. Biennials may follow on with their two-year toehold. Meanwhile perennial weeds are creeping around both under and over ground, steadily entangling themselves within and all around our own treasured garden perennials. Vegetative reproduction backed up by sexual reproduction now becomes the all-year, year-after-year driving force behind the relentless invasive threat of the garden spoilers.

Just what is it, then, about this army of troublemakers which bothers us so? How is it that, at times, weeds appear to become all too much for us, and in endless ways?

All too...

much of the wild
These are plants which have been left far behind those we have domesticated for our use, and now look uncouth and hopelessly straggly.

out of place
They may be in the wrong part of the garden, the wrong kind of garden or perhaps they should not be in any garden at all.

alien
They look too foreign or run amok when away from their homeland constraints.

obstructive
They get in the way of other plants, or even simply block our way, like nettles on a path.

harmful
They damage other garden plants or us with their bristling defences, making them too 'noxious and injurious', as the legislators put it.

charmless
They are unsightly, whether scruffily untidy or downright ugly.

insignificant
They are too slight in appearance or just insufficiently interesting, and so deemed to be without any 'garden merit' whatsoever.

out of favour
They are 'uncool' or rejected out of personal taste, whim or outright prejudice.

ready to appear
They spring up from endless reserves of seed in the ground, the soil bank which allows dormant seeds to remain viable for an average of seven years.

insolent
They seem to be there just to tease and taunt – forget me not forget-me-not.

quick
They are faster off the mark than most other plants and capable of spreading at breakneck speeds, a 'mile a minute', or so it sometimes seems.

pervasive
They are too ubiquitous, just too common – usually plants with exceptional reproductive and dispersal capacities.

invasive
And this is the ultimate fear – when nature's garden selection threatens to take over the garden, not to mention invading fields or even taking over the wild.

The last point brings us round to the big question. Which are the world's worst invaders? Grass? Moss? Bracken? Brambles? Bees? Flies? Ourselves? Fungi (which, incidentally, are more closely related to ourselves than to plants)? Uncomfortably, we can see where the finger may be pointing. Admit collective culpability for a start, and then collective responsibility for damage curtailment to our excessive onslaughts on our fellow species. Meanwhile the weeds in our gardens still need attention. In the garden it is warfare as ever – and there is virtually no escaping this. So we fight battle after battle after battle, knowing, as we have already pointed out, that each partial victory will be preparing the ground for the next weed comeback. But perhaps, just perhaps, we can step back for a moment and start to fight with a little more equanimity, possibly seeking a partial truce here and there.

Apart from employing the best possible weeding tactics, there is always scope for looking again at overall management strategies and consequent styles of gardening. How far do we go 'organic' and what are the implications for attempting to be more in harmony with nature and with our surrounds? How far can we even accommodate just a few weeds? Here we put a gentle spotlight on five very different gardens which have considered these challenges in a variety of ways.

Christopher Lloyd and Beth Chatto, two highly regarded creators of distinctive English informal gardens, both played with an edgy frisson by drawing in elements from their immediate surroundings. Lloyd, at Great Dixter in Sussex, introduced teases with teasels (among other frowned upon commoners) and had an entrance through a wild flower meadow. The Beth Chatto Gardens, in Essex, have visitors arriving through an extended

BELOW The gravel bed at the entrance to Beth Chatto's garden.
RIGHT The wild meadow at Great Dixter, Christopher Lloyd's house and garden.

gravel bed which virtually merges with the car park, and where mulleins (and much else) erratically flourish on the way to the main garden which is in a former gravel pit.

Even more daring was Derek Jarman, an avant-garde film maker, who retired to a shack on Dungeness, a desolate extensive expanse of shingle on the English South Coast. There was no definitive boundary to the space he adopted around his simple dwelling. Horned poppies, sea holly, seakale, purslane and other elements from the sparse local flora were welcomed in and enhanced among artfully arranged bits of driftwood, piles of old rope, beached flotsam and so on – a truly enchanting little garden emerging out of an almost empty wilderness, with local 'weeds' as its inspiration and sole floral content.

Jarman picked up, whether consciously or not, on the idea put forward by William Robinson in his 1870 book, *The Wild Garden,* where, to counterbalance his enthusiasm for 'naturalisation' (for putting imported garden shrubs around the edge of English woodlands, for example), Robinson advocated 'The Garden of British Wild Flowers'. He knew what he wanted: the elite wild flora as he saw it, brought into gardens. He had his prejudices and, dare we say, snobberies in a hierarchy of plants where his lowliest

wild plants are categorised as the weeds and included the tearaways like dandelions, daisies and so on. But to be fair to Robinson, when he set up his own garden at Gravetye Manor (in the Weald, barely twenty miles from Downe village), it set a new standard for sensitive informality, flirting with garden outsiders and, in particular, breaking away from Victorian ultra-contrived annual bedding schemes.

Moving on, there is a gardening movement in France (led by Gilles Clément) which advocates '*le jardin en mouvement*'. It defies garden designers who have fixed ideas that their gardens will stay put in the mould of their original plans, and opens the door to a more imaginative approach of playing with and adapting to what is actually happening, taking note of interesting weeds among everything else that is going on. Nicholas and Agnes Brückin, the creators of Le Jardin des Sambucs on a Cévennes mountainside,

LEFT Prospect Cottage and its garden as created by Derek Jarman on the bleak shingle of Dungeness. BELOW Le Jardin des Sambucs (the garden of elders) also sits sympathetically in a rough and ready locality, nestled among the scrub of a rugged hillside in southern France where Himalayan balsam and Japanese knotweed star.

adopt this approach with charming aplomb and originality. This garden was mentioned in chapter two at Weed 82 and Weed 85.

Finally, in this eclectic little round up of gardens which take on weeds and toy with them if only on the side, we should mention again that considerable space behind Down House. This was a homely, lived-in, family garden if there ever was one, not that different from the average back garden of today – with a lawn, flower beds, a greenhouse, a vegetable patch, paths, shrubs, a few trees – but all on a large scale. Weeds have thrived there and at the same time seem to have been kept under reasonable control, as in most other gardens. The principal nineteenth-century owner largely ignored them, except for a brief episode of bemusement as he was gathering together final bits of evidence to complete

BELOW A watercolour of Down House and garden by Albert Goodwin, 1880.

his epic tome. Of the five gardens just described rather sketchily, the Down House garden is probably the one with which most us will identify more strongly, being safely in the traditional English garden mode, while allowing for a bit of fun to be trying new things from time to time. Darwin's experimentation, of course, was essentially botanical. While wandering around this place, which has been restored with great care to how we know it must been in the Darwin family's time, we can feel mildly reassured that here is a garden every much as well-worn and weeds-fallible as our own back home.

In or out of our gardens, weeds are our natural companions, forever with us, whether we like it or not. Should we not admit, then, to a symbiotic relationship, one of long-term mutual dependency? Should not we also admit that there is no chance of our ever rounding up the enemy once and for all, nor of finding a magic potion to do the trick for us just like that? Furthermore, should we not acknowledge that our old sparring partners actually have us locked in a longstanding deep bond?

And then, in conclusion, we should recognise that our relationship with weeds may now include an extra dimension. As we have been discovering, if we are truly open to the wily ways of these plants they, in turn, are capable of throwing shafts of new light on the life and work of Charles Darwin, the all-time naturalist who was no gardener but a man of his garden like no other, and who concluded his major groundbreaking work with these words:

> There is grandeur in this view of life, with its several powers, having been originally breathed into a few forms or into one; and that, whilst this planet has gone cycling on according to the fixed law of gravity, from so simple a beginning endless forms most beautiful and most wonderful have been, and are being evolved.

Recommended reading

Mea Allan *Darwin and his Flowers*, Faber and Faber, 1977.

Edgar Anderson *Plants, Man and Life*, Little Brown, 1952; Dover, 2005.

Janet Browne *Charles Darwin, Voyaging*, Jonathan Cape, 1995; Pimlico, 1996.

Janet Browne *Charles Darwin, The Power of Place*, Jonathan Cape, 2002; Pimlico 2003.

Alfred W. Crosby *Ecological Imperialism – The Biological Expansion of Europe 900–1900*, Cambridge University Press, 1986.

Charles Darwin *On the Origin of Species*, Murray, 1859.

Charles Darwin *Journal of researches into the geology and natural history of the various countries visited during the voyage of H.M.S. Beagle round the world*, Henry Colbourne, 1839.

Charles Darwin *Autobiographies*, Penguin Classics, 2002.
For the full range of Darwin's publications, including his seven botanical books, readers are advised to look at darwin-online.org.uk/. Here are all the published works of Charles Darwin and a huge majority of his unpublished manuscripts and correspondence (including letters to papers like the *Gardener's Chronicle*).

Gareth Davies, Bill Turner and Bill Bond *Weed Management for Organic Farmers, Growers and Smallholders*, The Crowood Press, 2008.

A. A. Dudman and A. J. Richards *Dandelions of Great Britain and Ireland*, Botanical Society of the British Isles, 1997.

John Gerard *The Herball*, 1597; Thomas Johnson, ed., 1636.

Nicholas Harberd *Seed to Seed – The Secret Life of Plants*, Bloomsbury, 2006.

Thomas A. Hill *The Biology of Weeds*, Edward Arnold, 1977.

Randal Keynes *Annie's Box – Charles Darwin, his daughter and human evolution*, Fourth Estate, 2001.

W. John Kress and Shirley Sherwood *The Art of Plant Evolution*, Kew Publishing, 2009.

Christopher Lloyd *The Well-Tempered Garden*, Collins, 1970; Penguin, 1978.

Peter Loewer *Solving Weed Problems*, The Lyons Press, 2001.

Tim Low *Feral Future*, Penguin Books Ltd, 2001.

D. J. Mabberley *Mabberley's Plant-book*, Cambridge University Press, 2008.

Richard Mabey *Weeds*, Profile Books, 2010.

C. Neal Stewart, Jr. *Weedy and Invasive Plant Genomics*, Wiley-Blackwell, 2009.

R. Lloyd Praeger *Weeds: Simple Lessons for Children*, Cambridge University Press. 1913.

Jo Readman *Controlling Weeds Without Using Chemicals*, Search Press, 2001.

William Robinson *The English Flower Garden*, John Murray, 1883.

Sally Roth *WEEDS friend or foe?* Carroll & Brown Publishers Limited, 2001.

Sir Edward Salisbury *Weeds & Aliens*, Collins (New Naturalist series), 1961.

Menno Schilthuizen *Frogs, Flies & Dandelions – the making of species*, Oxford University Press, 2001.

Jonathan Silvertown *Demons in Eden – The Paradox of Plant Diversity*, The University of Chicago Press, 2005.

Edwin Rollin Spencer *All About Weeds*, Constable, 1957.

John S. Stephenson and James M. Churchill *Medical Botany*, John Churchill,1834.

Edward O. Wilson *The Diversity of Life*, Penguin Books, 1992.

Index

Italic pagination indicates illustration or caption

Numbers in bold refer to one of the one hundred weeds

Picture credits

All photographs are © the author unless listed.

The illustration on page 18 and the miniatures derived from it are based on the publication *The Art of Plant Evolution*, Kew Publishing, 2009.

© azure/Shutterstock.com 177
© Celia Berridge 7, 53
By kind permission of the Botanical Society of the British Isles – Publications 223, 224, 225
Illustrations reproduced with the kind permission of Brighton and Hove City Libraries 38, 86, 93, 153, 191, 220, 232
© Jonathan Buckley 273
Cambridge University Herbarium 147
Reproduced by courtesy of the Syndics of Cambridge University Library: MS.DAR.DAR. 271.1.1. Accepted by H M Government in lieu of Inheritance Tax, 2011 and temporarily allocated to Cambridge University Library pending a decision on permanent allocation 252; MS. DAR. 157a Darwin Collection 259; MS. DAR.DAR. 226.2.21 Darwin Collection 268
© Val Corbett 14
© Gillian Darley/Edifice/arcaid.co.uk 274
© English Heritage 12, 57, 253 (by permission of Darwin Heirloom Trust), 254 (by permission of Philip and Nell Trevelyan), 255, 256, 265, 276
© David Evans 64
© Robert Foster 4, 233
© Garden Organic 51, 62, 95 above left and above right, 102 left, 107, 114, 129, 135, 136, 160, 165, 167, 183, 202, 203
Archives of the Gray Herbarium, Harvard University, Cambridge, Massachusetts 10
© Rob Hainer/Shutterstock.com 126
© Mark Hereid/Shutterstock.com 219
© Tamara Kulikova/Shutterstock.com 157 above
© Sarah Last 93, 115, 120, 127, 137 below, 158, 169, 170, 181, 182, 189, 193, 204 top
© Gerald Legg BG020911 Booth Museum of Natural History, Brighton and Hove City Council 32
© Deborah Locke 111
© Graeme Lyons 69

© Carolyn Orchard 237
© Steven Paul Pepper/Shutterstock.com 2–3
Reproduced with the kind permission of the Director and the Board of Trustees, Royal Botanic Gardens, Kew 91, 99
© David Salter 33
© John Scholey 172
By kind permission of Search Press 234
© Russell Tuppen 45, 141, 214
© Steven Wooster 272
By kind permission of the Yale Center for British Art, Paul Mellon Collection 25
© Hazel Young 1, 5, 98 above, 104, 108, 226

We are fortunate to have three prime agencies of expertise, each of them welcoming enquiries and each also being a leading international institution.

THE ROYAL HORTICULTURAL SOCIETY, the centre of horticultural expertise, based at Wisley in Surrey, www.rhs.org.uk

THE ROYAL BOTANIC GARDENS at Kew is the international centre of botanical knowledge. One of its former directors, Sir Edward Salisbury, made a great contribution to our knowledge of weeds and their alien associates. This was summarised in what is still one of the most authoritative books, *Weeds and Aliens*, in the Collins New Naturalist series, 1961, www.kew.org

GARDEN ORGANIC, based at Ryton near Coventry, is especially helpful on the issue of weeds and their alien associates, www.gardenorganic. org.uk. It has a DEFRA sponsored database of 'Weed Information', which consists of ongoing collated summaries of scientific papers relating to agricultural and horticultural weeds and provides the most authoritative guidance available on nearly 150 different weeds. It demonstrates a desired shift from an overdependence on herbicides. The references for all of the statistics quoted in this book can be found here if they are not otherwise attributed, www.organicweeds.org.uk.

Acknowledgements

This book has come out of a lifetime of weeding gardens and from a mounting personal fascination with Charles Darwin. I am therefore indebted to a wide range of influences, encouragements and sources of expertise. So thank you especially to my late mother, Betty, who deftly sowed the seeds for an enduring love of gardening, and to Celia, my wife, who led the way in a joint quest after oddball plants like sundews, opuntias, asphodels and evening primroses. She has understood my distraction and supported this project all the way, no doubt seeing it as an honourable counterpart to her own passion for bantams. Thanks to her too for the excellent drawings.

Thanks also to the late John Cannon, former Keeper of Botany at the Natural History Museum, for setting me going with encouraging advice on my first scribbles about dandelions; to Maggie Boden who, together with the biographers Janet Browne, Adrian Desmond and James Moore, led me into this rich exploration of the life and work of Darwin; to Mark Chase, Director of the Jodrell Laboratory at the Royal Botanic Gardens, Kew, for answering my naive questions about the 1910 Kew 'Tree of Plant Evolution' and the work of the Angiosperm Phylogeny Group; to Rowan Blaik, Head Gardener at Down House, and Randal Keynes, of the Darwin Trust, for elaborating most illuminatingly on the goings-on of Darwin in his garden; to Melanie Newfield of the New Zealand Department of Conservation, for helping to give a picture of weed issues in New Zealand; to Andy Strachan, Head Gardener at Garden Organic for kindly informing me on weed issues at Ryton Organic Gardens, and Phil Sumption, Research Officer at Garden Organic, who oversees the Weeds Information section of the Garden Organic website, which has been a prime resource for this book. Phil has also been most helpful and generous in supplying photographs. Thanks too to Andy Wright, of the Health and Safety Executive, who helped with finding information on the historical development of particular herbicides.

Then I am especially grateful to some very helpful and welcoming librarians, notably Craig Brough and Julia Buckley, Library, Art and Archives – Royal Botanic Gardens, Kew; Adam Perkins, Keeper of Scientific Manuscripts at Cambridge University Library; Margaret Curson, Rare Books Librarian, Brighton Jubilee Library; and the staff of the Lindley Library, Wisley.

Rodmell Camera Club has enthusiastically pitched in with some fine photography. Many other friends, family members and gardening colleagues have chipped in with pertinent details which all helped to enrich the end result. Finally I have to express huge gratitude to Jane Crawley, my editor, who together with Anne Wilson the designer, has taken exceptional care in a long succession of challenging stages to bring this book to fruition.

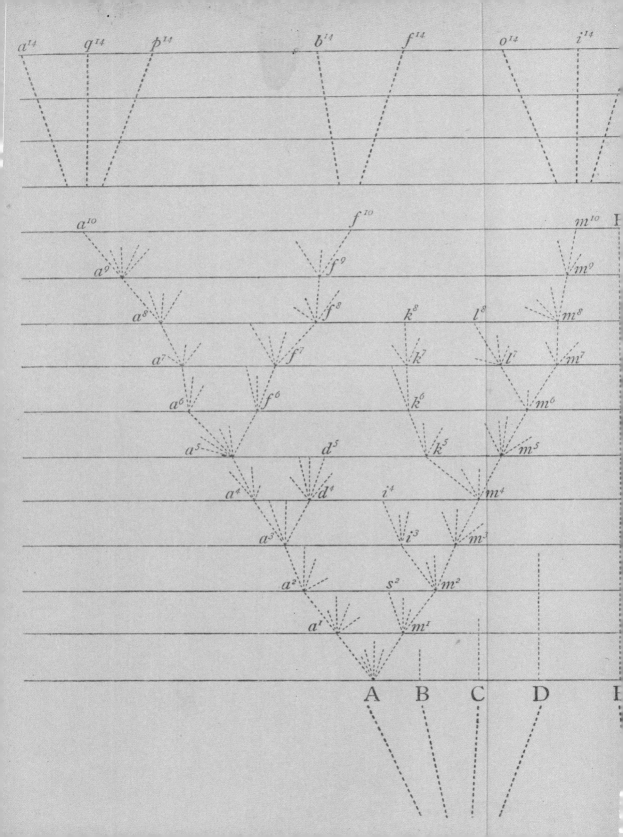